AN OUTLINE OF BOOK DESIGN

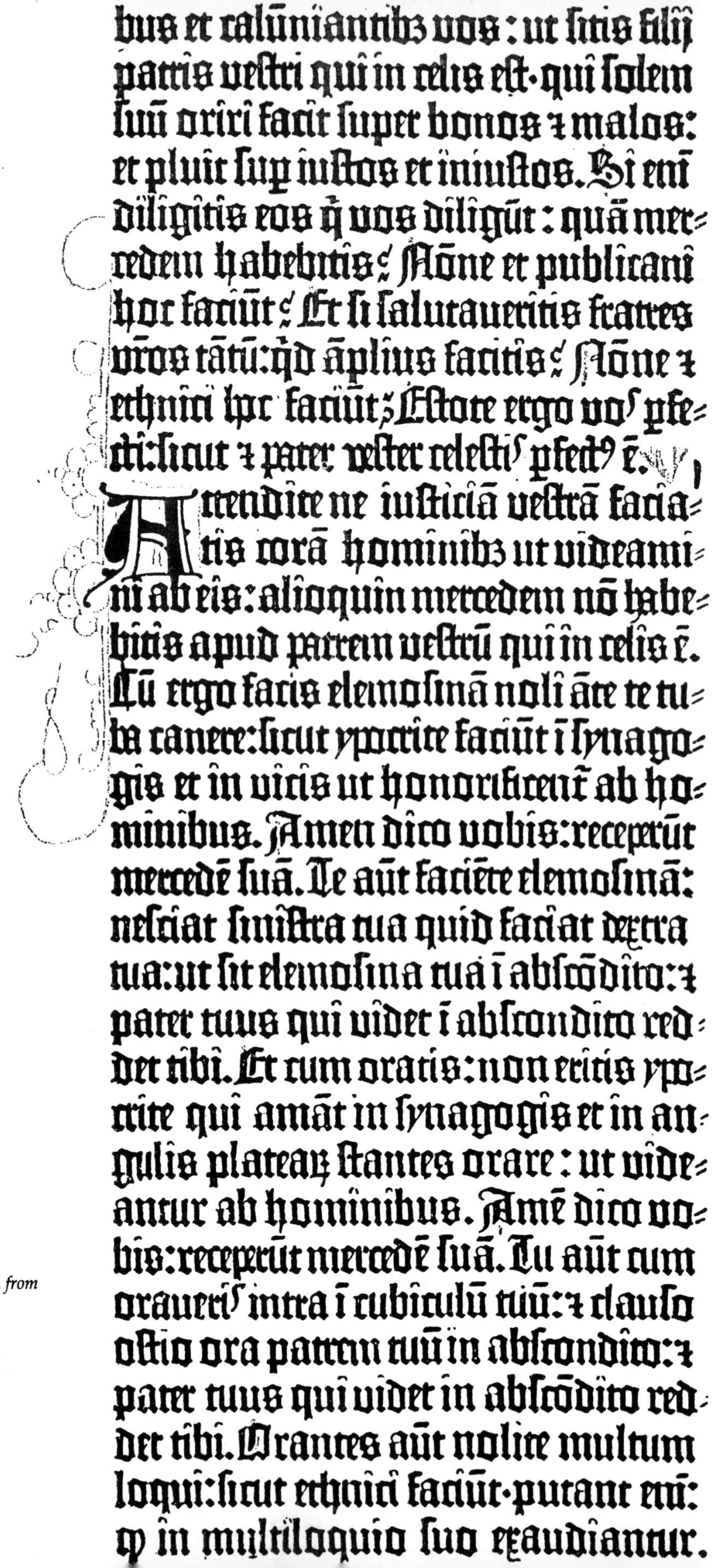

bus et calūniantibꝫ vos: ut sitis filii
patris vestri qui in celis est· qui solem
suū oriri facit super bonos ⁊ malos:
et pluit sup iustos et iniustos. Si enī
diligitis eos q̄ vos diligūt: quā mer-
cedem habebitis? Nōne et publicani
hoc faciūt? Et si salutaueritis fratres
vr̄os tātū: q̄d āplius facitis? Nōne ⁊
ethnici hoc faciūt? Estote ergo vos pfe-
cti: sicut ⁊ pater vester celestis pfect9 ē.
Attendite ne iusticiā vestrā facia-
tis corā hominibꝫ ut videami-
ni ab eis: alioquin mercedem nō habe-
bitis apud patrem vestrū qui in celis ē.
Cū ergo facis elemosinā noli āte te tu-
ba canere: sicut ypocrite faciūt ī synago-
gis et in vicis ut honorificent̄ ab ho-
minibus. Amen dico vobis: receperūt
mercedē suā. Te aūt faciēte elemosinā:
nesciat sinistra tua quid faciat dextra
tua: ut sit elemosina tua ī abscōdito: ⁊
pater tuus qui videt ī abscondito red-
det tibi. Et cum oratis: non eritis ypo-
crite qui amāt in synagogis et in an-
gulis plateaꝝ stantes orare: ut vide-
antur ab hominibus. Amē dico vo-
bis: receperūt mercedē suā. Tu aūt cum
oraueris intra ī cubiculū tuū: ⁊ clauso
ostio ora patrem tuū in abscondito: ⁊
pater tuus qui videt in abscōdito red-
det tibi. Orantes aūt nolite multum
loqui: sicut ethnici faciūt· putant enī:
q̄ in multiloquio suo exaudiantur.

Part of a single column, actual size, from the 42-line Bible, Mainz, c. 1455.

Douglas Martin

AN OUTLINE OF BOOK DESIGN

BLUEPRINT / THE PUBLISHERS ASSOCIATION

Published in the United Kingdom
by Blueprint Publishing Ltd
40 Bowling Green Lane
London EC1R ONE
Tel. 01 278 0333

First published 1989
Reprinted 1991

British Library Cataloguing-in-Publication Data

Martin, Douglas
An outline of book design
1. Books. Design
I. Title
686

ISBN 0–948905–40–9

Typeset by Matrix
Covent Garden, London WC2
Printed in Great Britain by
The Ipswich Book Company
Ipswich, Suffolk

CONTENTS

ACKNOWLEDGEMENTS

A heartsearching list of acknowledgements for a book of this kind would prove lengthy and tedious, for it seems that every scrap of an idea from the broadest historical generalisation to the most trivial practical tip is acquired from some source at one time or another, and that originality consists as much as anything in mishearing or getting things plain wrong.

The biggest thanks in any situation should be reserved for those who give out confidence or convince or compel one to produce things, and these are usually family, friends or publishers and in this case it took all three of each.

The world of book design is a small one and colleagues offer each other much unselfish assistance and encouragement, and I would like to express gratitude to those who have lent ideas or examples of work for this current venture: Max Caflisch, Adrian Frutiger, Rigby Graham, Michael Harvey, David Howells, Faith Jaques, Professor Dr Albert Kapr, Dr Peter Karow, René Kerfante, Ian Mortimer, Leon Urbański, Malcolm Harvey Young, Adrian Wilson and the late Prof. Horst Eric Wolter.

I am indebted to the staff of the following institutions for willing help with queries and for generous research facilities over the years: Bavarian State Library, Munich; The Olga Hirsch Paper Collection, The British Museum; Deutsche Bücherei, Leipzig; Gutenberg Museum, Mainz; Klingspor Museum, Offenbach; Nuremberg City Library; St Bride Printing Library; University of Leicester Library; University of London Institute of Ophthalmology.

Virtually all the illustrations have been deliberately held to line only, and this has posed some tricky problems; where possible, an office zoom photocopier has been used, but I am grateful to John Grant Studio, Leicester, for their perseverance with photomechanical copies of the more difficult subjects.

D.M.

Oadby, September 1989

1 INTRODUCTION

"Of making many books there is no end . . .", and, even if it remains forever unclear in which of several possible senses Ecclesiastes intended his remark, it holds true for most. The study and practice of book design is an activity for a lifetime, it is intriguing from the very outset and yet there is never a time to become bored with it. There is no set career route into it, and book designers certainly don't emerge fully-fledged from universities and art colleges – although one must be fair to the one or two institutions in various countries which are at any time striving to change this situation.

A good feature of the structure of book publishing, in contrast to some of the other arts and media, is that it makes allowance for this, and for people who would not normally describe themselves as designers but nevertheless care passionately about books to contribute positively to their appearance, sometimes almost without knowing. The specific job description on entering into publishing appears to be fairly immaterial for a while – today's secretarial assistant has a fair chance of becoming tomorrow's managing editor – and similarly the design content of an editorial or production post, or the whole direction of a career, may be developed freely according to personal motivation and innate or acquired skills. This study tries to take this situation into account and not just address the designer as professional.

1:1 What is design?

Design is the sum total of the decisions which make a product serviceable and attractive. Whoever takes these decisions or at whatever stage in planning or manufacture does not affect this view of the design process, in which everyone involved is capable of contributing to or detracting from the success of the venture. Design is not synonymous with making things, either on an artistic, craft or industrial basis; neither has it anything to do with the primary creative idea or the initiative to place a product on the market. It falls between the decision to make and the making.

The initial thinking about any proposition has to reach a briefing stage, that is to say aims and problems must be clarified, before design – and design should not be taken to imply the individual designer in this context – can begin to operate in drawing up a plan. Design is not something which is added on to the proposition from outside, it consists in resolving problems that are already present. It is the search for the simplest and most appropriate answer right down to questions of the smallest detail – a process of creating order out of muddle.

In this sense, questions about whether design is necessary or affordable are quite beside the point: design is inevitable. The alternative to good design is bad design, not no design at all. Everyone takes design decisions all the time without realising it – like Molière's M. Jourdain who discovered he had been speaking prose all his life – and good design is simply the result of making these decisions consciously, at the right stage, and in consultation with others as the need arises.

1:2 The book designer

A designer is a visually literate person, just as an editor is expected by training and inclination to be versed in language and literature, but to call the former an artist by occupation is as absurd as to refer to the latter as a poet. Designer or editor, most of us work in publishing and our professional concerns are shared ones. However, stereotypes persist, and a certain mystery attaches to other people's jobs even when you have worked alongside them for years.

No one in Europe or America made their living exclusively from designing books before about 1900, and yet masterly books were produced over the centuries by those for whom design as such was an unconscious attribute or minor preoccupation. Therefore if book designers have an ancestry it is to be traced back to the printing trades rather than to that of the printer's customer, the publisher; but if there should be a Valhalla for book designers it must closely resemble the workshops of Gutenberg and the early printers, when typography and publishing were still inseparable activities.

Until the demise of letterpress printing it was true that most of the best designers had either served part of their apprenticeship in the printing industry or had been trained in the printing schools. In 1956, Hugh Williamson sub-titled his treatise on *Methods of Book Design*: 'The practice of an industrial craft', and that comes close to the mark.

Writing as far back as 1943, the veteran American book designer, Bruce Rogers, explained how and why his profession had emerged in one of his *Paragraphs on Printing* that is worth quoting in full:

> It is still the practice in many publishing houses and large printing-offices for the elements of a book to be planned and ordered piecemeal by different departments. This is a regrettable procedure which can hardly result in satisfactory bookmaking. [On his first visit to England Rogers is reputed to have raised eyebrows by describing himself as a bookmaker.] The book should always be considered as a whole and all instructions for materials and design should emanate from one desk.

It is tempting to say that little has changed; whereas in fact a revolution is in mid-course. When the great book houses threw out their hot-metal composing departments, independent phototypesetters using transitional technology sprang up to fill the gap. Some specialised in book setting although the majority offered a more comprehensive service to advertising and industry, and it has become a battle for many publishers to maintain consistent standards from suppliers over a period of time. As the gap between word processing and professional typesetting has narrowed in all dimensions from cost of equipment to ease of operation, it has become clear that text composition and camera-ready page make-up will, at least to some extent, inevitably move in-house for publishers from the greatest to the least. The fashionable term for this is DTP, but this has an imprecise meaning and amateurish connotations, and I would prefer to talk of PIT – professional in-house typography. This progressive handing over of initiative for keyboarding from the printing industry to publishing needs to be accompanied by the transfer of five centuries' accumulated craft skill, and I doubt that this can be satisfactorily accomplished without an increased commitment to design on the part of management and the active involvement of numerous able designers.

If properly approached, full in-house typography should not only allow the book designer access to a personally selected repertoire of the finest type designs and typographic material available, but also place typographic house style and standards on a permanent basis and make the task of constantly retraining suppliers a thing of the past. As well as simplifying or eliminating some of the less productive tasks described in this book, above all it should confer an unprecedented control over the entire sequence of events from design visualisation to final copy.

1:3 Design responsibility

The book designer's duty is first to the author and then to the hidden client, since only in reconciling these will any service be rendered to the direct client or employer. These very different although related aspects of the same problem will be considered in turn. It would be false to pretend that the designer has either time or inclination to read each and every manuscript which comes along, but an ability to become rapidly familiar with the detailed pattern and method of the work is indispensable: it is not necessary to comprehend, but only to discern, those qualities which ultimately make each and every book unique as a proposition, and to be generally responsive towards literary and illustrative structure and voice.

In taking an initial look at the proposed verbal/visual mix, the designer has a common purpose with the editor, but will be expected to spot certain visual problems associated with the text and the range of means which may lead to their resolution. No one can be blamed where there is a mismatch between an author's verbal skill and the visual presentation with which he or she has been required by contract to support it, and in my experience of books where this may happen, the designer is frequently not involved at a sufficiently early stage. In addition to being able to help an author over the visual exposition and organisation of material, and in drafting-in any special picture research, artwork, illustration or photography that may be indicated, the book designer's involvement on the author's behalf should include formulating an approach to the kind of jacket and external appearance that will best get the book across. This is largely a marketing problem, and in many fields no one can help more than the author, not in the search for an idea but in the description of that specialist market.

The designer is beginning to locate the hidden client who will buy or borrow in order to read. Market research is fascinating but fragmentary – Peter Mann's which found that the Mills & Boon readership belied stock assumptions about it, and the discovery that gratuitous violence grafted on to a recent series of Agatha Christie covers was in fact damaging rather than enhancing sales, are examples that spring to mind. Above all it is rarely available or affordable to the book designer, in-house or freelance, at the stage at which it might be of some use. In default it is necessary for the designer to make up his own mind, and whilst there is never any trouble in picturing the reader for any particular title and getting things right in those respects, it is a different matter when it comes to visualising the purchaser. The hidden client is the person the author wrote for, and the designer has a fair share of the responsibility for putting them in touch.

The art of briefing is a neglected one to which the best publishers bring a charisma which sees them through, whereas designers on the whole need the facts of a situation rather than well-meant pointers as to how they might tackle their task – it can take time for them to disentangle the essential from the misleading, simply out of deference to the person seated at the other side of the desk.

There will always be a certain built-in difficulty in communicating visual matters through words and with people whose taste and acuity may be imponderable, and one of the hardest tasks for many in-house designers is to make the recurrent leap from text to jacket design and back, because of the speculative and unscientific atmosphere in which jacket decisions are taken. This mistrust can be mutual and it can be well grounded, and I don't think it hurts to admit openly that designers have to work at different levels with text and with jackets and that they can't all be equally good at both – this is closely paralleled with illustrators, of whom some are equally proficient in colour and in black and white, and some are not. This situation in my view is closely related to the recent policy on the part of a number of publishers to place high-profile jacket design and matters of corporate image with advertising agencies, where the focus on marketing and sales alignment creates confidence.

It seems to me that we are seeing a number of things happening as a result of this design group and agency intervention. Each decade from the 1920s through to the 1970s has been researched and raided for its fashionable, 'appearance design' tendencies. (Appearance design is the exercise of restyling for its own sake, without tackling any of the problems which design exists to resolve.) It is clear that the independent lettering, book design and illustration traditions within each European country have been studied; and the results brought together in a new synthesis and with a certain flair to give a new look to books and jackets, particularly in series. It is marvellous to be able to walk around my favourite Waterstone's bookshop in Bath and feel that a few years ago none of this would have been conceivable; neither the bookselling initiative nor the vitality and crisp appearance of the recently designed stock. Much has been accomplished by designers from outside the world of books, giving special attention to series and new marketing concepts, and one hopes that some of the best will get hooked and stay on. But fashion and appearance design generate a vocabulary of mannerisms, and everyone will quickly tire of these as less able designers keep facile and outworn ideas in circulation. Publishing design is in danger in the sense that where ideas are grafted on from outside – by those for whom it was a company report last week and tinned food packaging will be next on the horizon – books could lose out in the short term. Dedicated book designers require a long time in publishing houses and need to discover a training in all kinds of unexpected places: the last years in Britain have been unsettled ones for the industry and in training, and a new leading generation needs to emerge and open up a fresh forum for debate.

1:4 Design in interaction

The tale is told of a well-known publisher who took his first typescript to a large book printer and handed it over with the words: 'Make this look like a Bodley Head book.' At one time printers retained their contacts with freelance designers against just such eventualities, but it was certainly an expensive as well as a roundabout way in which to commission a designer.

Times have moved on, and it is possible to distinguish three functions – editorial, production and design – which no publisher large or small can dispense with. These functions may all be combined in a single person or each may be located in a separate empire, and the way the parts hang together will develop according to the needs of the kinds of book involved. It is difficult to generalise under these circumstances, but one or two points at which design and editing, and design and production, can come together are considered briefly.

Editor and designer

There are companies and situations in which a book's editor may have little or no direct contact with the design department, and where communication is intended to be taken care of primarily by means of well-prepared copy – but in practice it is rarely as straightforward as this. A designer usually needs to have some form of editorial briefing and feedback, in addition to a production framework, from which to set out along the right lines. It is difficult to assemble this information efficiently on a piecemeal basis or at second hand, and for this reason it is strongly recommended that briefing meetings of all kinds should be consolidated into a *written* brief for everyone's sake, and this becomes essential when working with freelance designers and illustrators.

Freelances often feel that they are having to work from insufficient information. It is comparatively rare to have a direct contact to editorial, production, and marketing or publicity departments should pertinent queries arise in the course of design, and in some British companies there appears to a degree of doubt or suspicion as to what a designer is entitled to know. As an example, it is only by knowing the publishing run and price that an experienced designer can discern to what extent a particular monograph is aimed towards a more general public as well as its specialised academic audience. Vital opportunities can be missed if the initial briefing on the editorial background and publishing aspirations for a new project fails to impart a sense of purpose: i.e. that which has to be achieved as distinct from how it is to be done.

A desk editor's *'notes to design'* should accompany the

material supplied to explain such matters as: levels of importance in headings and display; complexities occurring in the text; priorities for the treatment of notes, tables, figures or artwork; and a note of any missing material. In the absence of such a map there is no way of knowing about most of these things, and of giving them all due attention in the preparation of layouts.

Design in publishing is conventionally regarded as those stages which fall between the completion of a manuscript's editing and its delivery to the typesetter, somewhere between when the manuscript has been received and edited and before work starts in earnest on its production; but this is to overlook the visual help design can afford editor and author as an idea evolves and the text is written. Over the past few decades it has become commonplace for certain publications to arise from teamwork of this kind, so that the look of each spread is determined before a word of the final text comes to be written; however, the method does not have to be confined to those publishers who specialise in full colour co-editions, but has applications at all levels of budget and complexity. It is straightforward at any stage to calculate and provide a guide to show how copy and artwork may be prepared by author and editor to fit a given page area or allotted extent, and downright wasteful of time and money to leave the author to flounder unguided.

Designer and production

Design and production share a common task in eliciting the best results from a changing print technology and making the most of affordable ranges of materials – in fact an ability to improvise in the face of change is perhaps the factor which most unites practitioners in these two areas. Working methods and procedures have to be invented or adapted, and similar problems are tackled very differently from the way they would have been a few years or even months ago. Nothing, it seems, stays on the menu for long.

The freelance designer has to stay independently informed about available systems and materials, and to check the acceptability of recommendations and specifications with the client's in-house production team; whereas in-house design may be better placed to participate in such matters as

Mackintosh: **Poetic Worlds**

Notes for design

M Royal 8vo, approx. 80,000 words. Allow for typesetting in Linotron 202 by ABC Typesetters or Typos Ltd (you should have typeface lists for both). Printed on 80 gsm Standard Bookwove by John Smith Ltd (you hold samples). Casebound in Linson, blocked spine only, 2-colour jacket with photo supplied, laminated.

General:

This is a collection of 10 essays on twentieth-century poetry by different authors, with a Preface and Introduction by the editor. Most of the essays are very lively and there should be some general sales as well as to academics and libraries. We expect to have an American co-edition, but this is not yet finalised. So it needs to look inviting rather than heavy, with an eye-catching jacket - photo supplied herewith, but if you think a typographic approach would be better, please feel free to do a rough on those lines.

Specifics:

Contents: standard prelims, Preface, Introduction, 10 essays with notes (to appear at ends of chapters for offprint purposes; NB chapters must therefore start recto); select bibliography; allow 8pp for index.

Headings: A and B heads in most essays (it would be nice to emphasise the A heads to give the book a bit of shape).

Quotations: lots of extended quotations, both poetry and prose, marked in MS with blue vertical line.

Notes: mostly just finding notes, could perhaps go double column to save space?

Illustrations: no line, 8pp photo section with 12 subjects, all b/w. Captions attached. Quality is a bit variable, but this does need to look attractive - it's probably the first thing readers will look at! We could print on a matt art if you think it's preferable - please advise. No particular preference for position, designer please specify.

Many thanks.

SCM
9.5.89

A typical written briefing to accompany an MS for specification, detailing what the designer needs to know from editorial and production.

evaluating new suppliers and sources, and in fine-tuning the balance between product quality and cover price. These are central and ongoing issues for any company, and the key to imprint recognition.

If the Henry Ford syndrome – 'any colour provided it's black' – which begins with the manufacturer who supplies to printer and binder, who in turn rationalise their stock ranges on offer to the publisher, should be reinforced by the production department, then scant choice will remain by the time the book designer becomes involved. This can and does happen, but all the best production directors are prepared to follow up reasonable specifications for cost-equivalent alternatives made by their designers. Agreed that this cannot happen all the time, but there will always be the exceptional book which creates its own special requirements.

There is another way in which design and production together may influence standards, and that is by concentrating on one specific aspect of the book at a time. A typical weakness might be diagnosed as, say, case binding: every aspect might be reviewed and each title receive extra attention for a period, in order to innovate and make demands of suppliers and materials where appropriate, and to improve on the same minimal and dull formula that serves most British publishers at present. Attention is then transferred to another feature of design and manufacture, and as a result of such a policy the imprint will quickly begin to edge away from the crowd in these respects, and the books to be noticed for these qualities.

This raises the question of whether or not the public is aware of design at all, to which I believe the answer has to be both yes and no, but in precise circumstances which it is the designer's business to control. It is the purpose of this outline of book design to enlarge upon this reply, which may be summarised for the moment by contrasting the decision to purchase – where we have to assume a degree of visual judgement in weighing up a physical object as appropriate to its purpose and value for money – with the act of reading, in which the page design is there as an envelope for the author's message and nothing more.

2 THE TEXT PAGES

Many typewriter users must have set the margin tabs on a new machine for an A4 sheet and rarely found any later need to alter them: whereas word processing brings page layout and margin schemes under frequent scrutiny in relation to the page size to be output. When interfacing with phototypesetting, a working knowledge of the point system will prove invaluable. Even where documents are produced for desktop reproduction in a few tens or hundreds of copies, higher quality layout than ever before is expected, and printing standards should be matched in such matters as correct line lengths and spacing between words and lines.

It is recommended that dot matrix and daisywheel output should only be set 'squared up' or justified in exceptional circumstances. This extends to the typing of authors' manuscripts – the uneven spacing produced by justification makes the reading and editorial stages unnecessarily tedious and bedevils casting-off or calculating an extent. The philosophy of the typewriter from its invention onwards has never received the study it merits: it addresses the problem of the mechanisation of writing in a way which is not synonymous with typography. A product that is preferable in so many respects to the vagaries of individual handwriting is somehow taken for granted in everyday conditions of use, so that it becomes difficult to highlight its radical difference in nature from print – we read it effectively and so are inclined to equate it with print. At a time when the gap is actually narrowing, and the interfacing can at times look almost seamless, it is well to make an essential distinction which is likely to affect the development of DTP for a while to come.

Typewriting has a texture and evenness of rhythm which makes a naturally ragged and asymmetrical shape on the page, and which leads the designer to argue that this should be respected and point out that the typewriter is at its worst when it tries to emulate the right hand edge alignment which true typography was devised to attain. So one practice for

Virtually all the books in the Library are recorded in either the card catalogue or the microfiche catalogue. The main exceptions are the publications of the British Government and International Organizations. If you require any of these governmental publications go directly to the Official Publications section on the second floor, where staff are available to help you.

'Rivers' of white which result from gappy and uneven word spacing.

setting straight text in fairly standard measures – unjustified on the typewriter unless there are the strongest reasons to the contrary – may appear at first sight to contradict the earlier recommendation to justify in similar circumstances with any full phototypesetting system, but the case for it is a strong one.

Since most computer software functions quite well in the absence of the typographic point system, it may be felt that undue prominence is given to it here; but it is difficult to have any sustained contact with print or publishing without coming across routine skills based upon it, which, like wiring a plug or riding a bicycle, come to be regarded with exaggerated awe or suspicion by those who have never mastered them. Advanced typography and scientific copyfitting are unthinkable without the theoretical basis supplied by the point system, but this system also yields insights into instinctive and everyday procedures, which may be developed and extended with the help of a few simple tips and formulae.

2:1 Selecting a format

There are many points of view that are entitled to a hearing in the matter of deciding what shape and size to make a book, and it does frequently merit research and debate since a wrong choice can lead to the remainder shelves for a title which may be excellent in other respects. This was borne out several years ago in my experience when one publisher absolutely insisted on using demy 8vo (216 × 138mm) for an otherwise unsinkable combination of royalty, horses and award winning photography. The remainder shop is just the place to learn from the mistakes of others, notably in the ill-advised choice of title, format and jacket design. A better starting point is to look at what the opposition are doing at full price; in most categories there are usually several titles currently in contention for the market, and the key to success is usually to outflank them with better value for money, and never to imitate an apparently successful formula.

The next guide is the nature of the material and the treatment it suggests – the additional width of a quarto format for pictorial volumes, or less than the standard page width for a poet who uses a short metre. Decisions about the format are rarely made in isolation from those affecting the choice and usage of the typeface, or without their contributing vitally to the overall plan which is emerging for the book.

The attitude towards the use of standard paper sizes in publishers' production departments follows the ruling orthodoxy; at times the industry inclines towards restricted sizes and at others it seems that anything goes and no two books share an identical format. It is a province where production has the final say, since paper supplies and printing and binding facilities need to be located and booked in advance, and the designer has to learn to accept compromise on occasion; although in working for a smaller house or in freelance practice all the facts and figures need to be at hand in the form of the latest edition of *The Print and Production Manual*, so that no design proceeds before the feasibility of the format has been investigated, and this is particularly advisable for non-standard formats.

AO paper sizes are taught fairly exclusively on some design courses, but in my view they are only really applicable to bookwork in specific areas, such as architecture or engineering, where the decision has already been taken to adopt international sizes for all types of publication. In Germany, where there has been greater pressure to impose the DIN standard on publishing, it is not liked by many book designers who envy the British and Americans their traditional paper sizes: the AO page rectangle is uniformly boring and the elegant and practical range of effects that can be derived from alternating the quarto and octavo folds has been eliminated.

Page size has clear implications for the number of pages and the thickness and weight of the resultant volume, and the designer has to handle this equation sensitively wherever an author has turned in a manuscript that is under length for its genre, or has supplied so much material that there is danger of the work running to more than a single volume; situations in which a good understanding of paper and of the various cast-off methods will come to the rescue. Many books are produced which are simply too heavy to handle comfortably whilst reading, and international comparisons are revealing here – books from Switzerland and Japan in particular having an admirable preference for lighter weights in relation to format.

Sometimes a strong case can be made out for a square, landscape, or irregular shape, but unless there is a tradition so that the prejudice of booksellers and librarians has been eroded and there are facilities for housing and display – as would be the case for younger children's books – then such a decision should be approached cautiously. Again beware of letting an isolated element force an uncomfortable decision on the balance of the content; everyone knows that features such as fold-outs are very expensive, but not as expensive as a landscape book which does not sell. The designer learns to interpret and to value the feedback from the front line which the good representative can supply; it is the only market research base we have.

2:2 How reading works

Few adults are able to explain *how* they actually read. The child learns to recognise letters, words, phrases, sentences and books (and not necessarily in that order), but the mechanics of the process recede into the unconscious as the act of reading becomes more fluent; until the more literate and widely read a person has become, the less he or she will be able to describe what takes place in the course of reading or to remember anything of significance about the appearance of a typeface or page of text.

This situation has the widest implications for book designers and others involved in effecting printed communication between author and reader – for coming newly to the job they are likely to find themselves just as much in the dark as the man in the street – and so it may be found helpful to try to reconstruct the steps by which reading skills were first acquired, and to start to observe and investigate your own active reading habits, with the object of acquiring a sounder basis for taking typographic and layout decisions to meet specific requirements at various ages and reading levels. This has to be approached through memory and personal observation rather than applied theory, since the available literature largely fails to address the problem from our angle of interest, and departments of ophthalmology report that research has shifted reasonably enough to the newer problem of type legibility on VDU screens as opposed to the printed page. In practice this subjective study of reading habits which is proposed entails grasping how the eye uses the text page, in order to be able to make text pages that are fit for the eye.

All printed messages have to be sent in a code, and the design task is to encode and transmit in order that the reader may decode and digest in the way intended. The alphabet as a code is not something which should be taken for granted. Consider the various ends to which it can be put, frequently in combination with other means of graphic communication including pictures, colours, tactile values, and the whole battery of techniques for persuasion so consciously exploited in the advertising world. It is particularly useful to regard things in this light where, for instance, a book jacket is being designed, and a whole complex of associations relating to a unique product has to be got across.

Before looking at how the eye tracks the page, it may be useful to differentiate between three of the most common modes in which visual signals are received and interpreted. First, type may be used to store the equivalent of 'frozen' speech – this is exemplified by an actor learning a role – where sound rhythms and phrasings are re-activated, alternatively by reading out loud or by 'hearing' them in the mind. Second, type is a vehicle for pure, intellectual meaning – where the reader is put into undistracted contact with another's mind for long periods at a time – during which the typographic means become transparent or invisible. Third, the type on the page is perceived as a shape that is tracked according to a visual pattern which is independent of its semantic content – that is to say the reader is trapped in a mechanical reading loop, following the lines automatically but assimilating little or no meaning – this state can be induced by the author, tiredness, or, most commonly, through bad typography.

These three phases alternate one with the other in prolonged reading, resembling the changes in position and levels of consciousness to be observed in sleep. The third phase in particular should act as a prompt to the professional, when laying any book aside, to question whether this is done because incompetent typography is blocking concentration. The difference between good and bad typography is to be measured in terms of such vital factors as the comparative time taken to read a book (if it is completed at all); the degree of pleasure and profit derived; and considerations no less serious than care for the eyes. It is no exaggeration to claim that a page where type size and arrangement have been well judged can knock an hour or two off the time taken to get through a book and improve the quality of reading – I have never lost confidence in the idea that reading is only a relatively effective technique, and that typography has a great and inevitable bearing on the percentage of the author's message that is successfully conveyed; therefore if the activity of designing books has any significance it is for this reason alone.

In various ways, I have conducted tests over the years in which subjects were asked to attempt to indicate or even to mark with a pencil their reading-line through the test passage. An analysis of the results tends to confirm the view already stated that at a conscious level we just don't know or have forgotten, and that people subscribe in the main and without assignable statistical significance to one of the following common sense views: (a) that the eye ploughs straight on through the middle of the printed image, (b) that it travels as a kind of underlining beneath the line that is being read, or (c) that it travels along through the white channel above the line being read in arc-like spans.

The figure shows those hypothetical eye-movements in the course of reading a page of type which most closely accord both with psychometric findings and with those constants that may be deduced from five centuries of Western typographic practice and the earlier history of alphabetic writing. This shows (c) to be closest to the real answer, and the fact that the eye travels above (rather than through or below) the line has implications for letter design as well, which may be

summarized by stating that the recognition characteristics of a typeface are concentrated in the upper part of the x-height: proof of this is observable in that the upper half of a line can

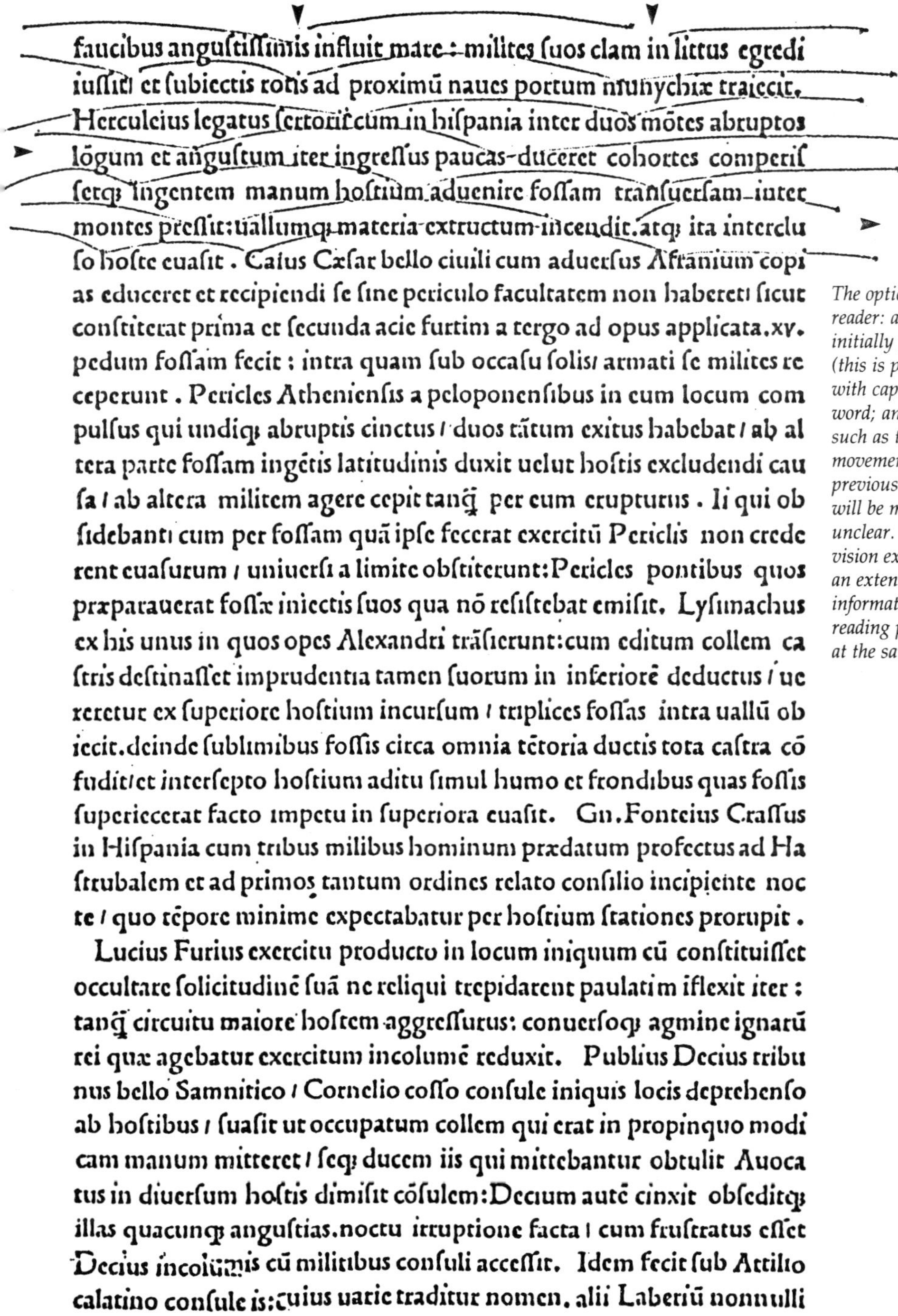
faucibus anguſtiſſimis influit mare: milites ſuos clam in littus egredi
iuſſit: et ſubiectis rotis ad proximũ naues portum munychiæ traiecit.
Herculeius legatus ſertorii: cum in hiſpania inter duos mõtes abruptos
lõgum et anguſtum iter ingreſſus paucas duceret cohortes comperiſ
ſetq; ingentem manum hoſtium aduenire foſſam tranſuerſam inter
montes preſſit: uallumq; materia extructum incendit. atq; ita interclu
ſo hoſte euaſit. Caius Cæſar bello ciuili cum aduerſus Afranium copi
as educeret et recipiendi ſe ſine periculo facultatem non haberet: ſicut
conſtiterat prima et ſecunda acie furtim a tergo ad opus applicata. xv.
pedum foſſam fecit: intra quam ſub occaſu ſolis/ armati ſe milites re
ceperunt. Pericles Athenienſis a peloponenſibus in eum locum com
pulſus qui undiq; abruptis cinctus/ duos tãtum exitus habebat/ ab al
tera parte foſſam ingẽtis latitudinis duxit uelut hoſtis excludendi cau
ſa/ ab altera militem agere cepit tanq̃ per eum erupturus. Ii qui ob
ſidebant: cum per foſſam quã ipſe fecerat exercitũ Periclis non crede
rent euaſurum/ uniuerſi a limite obſtiterunt: Pericles pontibus quos
præparauerat foſſæ iniectis ſuos qua nõ reſiſtebat emiſit. Lyſimachus
ex his unus in quos opes Alexandri trãſierunt: cum editum collem ca
ſtris deſtinaſſet imprudentia tamen ſuorum in inferiorẽ deductus/ ue
reretur ex ſuperiore hoſtium incurſum/ triplices foſſas intra uallũ ob
iecit. deinde ſublimibus foſſis circa omnia tẽtoria ductis tota caſtra cõ
fudit/ et interſepto hoſtium aditu ſimul humo et frondibus quas foſſis
ſuperiecerat facto impetu in ſuperiora euaſit. Gn. Fonteius Craſſus
in Hiſpania cum tribus milibus hominum prædatum profectus ad Ha
ſtrubalem et ad primos tantum ordines relato conſilio incipiente noc
te/ quo tẽpore minime expectabatur per hoſtium ſtationes prorupit.
Lucius Furius exercitu producto in locum iniquum cũ conſtituiſſet
occultare ſolicitudinẽ ſuã ne reliqui trepidarent paulatim iflexit iter:
tanq̃ circuitu maiore hoſtem aggreſſurus: conuerſoq; agmine ignarũ
rei quæ agebatur exercitum incolumẽ reduxit. Publius Decius tribu
nus bello Samnitico/ Cornelio coſſo conſule iniquis locis deprehenſo
ab hoſtibus/ ſuaſit ut occupatum collem qui erat in propinquo modi
cam manum mitteret/ ſeq; ducem iis qui mittebantur obtulit. Auoca
tus in diuerſum hoſtis dimiſit cõſulem: Decium autẽ cinxit obſeditq;
illas quacunq; anguſtias. noctu irruptione facta/ cum fruſtratus eſſet
Decius incolumis cũ militibus conſuli acceſſit. Idem fecit ſub Attilio
calatino conſule is: cuius uarie traditur nomen. alii Laberiũ nonnulli

The optical span of an experienced reader: a child learning to read will initially progress from letter to letter (this is particularly observable in tests with capitals); and thence from word to word; and eventually to word groups such as those indicated. Regressive eye movements from one fixation point to previous ones occur in any case, but will be more frequent where the sense is unclear. It is held that the vertical field of vision expands with the horizontal one to an extent that admits certain peripheral information about the structure of the reading passage from two or more lines at the same time.

still be made out easily when the lower part is covered up, but not conversely.

Gutenberg and other early printers must have taken their priorities from an analysis of the best features of the manuscripts which they were setting out to rival and supplant: to Gutenberg this meant close and *fixed* word spacing among other things. He went to extraordinary lengths actually to achieve this ideal for entire pages at a time, coming close to it throughout his 42-line Bible, and this he did by having a fount of no fewer than 290 characters so that word lengths could be adjusted rather than the spaces between the words. It would seem reasonably certain that a typeface and software could soon be devised to work in this way again: contractions would not be readily accepted, but variant set versions of many characters might well be, as they were in Gutenberg's day.

Eye movements focus attention on the importance of interlinear white space for continuous reading. The 'saccadic span' (the ophthalmologists' term for it) is in fact a double span separated by a micro-second, the first demarking, and the second absorbing, material. A fluent reading rhythm of two and a bit spans is found to be consonant with an ideal average line length of 10 to 12 words; in unusual formats as few as 7 or as many as 15 justified words a line may be averaged on the single column page, given skill and a good reason for doing so.

Looking at the desirability of close and even word spacing together with the need for adequate interlinear space, it quickly becomes clear that the eye will take the line of least resistance and follow the broader channel of white. Wherever the space between words exceeds the space between lines then there is a 'rivers' situation – in which the eye will wander off down the page following the pattern of wide, white gaps between words. This is one of the more commonplace faults and everyone will recall it having happened, but it is becoming less frequent now that typesetting software has tightened up spacing parameters and produced better hyphenation programmes. More than two successive hyphens at line endings can also halt the reader; this too is a universally-remembered experience, which can occur equally where words are broken incorrectly. Word breaks are normally avoided in ragged or centred setting, and care should be taken not to allow any feature of a programme to operate which will change the fit or letter spacing of characters or condense them within the line; this is bad practice and many readers spot that something is amiss even though they cannot put a name to it.

Many other aspects of page design can interfere with the process of reading fluently, and these are of a kind which it is difficult to spot where the native language is exerting a reading pull – it is always fascinating to see typefaces set in unfamiliar languages because in that way the page is being regarded purely for its abstract qualities of shape and texture; but this knack of distancing the content to appreciate the form in order to criticise or check decisions is soon acquired and often useful. Capitals, for instance, can appear large in relation to the lower case so that they give the page a spotted appearance where the incidence is higher than average, and some characters have peculiarities of design which draw attention to themselves.

An em of the text size is fairly standard for indentation, but more can be used where the measure is wide and the leading generous. Paragraphs should indent in ragged setting as otherwise they can disappear altogether. The opening paragraph after a heading should be full out so that there is not an awkward bite out of the top left corner of the text panel. Similar spacing situations can be caused through the interposition of artwork or other matter at set points in the text, and these will always call for individual consideration.

Lines of space should not be used as an alternative to proper indentation since this chops the text into discontinuous blocks. Many authors call for breaks in the text signified by nothing more than a line of white followed by a full out paragraph, and these can go missing in effect where they fall at the foot of the page, whereas any sign or ornament placed in the break can be intrusive – it is only possible to take extra care in this situation and perhaps to advise numbering if there is a structural call for it.

Widows, where the final line of a paragraph falls at the head of the page, are unsightly and good page make-up entails their elimination; on the other hand club lines (where the opening line of a new paragraph falls at the foot) have never troubled me greatly. Where folios are centred at the foot and the last page of a chapter falls well short, there can be a case for dispensing with the folio provided there is no index. Word breaks should be avoided as far as possible at page turnovers since concentration is apt to be thrown; in earlier centuries a catchword (the first word of the following page) was often printed at the foot – a civilised custom.

2:3 Typographic measurement

It is regrettable that several systems of measurement have to co-exist within the graphics industries in response to variations in training from one time, place or industry to another. There can only be a gain in precision and ease of working as millimetres come to replace inches for all paper and format measurements, but in England and America progress must remain slow whilst there remains an influential sector for whom – whether through age or attitude – the imperial system is still the mother tongue (as is apparent from the wide provision that has been made for it within computer stationery and software).

In theory the metric system should provide a universal answer to all typographic measurement, but when it comes to replacing by metrication the point systems that were devised to cope with these specific problems (the Anglo-American point system and the Didot system in Europe), there are a number of practical shortcomings which add up to a case – which will be presented stage by stage – for the rational retention of point and pica for certain purposes. At first sight it may seem odd to recommend to publishers that they should acquire a working knowledge of a measurement system that is related to an obsolete technology – and it has to be admitted that, even whilst it flourished, only a handful of people for whom it was not essential could be troubled with it – but now that so many editors are working hands-on with text origination, it has become a vital key in communicating about the nature of technological change both at a theoretical and at a practical level.

Pica and line length

The point system was invented by Pierre Simon Fournier in 1737 as a means of bringing order to a situation in which "there were almost as many diversities of size as there were printing houses", and the revision adopted by American typefounders in 1871, in which the typographic point was set at 0.013833 inches (or approximately 72 to the inch), was adopted in England in 1898. An earlier advance in parallel to the Anglo-American system had been made by François Ambroise Didot, and this still serves as the continental European point system; but it would be academic to enlarge upon it here since the only credible proposals for the unification of typographic measurement rest on a metric basis.

The 12pt multiple, of which there are roughly 6 to the inch, is called pica and acts as a kind of common denominator, notably where types of different point sizes are to be set to the same line length or measure. The 12pt calibrations can be used for specifying column widths, and a suitable plastic typescale can be obtained through a typesetter or an artist's materials shop.

It rapidly becomes familiar that a common measure in standard paperback format, for instance, will be about 20 picas and for a demy 8vo novel some 24 picas, give or take a pica or half that amount. Printers also call picas ems, but as ems come in all sizes, speak always of pica ems and you will be understood to mean precisely 12 typographic points: half this measurement is the 6pt or pica en. In the incredibly rich private language of the trade, British compositors shouted for 'muttons' when they wanted ems, and 'nuts' when ens would do. So all measures or line lengths should be specified in pica ems, for example: 'set justified to 24 picas', or 'set ragged right to maximum 16½ picas', or 'set centred line for line to 12 picas', etc.

Such specifications are straightforward to work out and yet they accomplish a great deal: it is true also that typesetters will accept these instructions in either pica, inches or millimetres, but remember that these systems of measurement do not convert without strings of decimals, and that there is imprecision in shifting between one and another: to throw out the point system at this juncture might cause a reversion to some of the chaos and anarchy it was brought into being to abolish.

Point size and type size

Printing from a flat lithographic surface eliminates one of the dimensions of printing from moveable metal types: that which is known as the 'height to paper' of a relief printing

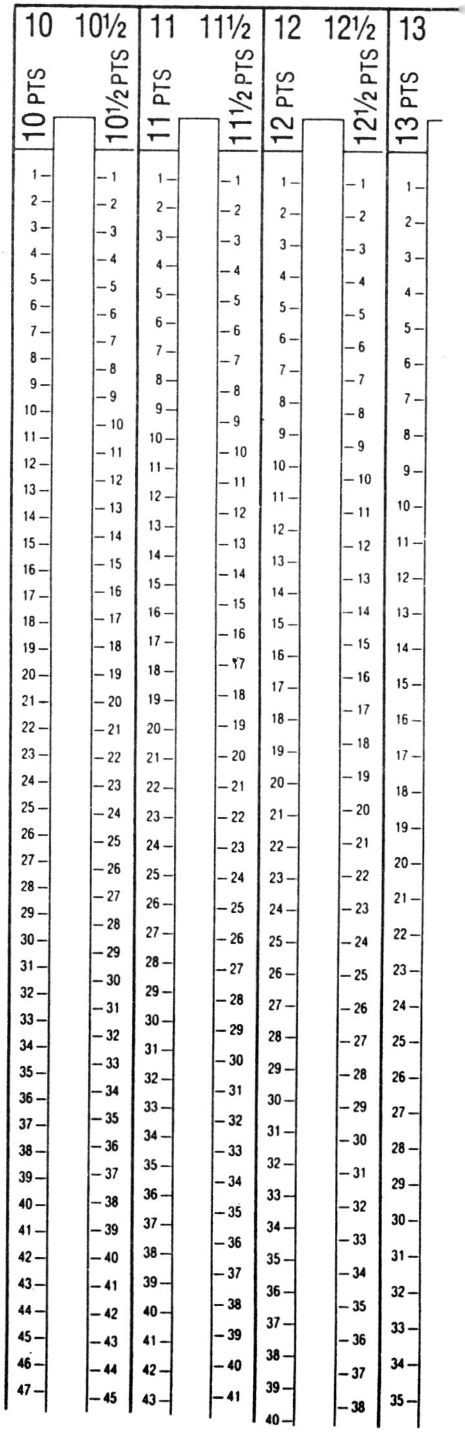

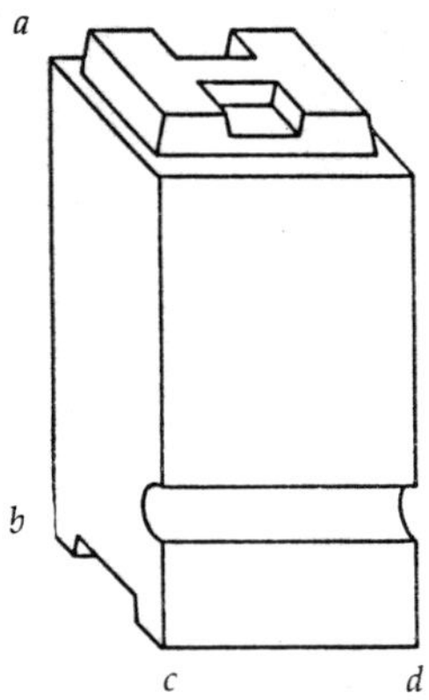

a–b height to paper

b–c height or body size of type

c–d set width

surface; the standard overall height of 0.918 inches from base to printing surface of letterpress types and printing plates. Each printing type was cast on the upper surface of a rectangular metal cube or 'body', and the size of this body is given in points: this is a measure of the body on which the letter is placed from top to bottom as distinct from the width of the character from left to right, which is called the 'set'. The set is a variable, enabling widths to be assigned to letters individually and in combination in word building, whereas height to paper and body size are both fixed dimensions in their original relation to metal printing types and their successors.

Point sizes denote the exact dimension of the body itself on which type designs are regularly placed – hence 8pt, 10pt, 12pt type and so forth – but this tells us absolutely nothing about the measurable size and appearance of the individual design which is to be accommodated on a particular body, and this in turn leads right to the heart of the dilemma which divides typographers world-wide into two opposed camps at present.

One group would have it that phototypesetting has done away with two of the three physical dimensions of the metal cube – namely height to paper and body size – and has seriously tampered with the third by making it more variable still through the facility to alter the fit of letters in combination and even to distort their basic characteristics digitally. From this it is argued that the body size has to be abandoned since it has become fictive or notional – a hypothesis which has to be supplanted by a concrete measurement that anyone can take from the printed page at any stage. The standard commonly advocated is the millimetric height of the capital 'H'.

This is persuasive, but I firmly share the opposed view that we should persevere with the notional point system (despite the risk that the reasons behind it may become less apparent to each rising generation), on the grounds of lack of sufficient faith in the ability of man or woman the measurer; how many people have the skill or the equipment to measure the printed image to tolerances of 0.1mm or so? Having a stepped series of nominal sizes permits identification by comparison, which is a more widespread ability than measurement.

And if the point system should be abandoned, with it would go the rationalisation into graded sizes that can be distinguished by eye, ease of cast-off and, not least, facility in ensuring continuity and standardisation in series and for reprint corrections. Worst of all may prove to be the co-existence of rival systems leading to the breakdown of all systems. At present most typographers and typesetters find themselves still able to communicate clearly and unambiguously through the merits of the point: the system may be an initial nuisance, but it does work.

To complete the picture it is necessary to mention in passing a third and minor school of thought which would retain the typographic point, but relate it only to what can actually be seen and measured on the printed page. There are several practical objections to this, but I would rest the case for the opposition on the need to avoid running twin systems in parallel for an indefinite period – the British experience in changing over from imperial to metric or from Fahrenheit to Celsius scarcely sets encouraging precedents.

Returning to the question of how the body size in points can help in a practical situation, the first thing that needs to be said is that the only way in which the size of a type can be identified even by the expert for much of the time is by matching it to an authenticated specimen. This detective work has become more exacting as systems have proliferated, and the plea entered in the preceding paragraph is intended only to prevent the further complications which would ensue from having no fixed size nomenclature at all. Where a comparison of characters, or word lengths, suggests that the type size may be an irregular one, then it may be best to ask the original typesetter to check this out rather than trying to formulate a match.

Once a type has been identified as, say, 10pt Palatino operating on the Linotronic 300 – according to the type catalogue, or following the typesetter's imprint on a printed book (and it has been suggested elsewhere that this is as important as that of printer and binder) – then it is possible to go on to establish anything else which needs to be known. If the 11pt calibrations of the typescale correspond line for line with the baseline of the face in question, then it follows that this type must be 10/11pt – i.e. a 10pt type plus 1pt of space or 'leading'. This may also turn up expressed as 10pt, 1pt leaded (archaic but understood); or as 10pt, 11pt line feed or film advance.

The information gained so far enables any text setting to be specified with total precision using the point system:

information to be given	*example of specification*
typesetting system	Linotronic 300
name and version of typeface	Linotype Palatino
point or body size	10pt
line feed [i.e. 1 pt leading]	11pt
justified or ragged?	justified
text measure	24 picas
lines of text per page	43

This specification will result in galley proofs if there are no complexities which should require special styling or layout. However, it is more efficient where possible to set a book straight into page proof, in which case the typesetter will require a margin sheet showing treatment for different levels of heading, position of folio, and any other necessary layouts to cover detail within the text and the setting of prelim and end pages. In the case of a straightforward book this information may be given on a specification form and through copy mark-up, but typesetters infinitely prefer to have a layout as well from which they can see the visual intention. An inaccurate layout is nothing but a pointless and misleading waste of everyone's time: but a good one will guide the typesetter in page assembly, and will result from honesty in making and showing calculations to ensure that the copy will fit the space available and in the specified size. The representational techniques involved to this end do not necessarily call for the skills of a trained designer or lettering artist.

Leading and the point system

As shown above, all typefaces in fact differ in general appearance and disposition within any given point or body size. This size is a relic of the metal body on which a type design would formerly have been accommodated, and it is retained as the best way we have of talking in general about size of type, and as a guide in considering any extra interlinear space a given type design may require to bring about the best conditions for reading.

Just as type can be produced at virtually any size, so leading can now be 'feathered' or adjusted exactly as required. But to avoid the anarchy which will ensue if everyone should go their own way with random enlargements or reductions calibrated according to percentages or in millimetres, some system is infinitely desirable. One involving $^{1}/_{2}$pt increments to type size (thus: 9pt, $9^{1}/_{2}$pt, 10pt) or $^{1}/_{4}$pt steps at the outside, and multiples of $^{1}/_{4}$pt for leading, would prove more than adequate in most conceivable bookwork applications. If this convention were to become established, it would still afford a far more flexible provision that any available in the past. Where measurements are expressed in a uniform manner over a period of time, these units take on meaning and it becomes possible to visualise and compare the effects that will be produced by certain sets of decisions.

The fitting and spacing of letters

The designer of a new typeface has a twofold task: to innovate within the strict discipline of individual letter design and to ensure that these letters will combine pleasingly into words, lines and pages. The preparatory drawings for this are always fascinating to study – freehand pencil or ink sketches lead on to technical drawings on an enlarged scale, and then proofs or photocopies are pasted into words or arranged like scrabble tiles to explore every possible letter combination. This process demands a sustained dialogue with the type manufacturer, who will be responsible for translating the designer's intention, via complex mathematics, into photographic or digital founts.

Whereas the disposition of the height of capitals, lower case and extenders on the fixed body for each point size is relatively straightforward, it is more tricky to determine the optimum set width for each individual character: i.e. the width of the printed image plus a little space to left and right to avoid touching and to fit correctly against others in word building. Once this had been accomplished in the case of a metal typeface, the lower case was fixed and immutable in this respect, but the capitals and small capitals were always expected to have a degree of extra letter spacing inserted in order to correct the inescapable unevennesses presented by the copy.

This concept of the predetermined fitting of the lower case, which was almost invariably well adapted – to continuous reading in the case of a book typeface, and in accordance with style and fashion for display – is of considerable historical and topical interest as it provides a record of the designer's true intent expressed as precisely as possible within the constraints of typefounding. Palatino, one of the most widely used of today's book faces, had its origin (1949–50) as a metal face, and the fitting should be regarded as an integral part of the design, in that rhythms and proportional relationships may be created between the partially enclosed parts of individual letters and the spaces between them. This is perhaps more immediately apparent in the schematic example, which draws on sanserif typefaces:

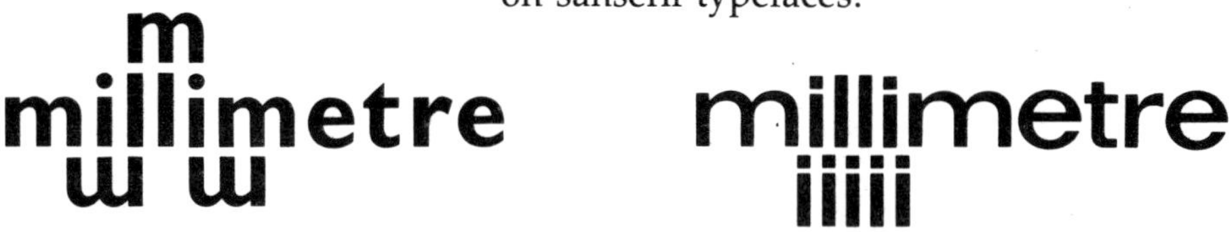

Space between letters may be made to echo both the width of the stem and that of the partly-enclosed areas of the letter design, as in Gill Bold (above). A different spacing rhythm is set up by contrasting the open counters of Folio (right) with close letter spacing to produce a 'ribbon' effect.

It is interesting to examine the fit of lower case in books of any period printed by letterpress, as certain constants emerge about the way in which types of different stylistic categories were destined for use by their makers. This situation was to change radically from the 1960s onwards as it was discovered that in computerised phototypesetting the spacing between letters could be closed up or opened out by degrees with no problem, and that the user was free to specify the set according to personal taste.

Fashion thrives on the ability to make things look different for the sake of it, and advertising typographers began to tighten spacing progressively, often sacrificing legibility to obtain a textural quality which looked impressive in the abstract and when set off against photographs. Book designers could not remain entirely uninfluenced and in several quarters this practice was allowed to become, quite literally, a headache for the reader. The anticipated pendulum swing can be traced back to a vogue, revived from the 1920s, for letterspacing capitals excessively – by as much as several times their individual widths – which also became a book jacket cliché for a while. From thereon it was clear that lower case would not escape similar attention for long, and the first examples of plus compensation text setting soon began to appear. The letter spacing of lower case is a disastrous practice, and must be allowed to advance no further into a book than its jacket at worst.

endangered tropical hardwoods in our furniture. In this way, we hope we can help the thousands of native people and wild species whose very existence is dependent upon the survival of the rainforest.

Kerning only

Yet there are also strong arguments

Kerning & letterspacing track 1

Yet there are also strong arguments

Kerning & letterspacing track 2

Yet there are also strong arguments

Kerning & letterspacing track 3

Yet there are also strong arguments

Increments of minus letterspacing compensation available on the Compugraphic system.

These trends – and the tendency to tighter fitting now has a good twenty years' history behind it – are naturally reflected in the concurrent adaptation of type production to the various composition systems, and so it is necessary to consult the associated specimen sheets each time before making a specification. Look critically at what has been nominated as standard fitting, and at the increments of plus and minus compensation to letter spacing and fit. It should rarely be necessary to depart from standard, except in special circumstances – and there is one curious exception: the labelling of artwork and maps for reduction to small sizes, where a fair degree of additional spacing to lower case in sanserif can improve clarity and legibility considerably. Kerning is a term which has shifted in meaning alongside changing technology and now refers to closer fitting in general as well as to the parts of a letter (such as the extremities of the italic '*f*') which can overhang the body of adjacent letters. Some systems have so-called aesthetics programmes which afford a number of optical refinements in recurrent spacing situations.

Many type specimens show only the minus increments to the letter spacing of capitals, whereas it is just the reverse which is needed. The lower case evolved through continuous writing, and its separate letter shapes became adapted to combine well in word building; whereas capitals sprang from formal inscriptional lettering, and from Roman times onwards have required careful letter spacing wherever they are to appear to advantage.

Letter spacing is achieved optically in dry transfer and photosetting, and often on a trial and error basis, except in stonecutting and wood engraving where the errors cannot be rectified. The practised eye can refine the differential spacing between letter combinations until the flow of space is perfectly even and harmonious (in the past pieces of paper and card as well as metal spaces were inserted between the types by craftsman compositors to achieve this), and optical letter spacing will always remain the standard on a title page and for a few key lines in display.

MILTON

M I L T O N

Samples Letraset in Garamond.

Mechanical letter spacing is available in the requisite increments of additional fixed space through the line at the press of a button, and this facility should invariably be used in bookwork: i.e. all capitals and small caps however large or small should take the same degree of letter spacing throughout the book. As a general rule, it is hard to improve on some 3 units for capitals and 2 units for small caps (of 18 units of set, or equivalent, as explained below). It is wrong, for example, to space out the titling on a title page and to leave the imprint in a smaller size of the same capitals, but unspaced, at the foot: the legend persists from times past, when it was a painstaking manual operation, that letter spacing is an additional expense and should somehow be used sparingly, but this is not the case and there needs to be a compelling reason to dispense with it.

There is another way in which good letter spacing benefits the look of the text page, and that is in the matter of tonal colour. Capitals are both larger and weightier than the lower case, and when they appear *en masse* they create an unsightly area which draws the eye, and this is why small caps are used in preference wherever feasible. Small caps themselves, whether appearing on a running headline or in the text, make a dense and closely-fitted pattern when set solid, but with 2-unit spacing they match the colour of the text perfectly: spacing in excess of this begins to lighten and weaken the even texture of the page.

Set on the Monotype 18-unit system; but similar specimens from current systems enable fixed letter and word spacing to be specified to individual taste with precision.

Small Capitals

1-unit letter-spaced

7-UNIT WORD SPACED
8-UNIT WORD SPACED
9-UNIT WORD SPACED

2-unit letter-spaced

8-UNIT WORD SPACED
9-UNIT WORD SPACED
10-UNIT WORD SPACED

3-unit letter-spaced

9-UNIT WORD SPACED
10-UNIT WORD SPACED
11-UNIT WORD SPACED

I leave the topic of letter spacing with the thought that it is just one of those regions of sound typographic practice where computer software could make higher standards universally available, once demand becomes sufficiently articulated: differential letter spacing between all possible character combinations is programmable.

The space between words

Close and even word spacing has already been mentioned as a desideratum for continuous reading, and the question here is: how close? A rather bizarre introductory experiment is suggested – try whiting out each lower case letter 'i' in a few sample lines of text setting and compare the gaps created with the word spaces which are actually present. If the setting is good there should not be much visible discrepancy, but in any case please try the same with the 'n', and then with the 'm'. My recommended rule of thumb would be that the fixed spacing within each line should fluctuate from line to line between 'i' and 'n', with the 'm' serving as a maximum outside tolerance. This may strike the reader as closer than would have been assumed previously, and if so reference to a specimen of your own handwriting may reveal gaps of up to a word in length; and whereas no necessary correlation between these separate activities is implied, the coincidence often serves to open up the topic so that spacing on the printed page can be studied objectively. Here is another instance where the knack of seeing the negative – that is the page as being a white (paper) image on a black (text) field – proves useful and is readily acquired with a little practice.

(see diagram at the foot of page 110.)

It is possible to make this generalisation about spacing in relation to character width, because spacing is proportional to the design of the typeface: narrowly-set and condensed faces, and some italics, will require relatively smaller gaps between words than those having a generous set width, resulting in a longer a-z length for comparable x-height. This is automatically taken care of on most phototypesetting systems, where the spacing is mathematically proportional to the set or width of the type design.

The parameters of spacing have improved immeasurably with computerised typesetting, and logic has largely supplanted the arbitrary standards of keyboard operators and mechanical systems. On the best systems, the programmes for spacing and word division at line endings are now first-rate, but good typography can only result where the conditions are reasonable: it is simply not possible to satisfy sound spacing requirements in justified setting where the length of line is inadequate for the size of type proposed. When it comes to ragged setting, then it is necessary to specify a fixed spacing value throughout, and this should be the closest sensible space, normally the equivalent of the lower case 'i'.

A trail is being laid down for the reader to follow – or perhaps it would be more accurate and realistic at times to say that white space is the thread which has to be followed in order to find a way out of the maze. The space between and surrounding letters, words, lines, columns and pages, and that which separates headings, text and commentary, is to be compared with the circulation areas of a great public building: it calls for masterly organisation along common-sense lines, in order that the user should never become bewildered or alienated. Excessive or irregular word spacing is a fundamental cause of poor concentration and reading fatigue.

Point size and the unit of set width

The above digression through spacing returns us to the point system and how it relates to the set width. Some of the practical implications for spacing in this dimension have already been discussed, and the further application of set width to copyfitting is considered in chapter four. Each typesetting system has a slightly different way of describing how its system of set measurement operates and so any brief unifying explanation must be theoretical and its practical usefulness limited. Each designer will need to come to terms with systems in regular use through the expert advice of suppliers, and the publications and measurement tables and scales issued by manufacturers, as necessary. In the design of many kinds of books there are few problems in this respect – a working knowledge of typography increases and is constantly updated. The Monotype, Linotype and Compugraphic systems are basically user-friendly; and it is only where the typographer chooses to specify complex matter using the individual terminology of, say, the Scangraphic or Berthold systems, that it is necessary to keep an instruction manual open on the desk.

Let's take the same starting point as for the other typographic dimensions, the individual type design, which presents unique mathematical problems in the course of transfer to the typesetting system. The theoretical basis for the em was that it was the square of the body size, and the pica em used for measurement – the 12pt calibrations on the typescale – as has been shown, is always 12pt in width and 12pt in depth.

The idea was that the em should carry the widest character called for, usually the capital 'M', and then be subdivided as necessary to carry each character width down to the thinnest, such as the comma. At the same time it should be the multiple of spacing, being divided in half to yield the en, and then traditionally into thirds, quarters, fifths and the single point (1pt) to give thick, mid, thin and hair spaces respectively, to be used in spacing and justification. This would be for pica or 12pt type, but as smaller and larger founts came to be produced, exactly the same thing would happen, and each point size would have its own governing em or square of the body size. Thus each character in a fount, and its related spacing material, would stand in direct proportion to all other sizes in the series. A solitary exception was made for the 1pt brass hair space which was left alone simply because it was not practical to produce thinner ones for use with the smaller sizes. Point and cicero (the continental equivalent of the pica type size) were taken by Fournier as the theoretical standard, and so it has remained.

In reality the physical em was rarely a true square, for there was no reason for it to be so, and nothing would go wrong if typefounders were to cheat on occasion and make it a little wider or narrower where the design as a whole, and of the 'M' and 'W' in particular, called for this. The em used for spacing and its derivatives remained standardised since these spaces were supplied in bulk for use with all typeface designs of the same size.

Mechanical composition brought about a need for the rationalisation of set width, and the Monotype Corporation devised a fundamental system along the following lines: first the em was assigned a set width in points, and this width could be slightly more or less than the body size according to the needs of the design to be accommodated. This entailed going down as far as increments of the $^1/_4$pt for adequate finesse, but it anchored the typographic dimension of set width mathematically to the point system, thus placing all kinds of copyfitting calculations on a firm basis, and to facilitate this the set always appeared alongside the body size in specimens, tables and specifications. The expressions 10pt ($9^3/_4$ set) or 10pt ($10^1/_2$ set) denoted the point value of the em in the cases of typefaces where the design tendency was respectively narrow or wide in relation to the body, and the $9^{3}/_{4}$pt or $10^{1}/_{2}$pt part of the typescale accordingly could be used to work in ems of set within the layout, in the precalculation of something as complex even as a railway timetable.

The term 'em of set' must refer always to the em of the type size in question since it is a physical measurement, and if this typesize should happen to be 12pt the need for the distinction that has been made between pica ems and 12pt ems of set becomes apparent – the former being the universal fixed measurement and the latter relating to the particular set of a specific typeface in its 12pt size (which might well be $11^{3}/_{4}$ points, or whatever).

The next stage must be to subdivide this em of set into an adequate number of units or bands to accommodate each and every character in the fount and to provide a range of proportionate spaces. This number of units will need to become the standard to operate the entire system, so that founts are interchangeable in their various sizes and from one typeface to another. Monotype must have thought long and hard about this optimum number, and the magic answer they came up with was, and for a long time remained, 18. Progress along the road that would lead eventually to digitisation led Monotype and other systems manufacturers to change over to an increased number of units to the em (usually and for obvious reasons when launching radically new equipment), in order to bring greater optical refinement and resolution to fount design.

Therefore the many systems on the market today adopt, and sometimes share, one or other of the following popular formats: 18, 36, 48, 54, 96, or 100, units of set to the em. The following table of spacing equivalents is intended as a guide only to optimum letter and word spacing and how this may be best specified:

Units of set	18	36	48	54	96/100
Minimal letter spacing	1	2	2/3	3	5
Letter spacing for small caps	2	4	5	5/6	10
Letter spacing for capitals	3	6	8	9	6
Fixed word spacing (close)	5	10	13/14	15	27
Fixed word spacing (medium)	6	12	16	18	32

The pocket calculator readily converts units or ems of set into pica so that they can be related to the text measure – just as the zoom copier will change a specimen from one point size into another – and such devices have eliminated much of the drudgery that was formerly involved in applying typographic theory to a range of practical problems.

The digital formatting of typefaces

Peter Karow is the authority in this field, and his seminal book *Digital Formats for Typefaces* is essential reading for the serious typographer. Rather than attempt a précis, I would like instead to draw an interesting parallel. The story begins with the deliberations of a commission appointed by the French Académie des Sciences into letter design and the

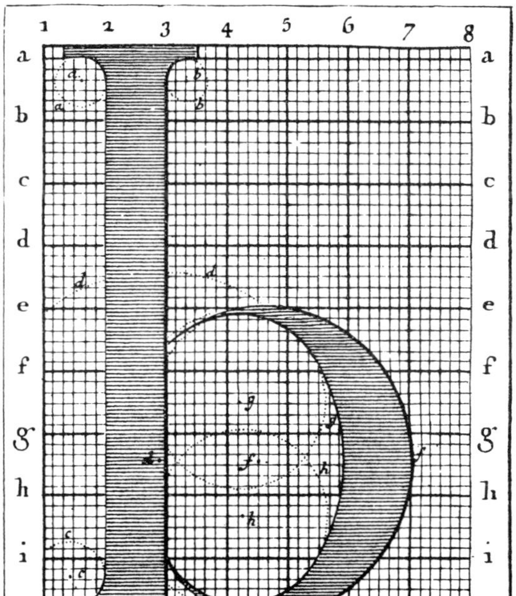

Detail from the plate XXVI for the romain du roi *project, engraved by Rochefort, 1718 or earlier.*

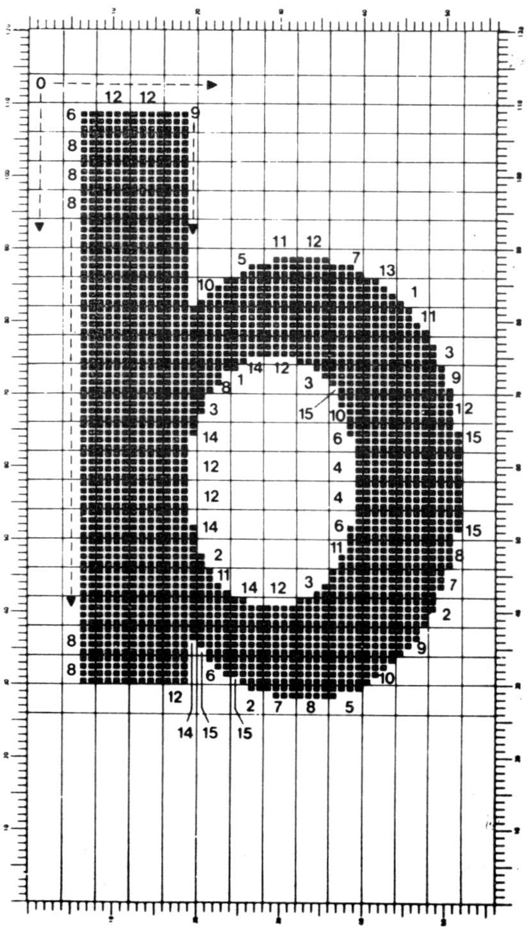

Preparation and calculation of a bytemap at a raster of 25×30 for the em.

plates it issued between 1695 and 1718, which were supposed to have guided the hand of Grandjean as he began to cut the *romain du roi* types, also in the year 1695. The model letters were designed on a grid of 2,304 little squares, and when these plates came to Fournier's attention, much later in the eighteenth century, as a practical typefounder he ridiculed the notion that such a grid – where *the twelfth part of an inch is divided into 204 parts*! (his italics) – could conceivably be taken into account by a punchcutter working to actual type size in steel.

The similarity in approach, spanning the almost three centuries which separate these two diagrams, is astounding. The principal difference is that the version on the right works, and because it works within an established framework there is again no need to take it into further account, other than to welcome the optical quality brought about through the high line-resolution offered by digitisation. It is perhaps inevitable, but nevertheless reassuring, that the raster used in digitisation is firmly linked to the printer's traditional system of measurement; to quote Dr Karow: "We [at UKW] are of the opinion that describing a letter according to its em is the best way of picturing the digitisation of type".

2:4 Margin schemes

There are many ways of looking at margin schemes; at a materialistic level they account for up to 40% of the paper bill, so they must have some function beyond preventing the text area from bleeding off or running into the binding. The value of white space – designers in many fields refer to its 'active' role – is a difficult concept for the layman to grasp. In the design of press advertising, it is evident to the client that he is purchasing an expensive rectangle of space, and commonplace for him to protest about waste and either attempt to cram in too much or to suggest that his copy be set in as large a size as possible in order to fill the whole area. It took a long time for advertising to progress from its Victorian state of development, and to recognise that the intelligent use of white space holds and directs attention within the format.

A forgotten nineteenth-century writer once suggested that margins were there to provide somewhere to put the thumbs whilst reading in order not to obscure the text. The Spanish philosopher, Ortega y Gasset, comes closer in his celebrated essay on the framing of pictures, and it is worth considering the parallel if only to note the universal practice of making the mount or margin deeper at the foot than at the head or sides. This follows from the observable effect that anything placed at the true centre in depth suffers from an apparent gravitational pull below that centre; and so designers speak of the optical centre, that point, often considerably above the mathematical centre, at which things look right. This can be seen in action as it affects book typography: throughout letter design (i.e. it is immediately apparent that the crossbars to 'A','E', 'H', etc. are placed deliberately high); as a major factor in title page design (where a good arrangement may be ruined simply by being positioned too low on the page); and above all in the traditional proportions of margins.

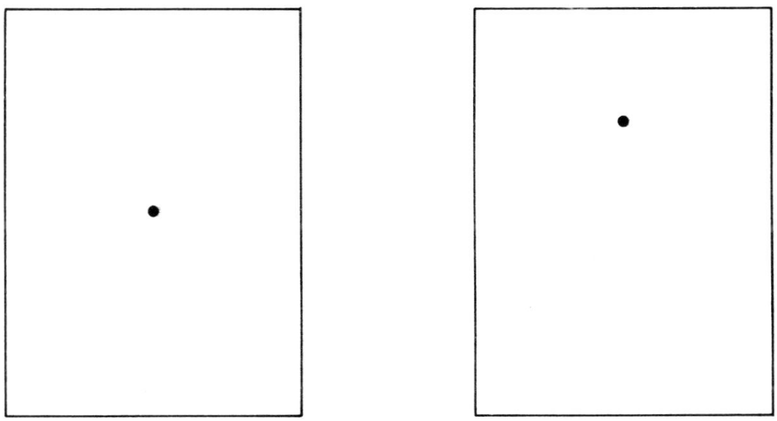

If, as I believe, our eyes and the basic habits of reading have remained unchanged over the centuries, then the historical constants in the layout and arrangement of a page of writing or typesetting represent a tradition in the finest sense. That is to say, we are free either to build new structures on these existing foundations, or alternatively to seek ways in which the classical laws may be successfully inverted or deliberately broken in response to what we see as new requirements. And so it makes sense to take a glance at traditional margin schemes, and then at some of the alternative approaches which have proved their worth.

Margins and grids (grid being a cult word for a slightly

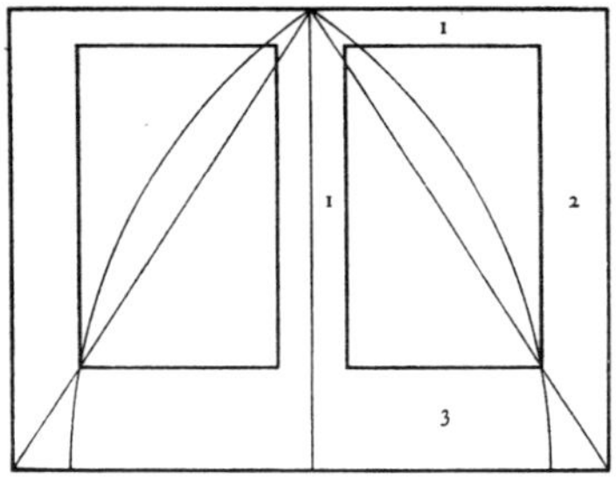

Ideal proportional skeleton of a pair of medieval manuscript pages. Page proportion 2:3. Margin proportions 1:1:2:3. Text proportion in accordance with the golden mean (q.v.). Only the outside lower edge of the written area is determined by a diagonal. (This and the following diagrams provide a glimpse into Jan Tschichold's seminal research of the 1950s.

more detailed margin scheme) are inextricably linked with the history of writing, and recent studies have proved fascinating and rewarding. Briefly, in the tradition of Western manuscripts, lines for writing were scribed blind into the vellum and pricked though at the corners of the writing area so that the lines on the other side of the leaf could be made to back up. The utility and aesthetic effect of the facing pair of pages when the bound book lay open (the double page spread) was the objective of the margin design. Valid systems of mathematical and geometric proportion were consciously used to relate the text area to the page format, a number of which correspond to those used by the early printers. A pair of examples are shown for their harmony and elegance as geometry and as applied design, but unfortunately such proportional canons can hardly ever be used in a pure form today because they tend both to require specific non-standard page formats as a starting point and to yield de luxe margins which are out of place in the modern world.

Type area and page proportion of the Gutenberg Bible, found to conform to Tschichold's rediscovered canon of the division of the diagonal of the single page into ninths. (After Rosarivo.)

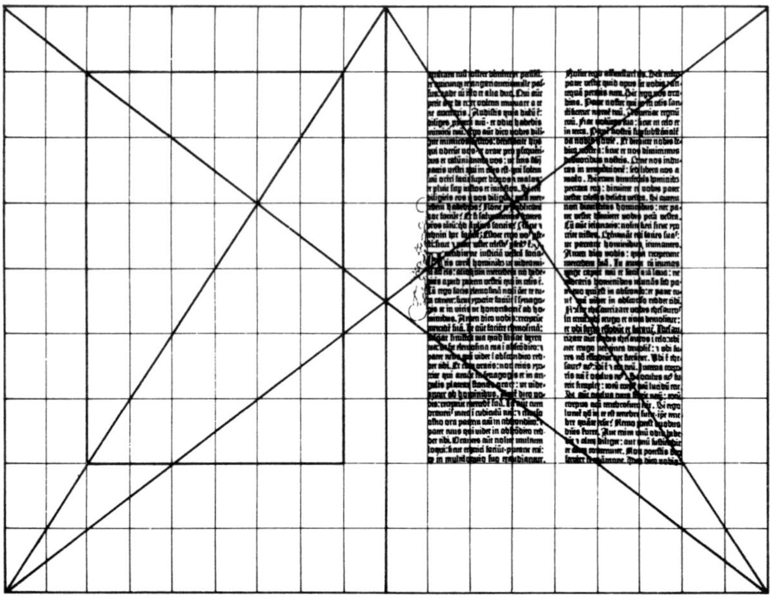

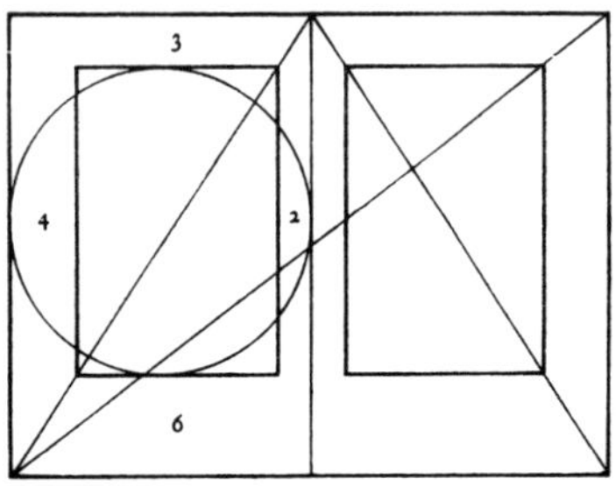

The secret canon, which underlies many late medieval manuscripts and incunabula. Discovered by Tschichold in 1953. Page proportion 2:3. Text and page area of the same proportions. Height of the text area equal to the width of the page. Margin relationships: 2:3:4:6.

What general conclusion may be drawn from these early examples and from the intervening centuries that still remains fundamental to sound book production? Maybe only that starting out from the single page back margin, there should be

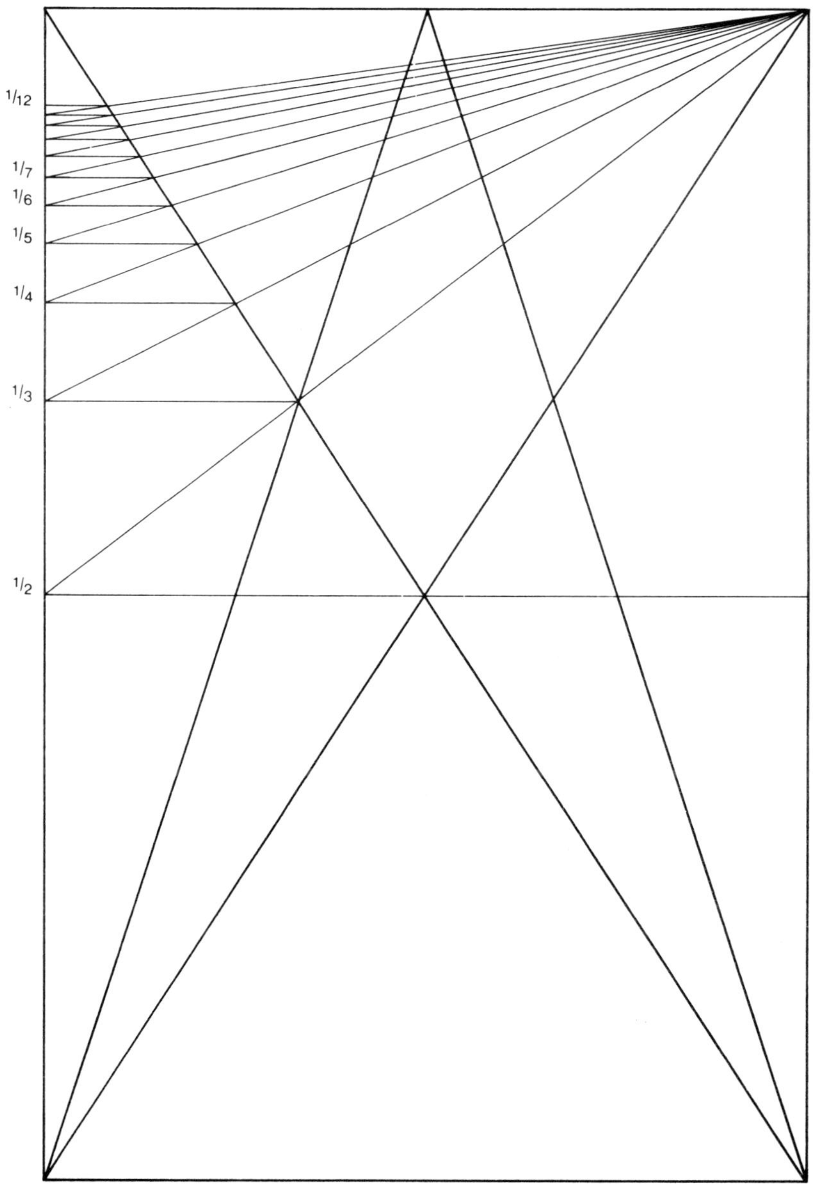

The Villard proportional canon applied to a rectangle of the proportions 2:3. The depth of the page is here divided down to a twelfth.

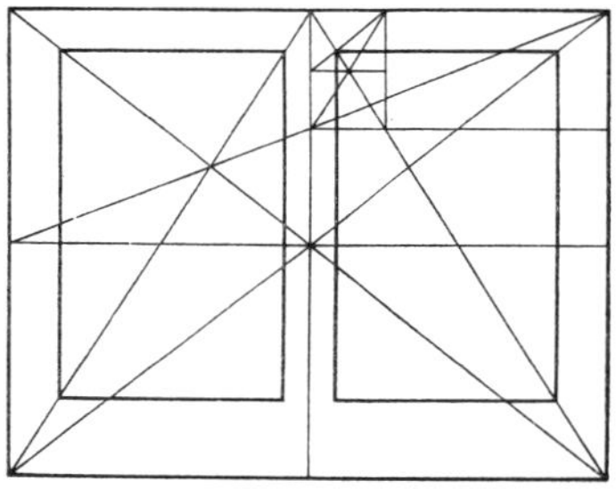

Page proportion 2:3. Paper height and width divided into twelve by means of the Villard canon shown on the left. (The French thirteenth-century architect, Villard de Honnecourt, whose manuscript sketchbook is kept at the Bibliothèque Nationale, records this canon with the aid of which any distance can be divided exactly into any desired number of parts without other measurements.)

slightly more margin at the head, more still at the foredge, and considerably more at the foot. Wherever this is not found to be so, then it can be confidently stated either that the margins are woefully incorrect, or that an 'inverted' scheme has been consciously used by the designer, and it is not hard to spot the difference.

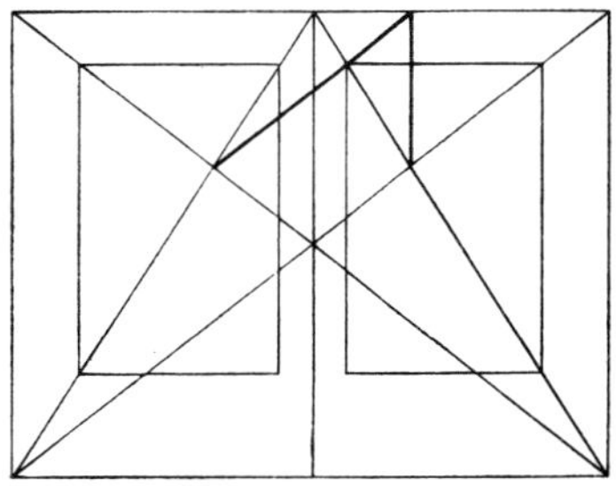

Division into ninths, illustrated on the page proportion 2:3. The simplest road to Tschichold's secret canon. Geometry replaces calculation. (After van der Graaf.)

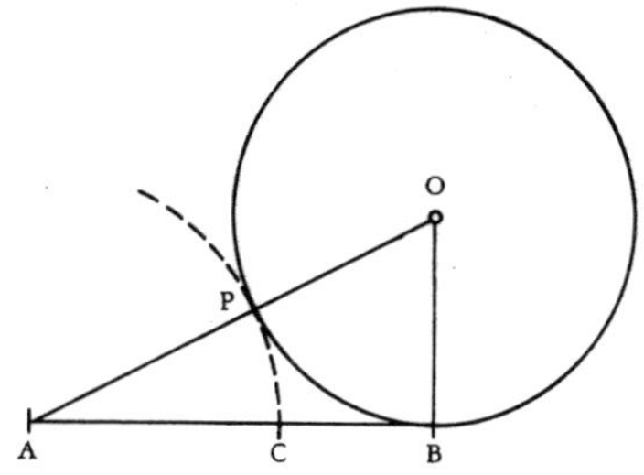

Construction of the golden mean. Construct on AB at B the vertical BO=$^1/_2$AB. Taking OB as radius describe a circle at O, and find the point P between A and O at which the straight line AO intersects this circle. Draw an arc of radius AP to intersect the line AB at point C, which divides AB at the golden mean. If the page depth is to be AB, then AC will be the width. If AB is to be the width then AB+AC will be the page depth.

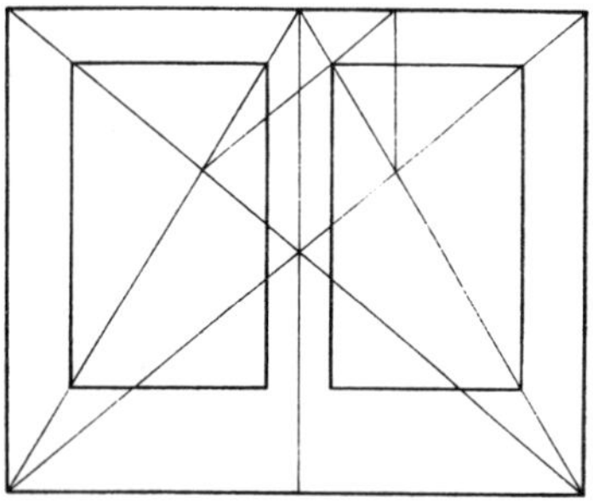

Page proportion of the golden mean (21:34). Paper height and width divided into nine.

It is broadly true that the combined back margins may be optically equal to the single foredge margin, having taken into account the consequences of the curvature of gutters into the spine and the splay of leaves beyond the foredge; although this will vary with format, binding method, and other factors. That is why it is so important to evaluate a layout or specimen page, not as it looks in the flat on the drawing board, but carefully inserted into a dummy to simulate conditions in handling and use. The running headline is another element to allow for: technically it is part of the head margin, which should be measured not to the running headline but to the first line of text; nevertheless it contributes to the visual effect of the drop in the sense that that the head margin would not be quite as deep if no running heads needed to be accommodated. (n.b. Printers have kept two ways of looking at the text area: exclusive and inclusive of running head and folio and, accordingly, the latter method would measure the head margin to the running head. As a designer I prefer the method already described, but all that matters is to stick to one procedure or the other, and to avoid any possible confusion through explicit layouts and specifications.)

This may sound complicated, but in practice the book designer's eye is trained to work to very fine tolerances (down to $^1/_4$pt in some instances) and to make such adjustments instinctively. Empirical judgement has to be relied on in the absence of mathematical or other rules of thumb, and no two titles ever present identical problems. This may be why many experienced typographers like to work within the framework of tradition for at least some of the time, partly because it is still a challenge to learn from and to practise well, and also because they know it to be the most responsive way to meet the reader's true requirements articulately and unobtrusively.

Thus the design process proceeds quite naturally: setting out from a reading of the author's text an appropriate format suggests itself; the selection of a really suitable typeface brings with it a sure indication of the size, leading and line length in which it will look best; the margins and a fine adjustment to the text measure are reciprocal; the number of lines of text on the page is conditioned by the ideal rectangle that will result in good margins.

If the operation described above has gone well, then the text page will at all events be eminently readable. The designer will know whether or not this is so – and just occasionally it can go wrong – and then the remainder of the design should follow on logically and effectively from this point. It is as inconceivable to me that a book designer could embark on the later design stages before this fundamental problem had been resolved as that the construction of a building should begin with the roof rather than its foundations. Traditional margins play a flexible and non-dogmatic part in this dialogue; they are the passive product of getting all the other decisions right and yet at the same time assert an active presence in the design.

Mid-twentieth-century publishing has witnessed the emergence of totally new categories of book to accompany developments in photography and colour printing, the arts and sciences, leisure and education. There has been a

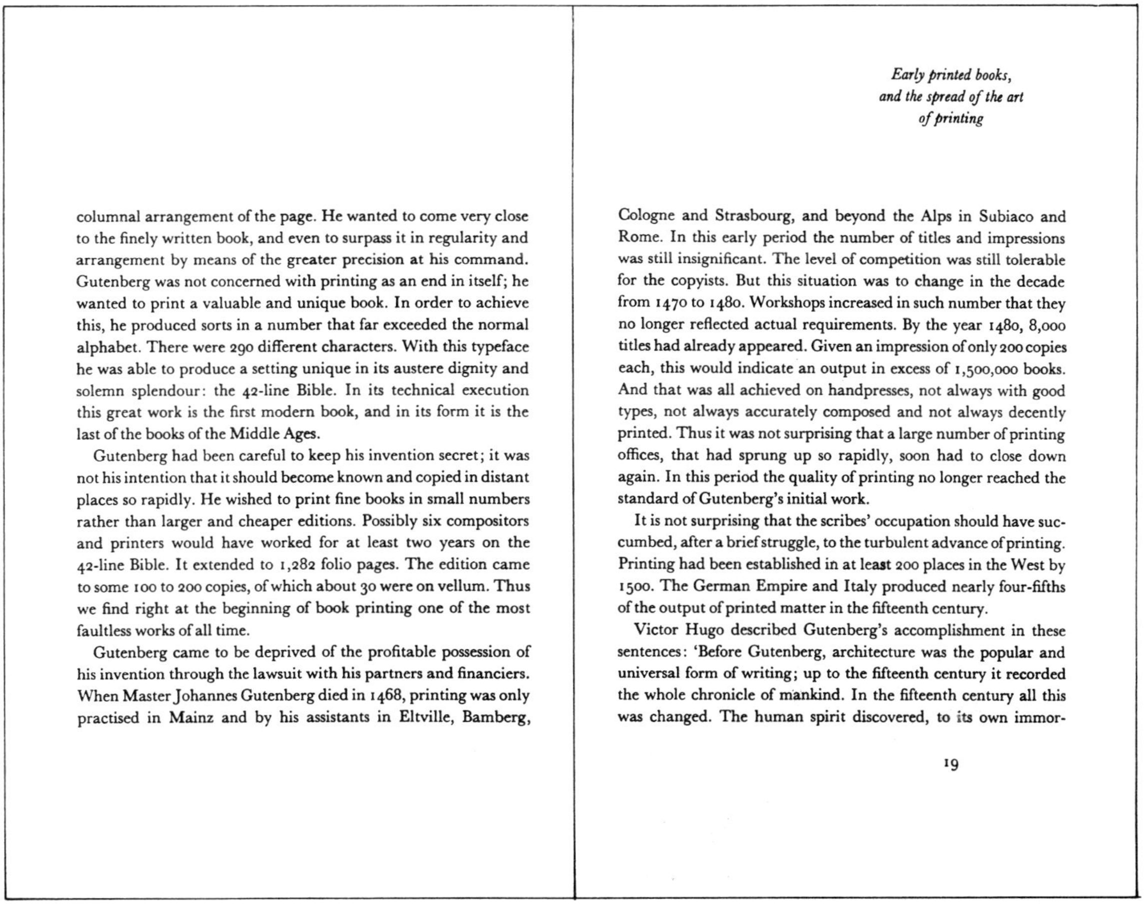

columnal arrangement of the page. He wanted to come very close to the finely written book, and even to surpass it in regularity and arrangement by means of the greater precision at his command. Gutenberg was not concerned with printing as an end in itself; he wanted to print a valuable and unique book. In order to achieve this, he produced sorts in a number that far exceeded the normal alphabet. There were 290 different characters. With this typeface he was able to produce a setting unique in its austere dignity and solemn splendour: the 42-line Bible. In its technical execution this great work is the first modern book, and in its form it is the last of the books of the Middle Ages.

Gutenberg had been careful to keep his invention secret; it was not his intention that it should become known and copied in distant places so rapidly. He wished to print fine books in small numbers rather than larger and cheaper editions. Possibly six compositors and printers would have worked for at least two years on the 42-line Bible. It extended to 1,282 folio pages. The edition came to some 100 to 200 copies, of which about 30 were on vellum. Thus we find right at the beginning of book printing one of the most faultless works of all time.

Gutenberg came to be deprived of the profitable possession of his invention through the lawsuit with his partners and financiers. When Master Johannes Gutenberg died in 1468, printing was only practised in Mainz and by his assistants in Eltville, Bamberg,

Early printed books, and the spread of the art of printing

Cologne and Strasbourg, and beyond the Alps in Subiaco and Rome. In this early period the number of titles and impressions was still insignificant. The level of competition was still tolerable for the copyists. But this situation was to change in the decade from 1470 to 1480. Workshops increased in such number that they no longer reflected actual requirements. By the year 1480, 8,000 titles had already appeared. Given an impression of only 200 copies each, this would indicate an output in excess of 1,500,000 books. And that was all achieved on handpresses, not always with good types, not always accurately composed and not always decently printed. Thus it was not surprising that a large number of printing offices, that had sprung up so rapidly, soon had to close down again. In this period the quality of printing no longer reached the standard of Gutenberg's initial work.

It is not surprising that the scribes' occupation should have succumbed, after a brief struggle, to the turbulent advance of printing. Printing had been established in at least 200 places in the West by 1500. The German Empire and Italy produced nearly four-fifths of the output of printed matter in the fifteenth century.

Victor Hugo described Gutenberg's accomplishment in these sentences: 'Before Gutenberg, architecture was the popular and universal form of writing; up to the fifteenth century it recorded the whole chronicle of mankind. In the fifteenth century all this was changed. The human spirit discovered, to its own immor-

19

A deliberately unconventional, but restful and effective, margin scheme.

These were designed to compensate for muscle shortening in the areas of the back, pelvis and thighs (see diagram on page 81). The intensive use of these and other daily stretching routines over a period of two years ensured that she not only compensated for these weaknesses but achieved above-average flexibility in the muscle areas concerned.

on developing endurance, having quickly realised that there was potential for improvement here. Boris's endurance programme between the ages of 13 and 15 consisted initially of long-distance runs at a relatively low speed (aerobic), leading eventually to shorter, more vigorous runs which brought him to the anaerobic threshold. These faster sessions were made up of two 3,000-metre runs with a ten-minute rest in between. At the age of 14, his pulse-rate at this speed was 180.

specific stretching exercises. These were designed to compensate for muscle shortening in the areas of the back, pelvis and thighs (see diagram on page 81). The intensive use of these and other daily stretching routines over a period of two years ensured that she not only compensated for these weaknesses but achieved above-average flexibility in the muscle areas concerned.

The results of extensive observation and analysis indicated a need for her to do some work on

observation and analysis indicated a need for her to do some work on her ankle and leg extensor muscles. She therefore included a set of step-ups in her training programme (see also page 81).

Westell uses a flannel glove with sport cologne to wipe away the grime on the face of one of his team, while another sips a post-race drink.

Frank Westell waiting at a race finish for his team to arrive. Each rider has his own race bag waiting by the team vehicle, with warm clothes and washing gear.

than men, with a smaller heart and a smaller heart-stroke, and as a result they have higher pulse rates at rest and under effort. But once again, with progressive overload training, there is no reason why they should not approach and sometimes better the typical male levels.

Particularly in the USA, where the female athlete is readily accepted, women racing against men have found that their performances improve greatly, with a consequent season. Are you happy just to be club champion? If not, then you'll need to train harder; if you want a division championship; then harder still; and if your goal is a world crown, then the intensity of training, the dedication, the concentration and the time involved all must increase accordingly.

So don't kid yourself, as so many do. So many riders just 'get the miles in' and reject speed training, interval training – all the areas of progression – because these require a greater commitment in effort. As a result, they just train themselves to a plateau of mediocrity. It is so easy to go out with training partners who aren't up to your level, so that you can ride them off your wheel when you please. It is easy, but it isn't the answer. If this is the way you train, then you are in fact relying haphazardly on the actual racing to really extend you and bring you some form. You are 'racing yourself fit', which means that the racing itself – not a progressive training plan – decides whether and when you will start to improve.

If you are to improve steadily, then you must systematically and regular extend yourself. Do it, and revel in the pain you cause yourself – because in the pain lies the improvement. At the same time, it helps you to assess whether you are following the right path within cycling – whether the particular speciality you have chosen is really right for you.

If you are a thin, weedy rider, unless you train for strength the top events just aren't for you. If you are heavy, you can rule out hill-climbs or stage races which include a lot of hilly terrain, because your power-weight ratio is wrong for them.

improvement in the performance of American women at world level. There is no reason why all racing women shouldn't seek to benefit in the same way, for by racing in the usually tougher company of men they can more easily recognise their own strengths and weaknesses in relation to future international competition. Many top racing women are hardly extended

A lot of the differences between men and women are usually brought about by social and cultural pressures during pre-adolescence and adolescence itself. In recent years these pressures have been decreasing, but they are still a factor.

Nowadays women and girls can do more of the things they want without any social restrictions, and hence many more are coming into sport. This will be a benefit for all sportswomen, because the more they participate, the more and deeper will be the research into the particular problems of women in competition.

As well as the social pressures which sportswomen have to contend with, especially when they are tackling sports which do not have a long tradition of female participation, they also have to deal with the hormonal differences. Men have higher levels of the 'male' hormones such as testosterone, which assist in strength and development. Women have less of this type of hormone, and as a result are at a disadvantage in track events and road sprinting where greater strength is important.

Women have a higher level of oestrogen, which is partly

Facing: Professional riders will 'peak' for the Tour de France, but this race in turn will sharpen their fitness for the world championship which follows some six weeks later.

resultant proliferation of formats for which traditional margin schemes will no longer serve.

The growing popularity of A4, square and landscape formats as alternatives to the quartos and octavos derived from conventional paper sizes has encouraged the use of multi-column setting, particularly for heavily illustrated publications. Similar problems had been confronted earlier in magazine design and other fields, and it was natural enough to look to the solutions which had evolved. These had been given a theoretical foundation in continental art schools such as Ulm and Zurich, which could in one sense be regarded as a coda to the rational and modernist view which Tschichold's *The New Typography* of 1928 had set in train.

At the same time this was a belated attempt to look at the essential nature of the technology of moveable metal type, and to find a design approach which would respond to this discipline, create virtues out of its limitations, and make the ailing process appear efficient, economical and progressive. With hindsight, it is possible to realize that during the years in which this initiative was mounted (in England the critical decade was roughly 1955–65), letterpress printing was already terminally ill. But the treatment devised and applied, known as the 'grid system', is not simply a matter for historians, since it changed the course of design for printing and enabled subsequent development along less dogmatic and regimented lines.

The basic procedure, as shown on the facing page, is to rule up the page area with a pica grid – like a piece of graph paper – and then to derive measures and sub-measures, margins and gutters, running heads and standard drops, as multiples of pica. All pages designed to this grid will be conditioned by its programme, and each element will conform to the permissible permutations of this set of horizontal and vertical co-ordinates. Type is set to the measures prescribed, generally ragged and in a sanserif face, and all photographs and other forms of illustration need to be planned for, or must be cropped to fit, the boxes allocated. The method is ideal for the control of series publications, since everyone in a team quickly becomes familiar with the parameters of word and picture content, and it is possible to settle into an easy routine from issue to issue. The biggest drawback is that in fact the grid may be found to be running the show, particularly if the original designer and the managing editor have not been entirely successful in anticipating the balance of future content.

Where a grid makes use of two or three equal columns on the page then the pressure is on the full *width*, and it is interesting to note the effect that this has on margin schemes. In a sense the side margins are being displaced, causing extra white space to find another home, and normally this has to be at the *head* of the page. I once christened this the washing-line effect, as should become evident from the diagram on page 50. The horizontal level will run consistently all the way from the half-title to the index – in the example shown this is placed low enough for small pictures and captions, as well as chapter and running heads, to be suspended from another washing line which is at the true head of the page. The merit of this formula is that the items hung on the line can vary in depth, which is by no means the case with all types of grid. A further variation – where the intention is to maintain fixed column depths throughout the text – is to distribute the space

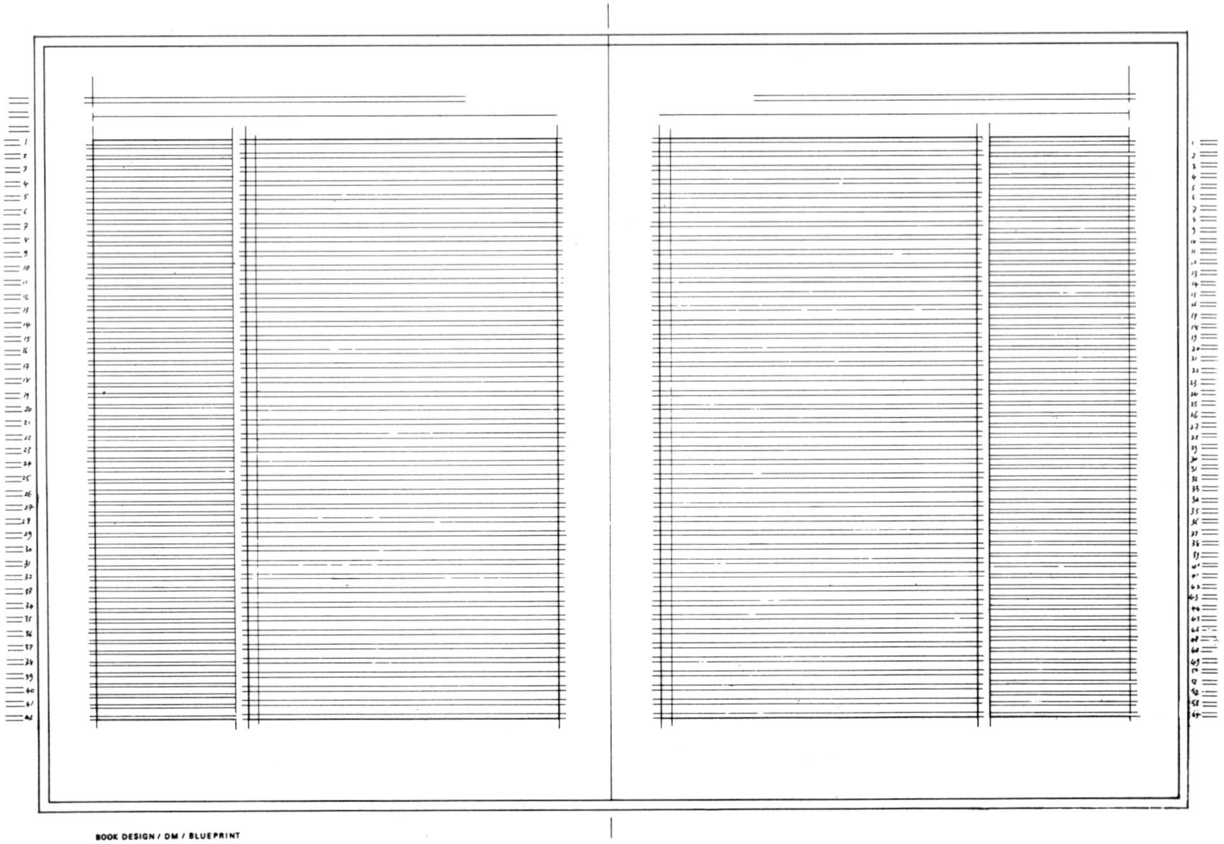

The grid used for this present book: ruling and numbering the lines brings speed and accuracy to the paste-up.

released at the sides between both head and foot margins to give the effect of a horizontal band across the page; this can be particularly effective in pictorial volumes where the page depth can correspond for at least some of the time to the illustration depth, and where running headlines and possibly caption lines can appear widely separated from the text.

Double column setting is as old as the 42-line Bible, and probably almost as old as writing itself. It can either follow traditional margin schemes or the scenario discussed in the preceding paragraph, where displaced space is brought together to give a generous margin at the head, which in turn can give the book an orderly structure and a sense of spaciousness. Double column setting has the property of accommodating far more words to any page, using a smaller typesize than would be feasible in the corresponding full measure, as evidenced by its long use for Bibles of every conceivable format. It has been left to journals to take advantage of this space-saving capacity in standard formats, and so for bookwork in general it only really comes into its own in landscape, square and outsize formats. Here, with single column measures in excess of about 35 picas, a considerable increase in both typesize and leading is indicated, and the case for double column setting should be reviewed – in relation of course to length of text, use of illustration and all the usual functional criteria.

Another grid variation uses thirds – i.e. a two-thirds column for continuous text, preferably justified, and with an unjustified side column available for small pictures and captions – or for shoulder notes or sub-headings. Take care before deciding to use the side column for more than one of these different types of matter that their demands for horizontal alignment with the main text will not conflict. Another snag is that this side column may fill up very unevenly from chapter to chapter or from title to title in series, for if it remains either empty or congested for too much of the time the scheme will be toppled; again page-turnovers in the side column can be maddening. This example is included to show how a scheme that looks attractive on paper could prove a disastrous choice for an on-going series; yet it is useful to know of as many such approaches as possible, because even variants of this one could provide the optimum solution for a project with special features.

The majority of grids are of the left-hand page equals right-hand page variety because until recently the production stages involved (of outputting copy 'blind' on the phototypesetter, pasting-up and over-running for correction), made the idea of placing marginal material to the left on versos and to the right on rectos quite unthinkable. As technology advances such restrictions gradually cease to apply, and suppliers are able to offer us, at no greater cost, facilities of a kind we

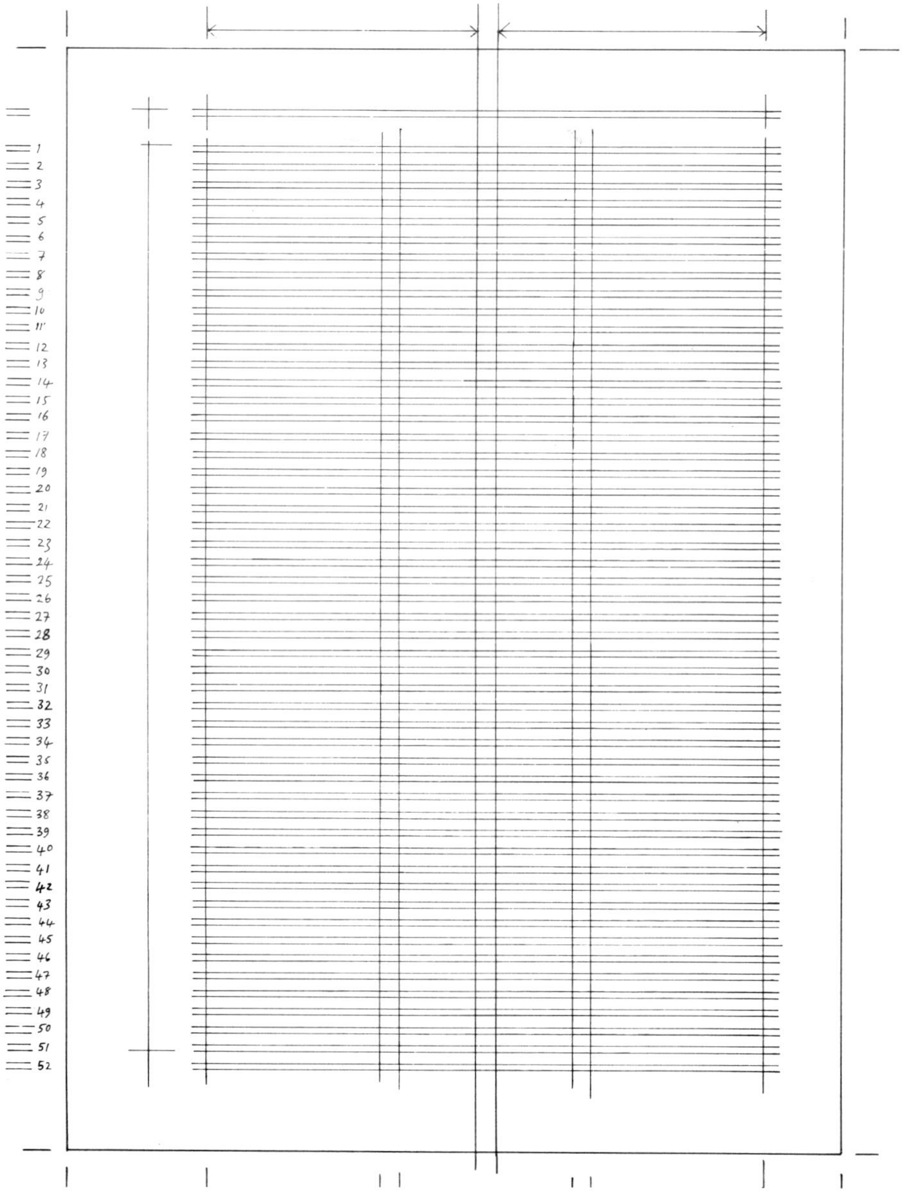

Left equals right for this grid which provides for single, double or triple column setting. The pages, however, would be mounted on the drawing board in facing pairs to ensure good flow and continuity.

have learned to manage without. Unless adequate production updates are received from suppliers, the designer can find himself living behind the times: in this context I had a recent opportunity to restore shoulder notes to their correct positioning in the outer foredge margins, ranged right and left respectively; in this way a return to a symmetrical design more appropriate to the project became feasible once again.

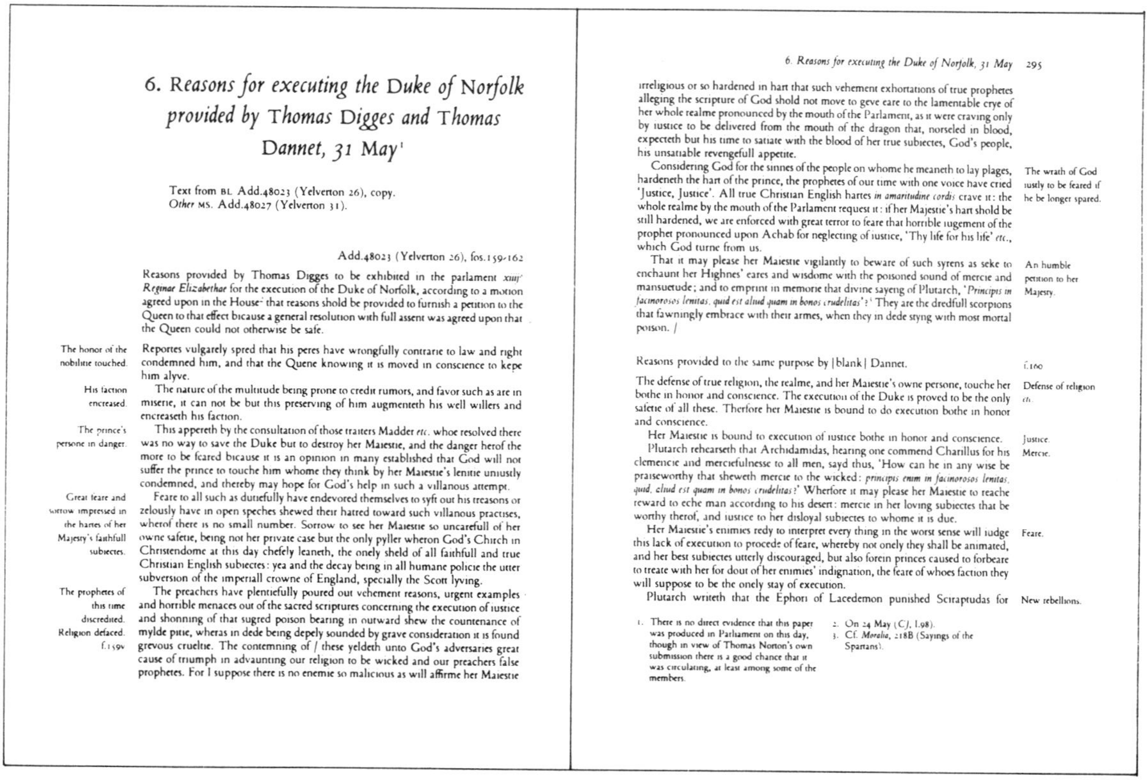

6. Reasons for executing the Duke of Norfolk provided by Thomas Digges and Thomas Dannet, 31 May[1]

Text from BL Add.48023 (Yelverton 26), copy.
Other MS. Add.48027 (Yelverton 31).

Add.48023 (Yelverton 26), fos.159–162

Reasons provided by Thomas Digges to be exhibited in the parlament *xiiij° Reginae Elizabethae* for the execution of the Duke of Norfolk, according to a motion agreed upon in the House[2] that reasons shold be provided to furnish a petition to the Queen to that effect bicause a general resolution with full assent was agreed upon that the Queen could not otherwise be safe.

The honor of the nobilitie touched. Reportes vulgarely spred that his peres have wrongfully contrarie to law and right condemned him, and that the Quene knowing it is moved in conscience to kepe him alyve.

His faction encreased. The nature of the multitude being prone to credit rumors, and favor such as are in miserie, it can not be but this preserving of him augmenteth his well willers and encreaseth his faction.

The prince's persone in danger. This appereth by the consultation of those traiters Madder *etc.* whoe resolved there was no way to save the Duke but to destroy her Maiestie, and the danger herof the more to be feared bicause it is an opinion in many established that God will not suffer the prince to touche him whome they think by her Maiestie's lenitie uniustly condemned, and thereby may hope for God's help in such a villanous attempt.

Great feare and sorrow impressed in the hartes of her Majesty's faithfull subiectes. Feare to all such as dutiefully have endevored themselves to syft out his treasons or zelously have in open speches shewed their hatred toward such villanous practises, wherof there is no small number. Sorrow to see her Maiestie so uncarefull of her owne safetie, being not her private case but the only pyller wheron God's Chirch in Christendome at this day chefely leaneth, the onely sheld of all faithfull and true Christian English subiectes: yea and the decay being in all humane policie the utter subversion of the imperiall crowne of England, specially the Scott lyving.

The prophetes of this time discredited. Religion defaced. f.159v The preachers have plentiefully poured out vehement reasons, urgent examples and horrible menaces out of the sacred scriptures concerning the execution of iustice and shonning of that sugred poison bearing in outward shew the countenance of mylde pitie, wheras in dede being depely sounded by grave consideration it is found grevous crueltie. The contemning of / these yeldeth unto God's adversaries great cause of triumph in advaunting our religion to be wicked and our preachers false prophetes. For I suppose there is no enemie so malicious as will affirme her Maiestie

6. Reasons for executing the Duke of Norfolk, 31 May 295

irreligious or so hardened in hart that such vehement exhortations of true prophetes alleging the scripture of God shold not move to geve eare to the lamentable crye of her whole realme pronounced by the mouth of the Parlament, as it were craving only by iustice to be delivered from the mouth of the dragon that, norseled in blood, expecteth but his time to satiate with the blood of her true subiectes, God's people, his unsatiable revengefull appetite.

Considering God for the sinnes of the people on whome he meaneth to lay plages, hardeneth the hart of the prince, the prophetes of our time with one voice have cried 'Justice, Justice'. All true Christian English hartes *in amaritudine cordis* crave it: the whole realme by the mouth of the Parlament request it: if her Majestie's hart shold be still hardened, we are enforced with great terror to feare that horrible iugement of the prophet pronounced upon Achab for neglecting of iustice, 'Thy life for his life' *etc.*, which God turne from us. The wrath of God iustly to be feared if he be longer spared.

That it may please her Maiestie vigilantly to beware of such syrens as seke to enchaunt her Highnes' eares and wisdome with the poisoned sound of mercie and mansuetude; and to emprint in memorie that divine sayeng of Plutarch, '*Principis in facinorosos lenitas, quid est aliud quam in bonos crudelitas*'?[3] They are the dredfull scorpions that fawningly embrace with their armes, when they in dede styng with most mortal poison. / An humble petition to her Majesty.

Reasons provided to the same purpose by |blank| Dannet. f.160

The defense of true religion, the realme, and her Maiestie's owne persone, touche her bothe in honor and conscience. The execution of the Duke is proved to be the only safetie of all these. Therfore her Maiestie is bound to do execution bothe in honor and conscience. Defense of religion *etc.*

Her Maiestie is bound to execution of iustice bothe in honor and conscience. Justice.

Plutarch rehearseth that Archidamidas, hearing one commend Charillus for his clemencie and merciefulnesse to all men, sayd thus, 'How can he in any wise be praiseworthy that sheweth mercie to the wicked: *principis enim in facinorosos lenitas, quid, aliud est quam in bonos crudelitas*?' Wherfore it may please her Maiestie to reache reward to eche man according to his desert: mercie in her loving subiectes that be worthy therof, and iustice to her disloyal subiectes to whome it is due. Mercie.

Her Maiestie's enimies redy to interpret every thing in the worst sense will iudge this lack of execution to procede of feare, whereby not onely they shall be animated, and her best subiectes utterly discouraged, but also forein princes caused to forbeare to treate with her for dout of her enimies' indignation, the feare of whoes faction they will suppose to be the onely stay of execution. Feare.

Plutarch writeth that the Ephori of Lacedemon punished Sciraptudas for New rebellions.

1. There is no direct evidence that this paper was produced in Parliament on this day, though in view of Thomas Norton's own submission there is a good chance that it was circulating, at least among some of the members.
2. On 24 May (*CJ*, I.98).
3. Cf. *Moralia*, 218B (Sayings of the Spartans).

Maintaining good margins is fundamental to obtaining acceptable results, even in areas of the market such as mass paperbacks, where standards are unnecessarily low; Penguins have demonstrated over the years that this need not be so. It was fascinating also to discover some years ago a Scandinavian series printed on bright yellow paper with excessively wide gutters into which the pagination was set, lacking running heads and with minimal margins to all the trimmed edges. An initial reaction was to suspect a fellow designer of mannerism, but the answer was irrefutable: "living near the Arctic Circle we spend many hours in bed during the winter reading paperbacks, let's be honest and admit that everyone folds paperbacks in half backwards because it's more comfortable to hold them like that particularly in bed; the paper stemmed from university level research into eye fatigue and paper tone under artificial lighting conditions".

Kohl ein bißchen rundherum in die Gegend fliegt: Priczkus, hier ist Vakarelis.

Priczkus, darunterhin, erzählt von anderen Hochzeiten, bei Salzburgern, also in den Dörfern nach Norden hinauf, die ihren Kohl nicht in Gefäßen aus Lindenholz säuern, eingestampft mit bloßen, sauberen Füßen, sondern ihn in die Erde vergraben, bei Deutschen, die sich die Jacken ausziehn und schamlos im kahlen Hemde tanzen, oder von den schrecklichen Speisen der Gutsherrschaft: von abgehangenem Wild, wo man die Maden einfach in der Küche herauskratzte, von schleimigen Wassertieren in flachen, breiten Muschelschalen, von schmutzig schwarzem Fischrogen, Fröschen, Schnepfengedärm, es wird einem ganz schlecht, wenn man das hört. Aber ich habe es mit eigenen Augen gesehen.

Einer erzählt von einem Wolf mit spitz gefeilten Zähnen, der aber gewiß kein Wolf war. Totgeschlagen hab ich ihn, tot war er und tot blieb er, aber ein Wolf war das nicht. Freilich, es ist in dieser Zeit hier keiner gestorben oder verschwunden, dann kam er wohl von weiter her, Sturnkats Großmutter kann es ja nicht gut gewesen sein. Und einer lobt seine Stute. Ein Tier, sag ich, mit einem Arsch wie ein Weib. Und dabei schiebt er den Unterkiefer vor, das bringt ein paar schräg aufsteigende Falten ein, zwischen Untergesicht und Augenpartie und dünnere an den Schläfen auch, wenn man genauer hinsieht. Und Lyne hat

156

Messer in der Hand. Ehe sie krepiert, wird er sie gleich abstechen. Sitzt bis Uhre fünf morgens, das, was der Mensch zuwege bringt, in Worten und Werken, darüber braucht man sich nicht viel aufzuhalten, sondern kommt bald zu den Strafen, dem Strafgericht, dem Sündenlohn, wo einem die Szenen, die Bilder, Farben, Vergleiche nur so wie Öl vom Munde gehn, immer hinab wie in Aarons Bart, Psalm 133, Vers zwei. Und zu den Strafen, was gehört nicht alles dazu! Frau Drescher hat Zahnschmerzen, rechnen die auch darunter? Aber wofür denn, wofür? So gerät man auf eine Rechtfertigungslehre: rechtfertigen wird sich der Mensch, dieser Sünder, er sagt zu seinem Gott, der eigentlich die Rechtfertigung übernommen hat, er habe doch gar nichts getan, oder: wenn man zum Beispiel sieht, was andere alles machen, und denen passiert nichts, im Gegenteil. Also kommt man aufs nächste: auf Unschuldig-Leiden, womit der Vater die Seinen väterlich züchtigt, auf diese Prüfungen, die er seinen Kindern bereitet. Ein ganz fixer Werdegang: von der heulenden Horde der Sünder zur friedevollen Gemeinschaft der Heiligen, vom Zähneklappern zum Halleluja. Das ist erbaulich, man weiß sich gerecht, ohne Federlesen, man hat etwas hinabzuschauen, auf die Sünder, die draußen sind.

Zum Abschluß hat Grinda noch seinen gedruckten Traktat: Große Wunder Gottes in den jetzt vergangenen Tagen, zwei Lit fünfzig das Stück,

157

2:5 Conclusion

If it is true that continuous reading, or the use of books for reference (as distinct from other applications of print), takes place as a private transaction between source and client, then the designer has no occasion to make his presence felt as a third party. So there are two antithetical attitudes to design for print, a functional and 'introverted' one that is in the service of pure communication, and an extroverted approach that draws attention to itself and to the rhetoric of advertising and packaging.

Typefaces themselves, which are the subject of the next chapter, are also similarly divisible into two kinds: text or book faces which must be unassertive, free of noticeable departures from the norm for the design of each of the distinct letters of the alphabet and their compatibility when used together – and display faces, a wide range of lettering styles which comes into play in the design of jackets and paperback covers and related publicity material.

3 TYPEFACES

The German word 'Schrift' denotes both the written and the printed letterform – calligraphy as well as typography – and this reflects current aesthetic and technological attitudes admirably. The Greek root for 'type' evokes the way in which punches are *struck* and cast in metal and then *impressed* into paper, and so the term remains tied through these associations to the old letterpress process and will gradually become archaic – although it certainly ought not to be supplanted by the misusage 'font'!

But five hundred years of evolution and thinking about a craft are not to be thrown out of the window lightly, and accordingly to review the present repertory of typographic material against an earlier yardstick may highlight both the immeasurable advantages of the new in some respects, and the ground that still has to be made up in others.

3:1 Choice of typefaces – basic working ranges

In a 'Desert Island Discs' situation I would be perfectly happy with only eight typefaces of my choice for text composition. Most publishers and printers, past and present, should find this ample, and it is doubtful whether any generation has produced on average more than that number of book faces of real and lasting quality. Ideally this selection should be allowed to range over both foundry type and matrices for mechanical composition, as well as the repertoire for digitised photocomposition; but this request would not be admissible since freedom of choice is governed by the technology which prevails at any given time. In other words it is possible to view the evolution of type design as a response to the constraints and potential of technical innovation: whether in the optics and precision of type manufacture, in printing methods and press construction, or in inks and papermaking.

Thus, when the letterpress process finally went under, it followed that all those typefaces that had been specifically designed to be mechanically cast in metal, inked and impressed, became historical source material almost overnight. Customers, however, continued to demand the names they were familiar with – Bembo, Baskerville, Plantin, and so forth – and numerous versions for photocomposition were rushed out to meet the demand. This was just a beginning; type manufacturers competed with each other to commission new faces and to compile those elephantine catalogues of digital founts which now overwhelm us for choice, and in this they were computer-aided in generating entire families of related weights from a single set of drawings. At the time of writing it is true to say that typesetters as well as designers are still adjusting to this onslaught and are engaged in quarrying the book faces of real distinction from all the ill-considered rubbish that came about for no better reason than that the technology for its production had become accessible at low cost – whereas in the late 1950s a leading typefoundry revealed that the cost of issuing a single trial size of a new design was then in excess of £20,000; a powerful incentive for the manufacturer to exercise taste, discrimination and foresight.

A range of eight typefaces has been selected with regard to those systems which are presently the most popular for text composition. Some of these typefaces may feature rarely on suppliers' broadsheets simply because, in the absence of expressed interest, typesetters – especially those with a 'mixed' business – tend to go in for typefaces with a higher personality profile than is often desirable for bookwork. These suggestions are advanced very tentatively and in the hope that one or two may prove of general interest; specialised areas of publishing would call for different or additional recommendations. There are several conflicting and confusing systems of type classification, and so terms will be explained as they occur.

Palatino

Aldus

An immediate first choice ought to be Palatino, but that is now so firmly established that a variant, Linotype Aldus, could well be nominated instead. Palatino harks back to early historical models, to Bembo's roman of 1495 and to the chancery italics current in sixteenth-century Italy. Although it has additional roots in the pre-war German schools of calligraphy and type design, in a remarkable way it also anticipated the requirements of photocomposition and digitisation – which were mere specks on the horizon when it was launched as metal type for hand-setting by the Stempel Foundry in 1950. Its designer, Hermann Zapf, has gone on to become the leading authority on design for digitised typesetting, with a number of distinguished later designs to his credit which have yet to become more widely known in Britain, such as Comenius for Berthold, Marconi on Hell Digiset, and Zapf Renaissance Antiqua for Scangraphic. It took Palatino a long time from its first appearance to consolidate its present position as one of the most widely used text faces of all, and it is fascinating to compare it with his Renaissance Antiqua, first shown in 1987, to see how the designer has returned to the same starting point to provide a new interpretation in the light of the changing nature of typesetting and printing and of his own thinking over this long interval.

hamburgefon hamburgefon

hamburgefon hamburgefon

Palatino left, Zapf Renaissance right.

Palatino is comparatively wide in set, and that is why German Linotype asked the designer to look at a revision that would accommodate more characters within the same measure. Compare the alphabet lengths of the two typefaces shown here in the same type size, and you will see why Aldus (1954) became a success story for paperback setting in Germany and why it offers scope as an alternative to Palatino in a whole range of situations.

ABCDEFGHIJKLMNOPQRSTUVWXYZ
abcdefghijklmnopqrstuvwxyzfifl,.-'';:()
ABCDEFGHIJKLMNOPQRSTUVWXYZ
abcdefghijklmnopqrstuvwxyzfifl,.-'';:()

ABCDEFGHIJKLMNOPQRSTUVWXYZ
abcdefghijklmnopqrstuvwxyzfifl,.-'';:()
ABCDEFGHIJKLMNOPQRSTUVWXYZ
abcdefghijklmnopqrstuvwxyzfifl,.-'';:()

Palatino above, Aldus below. Note that many italic alphabet lengths are traditionally shorter than roman, but that with Aldus they had to be equated to comply with the Linotype system constraints of the time.

Sabon

The next task must be to select a current version of the Garamond/Granjon/Jannon letter; one modelled on those typefaces of unsurpassed elegance and legibility which emanated from France during the earlier half of the sixteenth century, and which remained without rival until the ascendancy passed to the Low Countries more than a century later. Once again, history provided no more than a starting point for the typographer Jan Tschichold, whose Sabon typeface was commissioned as a joint approach from Stempel for foundry type and from Monotype and Linotype for their respective composing machines.

First released in 1967, Sabon is one of those rare, unassertive faces in which each detail is well judged in relation to the whole; and one would have expected no less of Tschichold's fastidious eye when it came to designing his one major typeface. Sabon has weathered the sea change to digitised phototypesetting better than many of the so-called Garamonds, but it is one of those faces – and typographers all agree that some typefaces are harder to work with than others – which will always demand considered design and printing; used with meticulous care and in accordance with its author's own precepts on compositional style, it is a classic.

ABCDEFGHIJKLMNOPQRSTUVWXYZ
abcdefghijklmnopqrstuvwxyzfifl,.-'';:()

ABCDEFGHIJKLMNOPQRSTUVWXYZ
abcdefghijklmnopqrstuvwxyzfifl,.-'';:()

Ehrhardt

Recent research has uncovered much new information concerning the Ehrhardt/Janson letter – always a favourite with working typographers – to the extent that it should now in fairness be credited to the Hungarian printer and punch-cutter Nicholas Kis, who cut the original in Amsterdam in about 1686. In many situations Monotype Ehrhardt or the Linotype versions of either Ehrhardt or Janson (redrawn by Zapf from the original founts) can be used as alternatives to Times New Roman, since there is a shared vigour of shading and colour, to which the former typefaces add an elegance of cut which has carried over well into the digital revampings.

ABCDEFGHIJKLMNOPQRSTUVWXYZ
abcdefghijklmnopqrstuvwxyzfifl,.-'';:()
ABCDEFGHIJKLMNOPQRSTUVWXYZ
abcdefghijklmnopqrstuvwxyzfifl,.-'';:()

Sabon and Ehrhardt are both taken from Linotron specimen sheets.

Following a broad progression, a point in the historical development of type design has now been reached where the technology that brought about changes in type design in the first place will be found to be at odds with the present technology for digitised photosetting. This covers the majority of those typefaces which classification systems would concur in describing as transitional into modern faces, representing the progressive tendency in the later part of the eighteenth century and becoming the dominant one throughout the nineteenth century. Baskerville may represent the earlier, and Bodoni the fully developed, state of affairs.

Prior to the industrial revolution which affected the state of printing within individual European countries at various rates, a series of advances went hand in hand. The fact that these developments were in the initial stages patronised for reasons of state and sponsored by the aristocracy and by vastly successful entrepreneurs (and only subsequently adapted and mechanised for the benefit of the populace at large), is not without significance for the entire direction in which type design was deflected. The first phase of technical innovation consisted in making smoother paper surfaces through hot pressing, and in constructing improved hand-presses to give more precise control over impression.

As a practical printer, John Baskerville was absorbed by these developments; and his typeface (1757) was devised over a number of years to work to best advantage in conjunction with a set of fine adjustments to inking, impression and paper surface over which he could exercise direct control. The new style of letter design favoured by Baskerville and his contemporaries involved developing a marked contrast between thick and thin strokes, which was aided by a displacement of the traditional oblique stress. This tendency was arrested short of its logical consequence in the 'modern' letter of Didot and Bodoni in the interests of retaining something of the spirit of Georgian elegance in its design, and hence it appears in many type classifications as a 'transitional' face.

The transition from old face to modern face is exemplified, from top to bottom, by Bembo, Baskerville and Bodoni.

ABCabc

ABCabc

ABCabc

Baskerville

With Baskerville there is still a gentle transition from thick stroke into thin, and from the stems of letters into the finely bracketed serifs, but already these fine strokes can be seen to be at the root of the problems experienced in recent adaptations of these faces. Even the lightest of letterpress impressions established the image on the page in a way not possible by offset, which results in a dazzling or flickering optical effect under many conditions. The relief impression causes ink squash – or a slight thickening of the impression, especially that from the fine strokes – whereas photographic stages in filmsetting and platemaking will have the converse effect of attenuating or eating into hair lines, so that even where these do not break down, the optical resolution remains poor. Attempts to compensate for this effect through redrawing the hair lines and serif structure more positively, result in an immediate loss of design identity, and one is forced to the reluctant conclusion that the true transitional and modern letters are inherently slightly less readable than other romans under many conditions. This does not imply by any means that they should be shunned, but rather that they should be carefully chosen and deployed for the job in hand.

This lengthy explanation is intended to account for something of the disappointment which book designers since have felt with those types named after Baskerville that have been made available – and there are currently at least a couple of dozen or so in the repertoire. The conclusion is that a version of Baskerville is indispensable, but that which one to use – once the clearly debased versions have been excluded – must largely depend on the sizes and circumstances. The range of choice is well exemplified by the Linotype repertoire which includes Linotype Baskerville, Baskerville No. 2, and ITC New Baskerville as well as a useful version of Fry's Baskerville (after Isaac Moore's type of c. 1768). For all-round general use and where historical connotations are unimportant, the ITC family has a number of advantages.

Håmbûrgefönstiv iam admodum mit

Fry's Baskerville above, ITC Baskerville below.

abcdefghijklmnopqrstuvwxyz
ABCDEFGHIJKLMNOPQRSTUVWXYZ
abcdefghijklmnopqrstuvwxyz
ABCDEFGHIJKLMNOPQRSTUVWXYZ

The modern face – which had been carried to its logical extreme in the types of Didot and Bodoni late in the eighteenth century – influenced the standard typefaces in use from the beginning of the following century when papermaking and printing presses first became mechanised, until its close by which time mechanical composition was firmly established. The best vernacular adaptations of late transitional and modern faces, Bell, Bulmer, Didot, Fournier, Modern No. 20, Scotch Roman, and Walbaum among others, were subsequently revived for letterpress bookwork, but as the category least amenable to filmsetting they are poorly represented in the current repertoire.

Bodoni Antiqua mager / *Bodoni Kursiv mager*

ABCDEFGHIJKLMNOPQRSTUVWXYZ
abcdefghijklmnopqrstuvwxyzfifl,.-‘’;:()
ABCDEFGHIJKLMNOPQRSTUVWXYZ
abcdefghijklmnopqrstuvwxyzfifl,.-‘’;:()

Haas Bodoni (above) and Bauer Bodoni are fine versions, but not to be recommended for everyday use.

Recent trends have pointed away from moderns as well as sanserifs and all other types with a rigid geometric or mechanical cast, and towards a softer look that accords well with offset printing. This friendlier style is part of a quiet revolution which has readmitted the calligraphic basis of letter-forms. This can be seen to affect the design even of modern faces, as in the case of Zapf Book, shown in comparison with the same designer's Marconi (at present only available on Hell Digiset), which has to be my final choice as it indicates a clear future path for the setting of scientific texts or tabular matter. Basilia, designed by André Gürtler for Haas in conjunction with Bobst for filmsetting, and now licensed to several manufacturers, is also a strong contender.

Zapf Book Light

abcdefghijklmnopqrstuvwxyz
ABCDEFGHIJKLMNOPQRSTUVWXYZ
abcdefghijklmnopqrstuvwxyz
ABCDEFGHIJKLMNOPQRSTUVWXYZ

Marconi

Marconi

Marconi Text

Schriften ändern sich
Nicht nur die Technik
und Druckmaschinen
auch heute im Lichtsatz.
len kleinen Lichtlinien
seine eigenen Gesetz

NG

The Vendôme capitals show a pronounced form of this serif structure.

Meridien

Trump Mediaeval

Vendôme, Meridien and Trump Mediaeval first appeared for hand composition in the 1950s; they shared a robust construction and sharpness of cut brought about through the introduction of a triangular, wedge-shaped serif structure (known as 'Latin' to nineteenth-century typefounders) to well-proportioned roman alphabets. Vendôme was the winner in the fashion stakes at the time and remains popular for display and packaging, whereas the other faces remained relatively obscure; although Trump in particular had inadvertently resolved many of the problems associated with producing a text face for digital photocomposition. As soon as it was reissued for this purpose by Compugraphic and Linotype, some book typographers were quick to perceive its merits, which include exceptional clarity in the smaller sizes, admirably contrasted italics of the 'sloped roman' variety, a useful related bold and true small capitals.

ABCDEFGHIJKLMNOPQRSTUVWXYZ&ÆŒ
ABCDEFGHIJKLMNOPQRSTUVWXYZ&ÆŒ
abcdefghijklmnopqrstuvwxyzæœ
.,;:!?''-()£$– 1234567890 1234567890

ABCDEFGHIJKLMNOPQRSTUVWXYZ&ÆŒ
abcdefghijklmnopqrstuvwxyzæœ
.,;:!?''-()£$– 1234567890 1234567890

ABCDEFGHIJKLMNOPQRSTUVWXYZ&ÆŒ
abcdefghijklmnopqrstuvwxyzæœ
.,;:!?''-()£$– 1234567890 1234567890

An inviting-looking page results from using the normal character fitting, whilst extra close letter spacing (minus compensation), to advertising agency tastes, will yield an unsightly as well as an unreadable product as the robust serifs of adjacent characters fuse together.

Berthold-Schriftweite weit
Berthold-Schriftweite normal
Berthold-Schriftweite eng
Berthold-Schriftweite sehr eng
Berthold-Schriftweite extrem eng

Garth Graphic

The letters of an alphabet may add up to more than the sum of their parts when combined into a text or to produce a texture; and it is no accident that the words text and 'textura' – as the appellation of a group of early typefaces – share a common root with the word 'textile'. I have this very much in mind in introducing Garth Graphic (at present exclusive to Compugraphic). In the course of studying each new typeface family as it is released internationally, book designers are reluctantly drawn to the same general conclusions: that a promising candidate has to be failed for text composition since the design is over-endowed with personality and can readily be seen to be striving for so many other markets as well as books, or that the colour and texture of the page setting is not acceptable, or that the ensemble is flawed by the behaviour of one or two eccentric sorts.

ABCDEFGHIJKLMNOPQRSTUVWXYZ&
abcdefghijklmnopqrstuvwxyz1234567890
ABCDEFGHIJKLMNOPQRSTUVWXYZ&
ff ffi fi ffl fl 1234567890

ABCDEFGHIJKLMNOPQRSTUVWXYZ&
abcdefghijklmnopqrstuvwxyz1234567890

ABCDEFGHIJKLMNOPQRSTUVWXYZ&
abcdefghijklmnopqrstuvwxyz1234567890

In its basic weight and with its small capitals and italics, Garth seemed to pass all the tests, except for an initial reservation about the design of the lower case 'y'. Although the originality and strong calligraphic rhythms of the design are evident in the larger point sizes, when reduced to text sizes it assumes a softer effect of the kind already described for Zapf Book and which is proving to be so readable and easy on the eye. The bold and condensed relatives are less so, but then such weights are infrequently called for in practice. I have now specified Garth for several books of quite different kinds and formats and am delighted with the way it looks in proof and in print. It doesn't happen all that frequently that a typeface comes along which proves to be a natural addition to the repertoire for book composition, but the designers of this one should certainly be congratulated on their achievement: it originated with John Matt as a project for American Typefounders in the mid-1960s but, after that company withdrew from phototype manufacture, it was revised and completed as a family by Renée LeWinter and Connie Blanchard at Compugraphic between 1979 and 1982.

The roman has a feeling of openness

Will do the best job of

Flowing

With one final choice to go, I have to admit to a change of plan: it was to have been Monotype Photina, but that would have had the effect of turning what is intended as a balanced review of the present catalogue of available typefaces into a bias in favour of the calligraphic tendency already described. In the quest for this eighth typeface, the revised brief became to find a functional, down-to-earth workhorse; and that in turn suggested several design categories which might be progressively eliminated on a reasoned basis.

Until quite recently it would have been *de rigueur* to include a sanserif in any range of typefaces for text setting, but this usage is increasingly being recognised for one of the cardinal design sins of the 1960s, quite worthy to be placed alongside residential tower blocks in its arrogant refusal to address human needs and preferences, expressed or implied. There would be more gain than loss if it were to be resolved to ban the use of sanserif for continuous reading purposes, as distinct from its role as an ancillary to the seriffed face for such purposes as captions, tables or headings where appropriate.

A small group of typefaces followed Optima along a promising line of development in attempting to unite roman and sanserif characteristics within the same design; that is to say to bring roman proportions, roman forms of 'a' and 'g',

Optima

abcdefghijklmnopqrstuvwxyz
ABCDEFGHIJKLMNOPQRSTUVWXYZ

Edgar Allan Poe

and the hint of a serif structure to the open simplicity and clarity of design of sans. Digitised photocomposition dealt as unkindly with this group of typefaces as with the so-called moderns with their notorious hair-line serifs. An emerging law governing the behaviour of type designs under digitisation might run along the following lines: that which is precisely and subtly finished will lose those qualities in the smaller sizes, whereas that which is vigorously stated and accentuated in a large drawing may gain in finesse and retain its liveliness on reduction.

Another group, exemplified by Melior and Candida, adapt the Egyptian or slab-serif to text face design. The design is robust enough for successful digitisation and the page appearance can be particularly open and inviting. A colleague used these faces extensively until he discovered that the hidden snag lay in the monotony induced over prolonged reading periods. That near-monoline weight, combined with squareness both in the rendering of 'O'-derived curves and in the detail of serif structure, should induce reading fatigue is hardly surprising; and yet, whilst urging caution in their use for running text, that still leaves a variety of valid reference applications for these interesting faces.

Candida

abcdefghijklmnopqrstuvwxyz
ABCDEFGHIJKLMNOPQRSTUVW
XYZ 1234567890 .,;:''«»&!?

abcdefghijklmnopqrstuvwxyz
ABCDEFGHIJKLMNOPQRSTUVW

Melior

abcdefghijklmnopqrstuvwxyz
ABCDEFGHIJKLMNOPQRSTUVWXYZ

abcdefghijklmnopqrstuvwxyz
ABCDEFGHIJKLMNOPQRSTUVWXYZ

abcdefghijklmnopqrstuvwxyz
ABCDEFGHIJKLMNOPQRSTUVWXYZ

Times

I turn finally to a handful of types which have in common little more than their proven utility: these include Plantin, Imprint, Concorde, and Times. Having looked at them afresh in all available versions and in a wide range of uses, my eventual choice was for Times New Roman. The best reason that can be offered is that whilst it will yield a serviceable result under most conditions, it is also possible for it to appear to finer effect than ever before when photoset and printed offset – perhaps set a size down from that which would normally be selected, and with commensurately greater leading.

ABCDEFGHIJKLMNOPQRSTUVWXYZ&ÆŒ
ABCDEFGHIJKLMNOPQRSTUVWXYZ&ÆŒ
abcdefghijklmnopqrstuvwxyzæœ
.,;:!?''-()£$– 1234567890 1234567890

ABCDEFGHIJKLMNOPQRSTUVWXYZ&ÆŒ
abcdefghijklmnopqrstuvwxyzæœ
.,;:!?''-()£$– 1234567890 1234567890

ABCDEFGHIJKLMNOPQRSTUVWXYZ&ÆŒ
abcdefghijklmnopqrstuvwxyzæœ
.,;:!?''-()£$– 1234567890 1234567890

ABCDEFGHIJKLMNOPQRSTUVWXYZ&ÆŒ
abcdefghijklmnopqrstuvwxyzæœ
.,;:!?''-()£$– 1234567890

Making this selection proved an interesting exercise, since unexpected patterns are discovered in re-evaluating the whole scene as distinct from reeling off personal favourites – which tend in any case merely to reflect the demands of the kinds of book one is presently working with as well as the constraints imposed by suppliers. Beyond this immediate framework, the designer always has a considerable background knowledge of those typefaces from which it is possible to draw apposite solutions to unusual problems, and it has been salutary on this occasion to realise the rate and extent to which much of that repertoire is receding into an unrecoverable historical past, as the text typefaces of our own time and technology consolidate their presence.

3:2 Factors in selecting a typeface

A favourite theory of the late Beatrice Warde was that there are good typefaces and bad typefaces and that the practice of typography starts after the bad ones have been eliminated. This is particularly true of restricted systems, from manual typewriters through to daisywheel printers and the budget end of photocomposition; where the advice would be to isolate those one or two faces – and there are rarely more

– which provide a pleasant and legible reading page on the system in question and to ignore the rest. It was the work of a few moments to reduce a recent chart of fifteen daisywheel founts to a single selection – four sanserifs, three italics, one script and a bold face went out at once. Four of the remaining romans showed no real advance on the 'Remington' style, possibly because they had not been designed for proportional spacing pitch, thereby reducing 'jumpiness' and improving the spacing of words – and there was no difficulty in spotting the superior of the two PS pitch romans which remained.

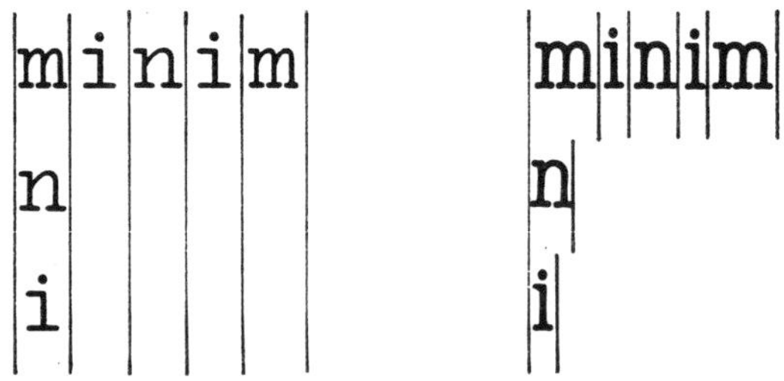

Standard pitch, where the design of each character has to be modified to fit an en body (left), and proportionally-spaced character widths (right), for typewriters and printers.

In a similar way it is quite easy to reduce the field to a very short list of typefaces, to suit any specific set of publishing requirements, and the degree of optical resolution offered by the system under consideration. There is widespread optimism that the quality gap is narrowing all the time between DTP resources and professional phototypesetting equipment, and that soon there will be more acceptable versions of worthwhile typefaces available for most low-cost systems; but already there have been striking improvements in this field, and the library of typefaces has grown to keep pace with the spectrum of demand from all sectors of advertising, promotion, in-house printing and routine commercial applications, as well as from book publishing.

Selecting a typeface involves thinking about the way in which it will be used, and in this connection the old maxim 'one type for one book' continues to provide a useful starting point: can all the levels of heading and emphasis in display be derived from larger sizes of the text type with its related italics, small capitals and perhaps bold? The answer is that this will almost invariably be possible and in many cases desirable, but the door should never be closed to alternative approaches. Try the simplest means first, you may be surprised and delighted at how naturally and rightly everything falls into place; a sure indication that it is likely to do so for the reader as well. The book designer is not called upon to do anything clever or novel or to seek to draw attention to the layout; on the contrary this should come about in response to the internal logic of the manuscript, as a series of decisions which articulate degrees of structural emphasis or importance through the 'voice' and size of the type and its spacing and arrangement.

Close attention to the manuscript will show where a more adventurous approach is needed in order to bring out the functional relation of its parts, or where qualities in the writing or illustration call for livelier typographic treatment. This can arise for example in highly illustrated books for schools where a magazine-like treatment is planned, and large format pictorial volumes in general often benefit from contrast in scale and character between text and display. Just occasionally the designer will anticipate that the text page – although correct – may prove boring and unrelieved in texture and that something by way of seasoning or styling to the detail may bring it to life, and perhaps even make a difference to apparent value for money for a slender title that has of necessity to be highly priced. Design should involve a dash of fashion or fun in addition to its functional purpose, but the designer has to guard against intrusive mannerisms which distract the reader when they occur in the wrong context.

A further indicator in the choice of typeface is provided by any unusual typographic requirements for an individual title or series, such as a need for tabular or mathematical setting; special language sorts or scientific symbols; high incidence of italic; or an editorial decision to set extensive notes down in size. Detailed specimens may have to be compared to reach the best solution, and in rare cases a mixture of typefaces may have to be considered, as where tables are set in sanserif to appear against roman text both for contrast and for the clarity which sanserif figures have in diminutive sizes. Sans is also one of the natural choices for the labelling of maps, charts and graphs that are to be supplied as separate artwork.

Illustration may influence the choice of typeface very directly, so that the designer may need to make adjustments until satisfied with the affinity of style, and the harmony or contrast of weight of line, that obtains between type and illustration. Until quite recent times, type and illustration had to be taken into consideration for the effect they had – either jointly or separately – on the selection of process, paper, inking and impression. Things are so much simpler now that offset lithography has become the dominant process to the point that alternatives to it are rarely encountered; and that the complexities of creating a balance between inking, paper and impression which were fundamental to the letterpress process do not arise in the same terms or involve the designer to the same degree. For example, it is unusual any longer for type and illustration to have to be printed on different papers with consequent constraints on colour distribution or the placing of plates sections. Many aspects of paper qualities remain of prime concern to the designer; although as a factor in the choice of typeface it is of diminished importance, since the planographic offset image of type undergoes far less modification in relation to a variety of paper surfaces than the letterpress relief image.

Of the remaining factors which influence the selective process, the parameters of page size and extent are the most important. Formats vary in accordance with use from one category of book to another, and there is little correlation to be found any longer between size of type and page size; this is largely because the variety, resourcefulness and sophistication of page layout and make-up schemes have increased vastly. The copyfitting methods which are discussed below enable the copy content (words and pictures) to be worked out for all such schemes, but at the typeface selection stage the concern is with how type will look in action. Apart from evident dissimilarities in overall style, types of the same nominal size may vary in relative appearing size (x-height), and in relative alphabet length (a-z length).

These are all 18pt types set on Linotron 202:
Goudy Old Style
Baskerville
Times
Trump Mediaeval
Aster

abcdefghijklmnopqrstuvwxyz
abcdefghijklmnopqrstuvwxyz
abcdefghijklmnopqrstuvwxyz
abcdefghijklmnopqrstuvwxyz
abcdefghijklmnopqrstuvwxyz

The variation in these characteristics, as shown above, in turn affects suitability for use in given measures and the amount of additional interlinear space (leading) they may require in those measures. Other design characteristics affecting the suitability of type in a particular setting include relative weight (some types are darker in 'colour' and exert a stronger presence on the page), and some may have a structure that imparts a slight horizontal or vertical bias to the text page:

Excellence in typography is the result of nothing more than an attitude. Its app
eal comes from the understanding used in its planning; the designer must care
In contemporary advertising the perfect integration of design elements often d
emands unorthodox typography. It may require the use of compact spacing, mi
nus leading, unusual sizes and weights; whatever is needed to improve appeara

Excellence in typography is the result of nothing more than an attitude. Its appe
al comes from the understanding used in its planning; the designer must care. I
n contemporary advertising the perfect integration of design elements often de
mands unorthodox typography. It may require the use of compact spacing, min
us leading, unusual sizes and weights; whatever is needed to improve appearan

A contrast in 'colour': ITC Veljovic Book and ITC Zapf International Light.

Excellence in typography is the result of nothing more than an attitude. Its appeal comes fr
om the understanding used in its planning; the designer must care. In contemporary adve
rtising the perfect integration of design elements often demands unorthodox typography. I
t may require the use of compact spacing, minus leading, unusual sizes and weights; whate
ver is needed to improve appearance and impact. Stating specific principles or guides on th

Excellence in typography is the result of nothing more than an attitude. Its
appeal comes from the understanding used in its planning; the designer m
ust care. In contemporary advertising the perfect integration of design elem
ents often demands unorthodox typography. It may require the use of com
pact spacing, minus leading, unusual sizes and weights; whatever is needed

A contrast in vertical and horizontal bias: ITC Weidemann Book and ITC Zapf Book Light.

In selecting a typeface for a specific title, there are, then, a number of functional and common sense ways in which the field will narrow itself down; and if there are should still be more than a single contender meeting all the conditions, then let the final choice be a subjective one!

3:3 The display sizes of text faces

Once the outlines of a proposed new typeface design have been established as coordinates, it is modern practice to generate an entire family complete with italic, bold and condensed, rapidly and inexpensively, through CRT-screen and computer. The resultant founts (or 'fonts' if you will) can be used for phototypesetting at any desired enlargement or reduction.

It is remarkable that a handful of excellent types should have arisen in this climate; and this has come about largely because Hermann Zapf and one or two other designers met Fournier's (1764) definition of a typographer as 'one who combined the knowledge to cut, cast and print [metal] types', and thus had a unique historical vantage-point from which to assess the nature of these changes and the extent to which the computer could be made to serve. Against the few really fine typefaces available for contemporary bookwork, it is necessary to contend with thousands that are unfit for that purpose. Book designers are beginning to reach a fair consensus in these matters, but in order to see the way ahead it is frequently necessary to step back to view things from a kind of time-warp, from a long but recently defunct tradition that has not yet been properly related to the new.

From the earliest times, a metal typeface was originated in the size for which it was most immediately needed, and the engraving of each steel punch for a single character continued to require at least a day's painstaking work. If the first size proved successful, then work on a related size might go ahead; the engraver's trained hand and eye introduced subtle variations as further sizes were issued, and the design would be modified in an organic way from the basic qualities established in the cutting of the first size. Different craftsmen would undertake individual sizes, particularly as these were added at the extremes of the range of sizes: greater contrast between thick and thin strokes and refinement to detail in the cutting became possible in the larger or display sizes; whereas the optical requirements of keeping the letter clear and open in diminutive sizes posed different problems. A design would rarely be reduced or enlarged beyond the range of its technical or practical utility, and the level of investment involved imposed critical standards and a rational evolution of the type repertoire. After the pantographic punchcutting machine was invented in 1884 there was an initial tendency to cut corners and to work from a single set of drawings, but typographers came to insist that separate sets should be prepared for each small group of neighbouring sizes within a series in order to incorporate the optical adjustments which experience had shown to be necessary, and this remained the norm throughout the remainder of the period of mechanical composition.

These historical lessons were swept to one side when it came to the development of typefaces intended for photo-setting. Competing phototypesetting equipment manufacturers found themselves in a position – given the available technology, and in the absence of international design copyright protection – to back up their systems with massive typographic software programmes. Companies of integrity and pirates alike were caught up by the same imperative to generate a new type catalogue virtually overnight, and so their efforts converged in a common direction: to allow a single set of drawings to govern the manufacture of the basic roman and to propound all its family derivatives; and to leave it to the customer to decide for himself which of these variants are valid and usable, and the parameters of enlargement or reduction which should apply in each case.

This removal of constraints or guidance for the use of the product is welcomed by most book typographers, who can exercise personal taste and discrimination in a land where the only curse is one of over-plentifulness, and for whom any disadvantages are outweighed by the sophisticated methods now offered by some manufacturers. These have abolished the concept of fixed type sizes and increments of spacing, so that any intermediate size can be selected in a situation where previously the 10pt would be judged too small and the 11pt too large for a given page; similarly questions of working to a specific extent, or adjusting the precise balance of a title page, are much simplified. Book typographers have found a lot of common ground with the designers and manufacturers of typefaces after a few initial misunderstandings; and the areas of concern which remain spring from different rates of adaptation to these recent developments, and from the fact that the typefaces and resources needed in designing books differ from those used in advertising, packaging, and the newspaper and magazine industries.

The table on p.76 shows how some of the body sizes that were standard prior to photocomposition are normally used in bookwork:

point sizes	*general application*	*presumed reading distance*
5, 6, 7, 8	pocket Bibles and dictionaries; ancillary setting of notes, appendixes, indexes, etc.	25-30cm (10″-12″) = slightly closer than customary reading distance
9, 10, 11, 12, 13, 14	range of text sizes for continuous reading; minor headings and extracts within text	35cm (13″+) = optical distance from page for normal reading
14, 16, 18, 20, 24	range of display for chapter and major sub-headings; text use confined to books for youngest children, large print books for the partially sighted, and outsize formats such as lectern Bibles	35-50cm (13″-20″)
24, 30, 36, 42, 48	main line on title pages, binding cases, etc.	50cm (20″) = held in hand
as above	jacket design	50cm+ (20″+) = held in hand or viewed spine-on
56, 60, 72, 96	jacket design	90-180cm (3′-6′) = table, dump-bin, small window display
as above, and larger	jacket design	? = seen across large bookshop or busy street

These guide figures will vary slightly with the format and function of the book, as well as with the reader's age and physique: they highlight that there are certain changes in use – gear-changes in effect – and the skill is to make these smoothly and at the right time. Printers term sizes below 14pt as text and above 14pt as display; clearly this must depend upon the particular typeface and the context in which it is used, but as a general rule text sizes are to be read but not seen, whereas display sizes are there to be seen as well as read. This is further emphasised in the next section which looks at classes of letter design that were never intended for text setting at all, and which may be used sparingly for titling in books and to greatest effect on jackets; but for the moment the focus is on using one and the same typeface appropriately for all the parts of a book.

Designing a book is basically a matter of setting out and signposting the reader's path through a document; the visual editing of a text. A good typist will achieve this and provide an adequate variety of levels of emphasis, simply through a judicious use of the capitals and underscoring available within the text size, in conjunction with straightforward degrees of spacing and indentation. To move on from the fount-resources of the old-fashioned typewriter to typesetting or the DTP keyboard is to liberate a whole new range of alphabets and permutations within the text size:

Manual typewriter keyboard	*Typesetting and (some) PC keyboards*
roman lower case alphabet	roman lower case alphabet
roman capital alphabet	roman capital alphabet
underscoring	italic lower case alphabet
	italic capital alphabet
	bold roman lower case alphabet
	bold roman capital alphabet
	bold italic capital alphabet
	bold italic lower case alphabet
	roman small capital alphabet

The enhanced resources displayed in the right column shows what is possible even before any increase of typesize has to be thought about. Note that underscoring has not been entered in the right column, since the contrast between different tones of voice within the same typeface has taken its place; i.e. underlining is merely a way of asking for the italic contrast or bold emphasis unavailable on the traditional typewriter. Typists will continue to use single and double underlining within documents to be circulated from dot-matrix and daisywheel output for a while, but as better laser founts become commonplace the redundancy of underlining will become apparent here too. Until then, editors and designers will continue to translate essential distinctions in terms of the wider possibilities of print.

Wherever there is to be a complex hierarchy of headings, experienced designers often start by working upwards from the slightest sub-sub-sub-heading distinction that needs to be made towards the major part or chapter division, looking carefully at the incidence of each type of heading and asking each time just how much differentiation will suffice to make the necessary distinction within the structure as a whole. In this way there is no danger of running out of levels of importance, and it will often be found that all the requisite differentials can be made without recourse to bold – which can be an advantage for some kinds of book.

Certainly economy of means tends to result in a clean, restful and well-ordered text for the reader, and this should be the designer's aim. There are circumstances in which a whisper is more effective than a shout – one has the reader's captive attention in any effective reading situation – and the use of over-emphatic headings can result in upsetting this concentration and in making it difficult to follow the structure of the book. When the first increase or decrease from the text size is called for, then a step of two point sizes should be the natural choice, from 10pt text up to 12pt to trigger a whole new set of heading levels, or down to 8pt to save space with extensive notes or extracts. The single point size shift, from 10pt up to 11pt or down to 9pt, should be avoided, since the distinction may be too fine for the average reader's eye to spot.

Unless the structure of the book presents unusual features, then all levels below part and chapter heads can almost certainly be met without recourse to any further increase in typesize for the headings. If this can be achieved, then all gradations of emphasis are likely to take effect without interrupting the progress of continuous reading.

An appreciable contrast in size or style becomes possible and often desirable when it comes to the articulation of the major sections into which a book is divided: the chapter headings and perhaps also the part titles; for these are not just encountered in the normal course of reading, they also serve as navigational aids and should be visible in all conditions. Each case has to be judged on its merits, and if there should be a high incidence of chapter heads that leave the reader

352 *Judith Turner*

Table 12.10. Results of principal components analysis: CF5b.

Mean frequencies	*Betula*	*Pinus*	*Ulmus*	*Quercus*	*Tilia*	*Alnus*	*Fraxinus*	*Corylus*	*Salix*	Herbs
Teeshead 2	8.30	0.57	0.85	11.95	0.14	14.09	1.00	23.53	0.33	39.23
Cross Fell South	11.04	0.40	1.01	13.86	0.07	12.38	2.49	26.04	0.34	32.37
Cross Fell Summit	11.45	0.54	0.43	9.87	0.14	9.94	0.79	21.28	0.47	45.08
Cross Fell West	20.78	0.18	1.39	8.49	0.00	11.54	2.77	14.59	1.39	38.87
Cross Fell East	8.34	0.54	1.08	13.83	0.07	17.15	1.69	31.39	0.07	25.83

	1st principal component	2nd principal component	3rd principal component
% variation	59.3	34.9	4.6
eigenvalue	5.93	3.49	0.46
Component loadings			
Betula	−0.994	−0.002	0.020
Pinus	0.952	−0.278	0.126
Ulmus	−0.571	0.779	0.199
Quercus	0.756	0.569	−0.291
Tilia	0.746	−0.647	0.008
Alnus	0.535	0.718	0.445
Fraxinus	−0.672	0.674	−0.301
Corylus	0.872	0.460	−0.095
Salix	−0.984	−0.116	0.129
Herbs	−0.337	−0.934	0.008
Component scores			
Teeshead 2	0.585	−0.454	0.815
Cross Fell South	0.096	0.584	−1.609
Cross Fell Summit	0.203	−1.474	−0.324
Cross Fell West	−1.710	0.238	0.466
Cross Fell East	0.827	1.107	0.652

with the high frequencies for herbaceous pollen at Cross Fell Summit and the low values at Cross Fell East. *Fraxinus* does not have particularly high loadings on any of the principal components although its frequencies are much higher at Cross Fell South and West than at the other sites.

CHANGES DURING THE COURSE OF CF5

The changes that took place in the pollen assemblages during the course of CF5 are summarized in table 12.11 which gives the (CF5b mean frequency – CF5a mean frequency) for each taxon.

14 Late-Quaternary pollen and plant macrofossil stratigraphy at Lochan an Druim, north-west Scotland

Hilary H. Birks

Introduction

PROFESSOR WINIFRED TUTIN made the first extensive investigation of the vegetational history of north-west Scotland (Pennington *et al.* 1972, Pennington 1975, 1977a, 1977b). She has published pollen diagrams from late- and post-glacial sediments from Loch Sionascaig, Cam Loch, Loch Borralan, and Loch Craggie in the Inverpolly area (see fig. 14.1) in conjunction with studies on sediment chemistry and diatom stratigraphy. Her work extends south to Loch Clair and Loch a'Chroisg in the Torridon area, where in addition, she made my work on Loch Maree possible (Birks H.H. 1972). To the south and west, the late- and post-glacial vegetational history of the Isle of Skye and the adjacent mainland has been reconstructed by H.J.B. Birks (1973a) and Williams (1976) (see Birks and Williams 1983). To the north of Inverpolly, Pennington (1977a) has presented a late- and post-glacial pollen diagram from Lochan an Smuraich. There are also post-glacial pollen diagrams from near Loch Assynt, Lochan an Druim (Birks H.H. unpublished data), and Duartbeg (Moar 1969a). The pioneering late-glacial pollen diagram from Loch Droma (Kirk and Godwin 1963) is associated with some macrofossil and moss records.

The present study was designed to investigate the late-glacial vegetational history of the far north-west of Scotland, thus extending Tutin's work northwards. To provide a contrast with the large lakes studied by Tutin, a small basin was chosen. It was hoped that this would provide a detailed picture of the local and nearby upland vegetation around the site. To further this aim, plant macrofossils were studied stratigraphically in conjunction with the pollen. The site chosen, Lochan an Druim beside Loch Eriboll, is of considerable botanical interest, as it is situated on Durness limestone, nearby outcrops of which today support a rich calcicolous flora, including an abundance of *Dryas octopetala* growing near sea-level (Ratcliffe 1977).

none the wiser, then clearly this ought to be underplayed. The design treatment of these headings will also depend upon the pattern of line lengths they exhibit, and how line-divisions will work out in one size as compared to another. Contrasting sizes of the same roman upper and lower case will sometimes complement each other in a given format and nothing more may be needed to give the page sufficient character; at other times the italic upper and lower, or roman capitals, may provide the better foil; on another occasion bold may provide a better strength of colour, particularly if long chapter titles indicate a small typesize.

There are endless ways of designing something as simple as a chapter heading, but usually only one way that works best for a particular title. If it is well designed, it will be accessible when looked for, and also provide a breathing space when reached in the course of reading. It is one of the few parts of the typography of a book which tends to be looked at as well as read; there is only one place where this is more so – the title page itself – to which it must always remain subservient. For this reason the seasoned designer will turn his or her attention to the title page before making a final decision about styling the chapter heads; that pattern of words which is allowed to determine the size used for the titling on the title page will act as a keystone to the whole structure of the book, and in turn suggest a suitable scale for part and chapter titling.

3:4 Faces intended for display use only

If printing types for text composition reveal the classical face of letter design, it certainly has a popular aspect as well. Before the rise of advertising in the early nineteenth century, the main display groups used by book printers are what might be described as failed or eccentric renderings of those current writing hands that had not found lasting favour for text setting – black letter, civilité, copperplate script – in addition to a handful of early decoratives. This was the stuff of tradesmen's cards and early ephemeral jobbing printing, as well as of the signwriter and monumental mason. Nineteenth-century typefounder's catalogues contributed robust new categories of display letter – the grotesque or sans serif, the fat face or *reductio ad absurdum* of the modern face tendency, the egyptian or slab serif – and a wealth of open, shaded, decorative or distorted elaborations on these basic themes. Art nouveau, functionalist, art deco, and more recent popular idioms have continued to swell the catalogues. These developments have all been well documented in readily available form, so it seems better to concentrate here on those forms most closely related to the history and recurrent requirements of book design.

Fitted initials

Illuminated initials are one of the earliest forms of display lettering, and spaces were left in the first printed books for their insertion by hand. Schoeffer's *Mainz Psalter* resolved the colour printing and typographic aspects of the problem at a stroke, and it can be seen how depths need to be related to

Variations from the dry-transfer lettering catalogues. Children learning to read are fascinated at the variety of signs for the same sound, but score well at identifying flash-cards of all but a handful of the worst designs.

lines of text: here are what can be described as single-line, two-line, and six-line initials in action, but note in addition how carefully the marginal flourishes have been made to correspond to multiples of text lines. Schoeffer's slow colour process (of removing each initial, inking it separately and replacing it within the forme between each impression) was soon dropped, but his typographic solution has conditioned all later developments in metal type. There has scarcely been a generation since the invention of printing that has not in some way added to or found appropriate uses for the rich repertoire of decorative or display initials. Modernists reacted strongly against the equally debased mediaeval and art nouveau models on offer at the turn of the present century, and, although there was an eclectic vogue for initials in the inter-war years, printers became keen to axe yet another craft operation that ran counter to mechanisation, and increasingly designers were brought up to regard initials as a bad thing.

Space prevents further demonstration of the versatility and potential of initials; but in confidently predicting their wider revival, I do not have in mind what might result from a stampede towards obsolete, off-the-peg examples so much as a return to the correct, unassertive use of 2-line capitals of the text fount and an exploration of specially drawn letters that the convergence in outlook between calligraphers and typographers will facilitate. Initials do not need to be fancy or elaborate in design, but they do need to be skilfully and intelligently fitted, although this is a simpler matter now that the constraints of type-metal have been removed. Schoeffer's initials are Lombardic capitals printed in red and beautifully fitted to the remainder of each initial word, which is set in the textura. The CRT-screen restores comparable optical control over the opening initial of each chapter and the word of which it is a part.

Affinities between text face and display

Typefaces are products of the time and place in which they were first introduced, and share style characteristics with contemporaneous art, architecture and fashion. The title page to Fournier's *Manuel Typographique* (1766) is one such an expression of its age, in which rococo ornament spills over into the decorative lettering of the top line as well as the delightful unit border; here the same typefounder provides text, display and ornament designed to work together. In total contrast, Bodoni's neo-classical manner, which had evolved by the turn of the century although his *Manuale Tipografico* only appeared posthumously in 1818, depends as much upon the elimination of decoration from the border as Fournier's page benefits from its inclusion. [Both title pages appear with no indication of their generous original margins]

Such examples of how a typeface was used at the time of its introduction are helpful in recreating an atmosphere of

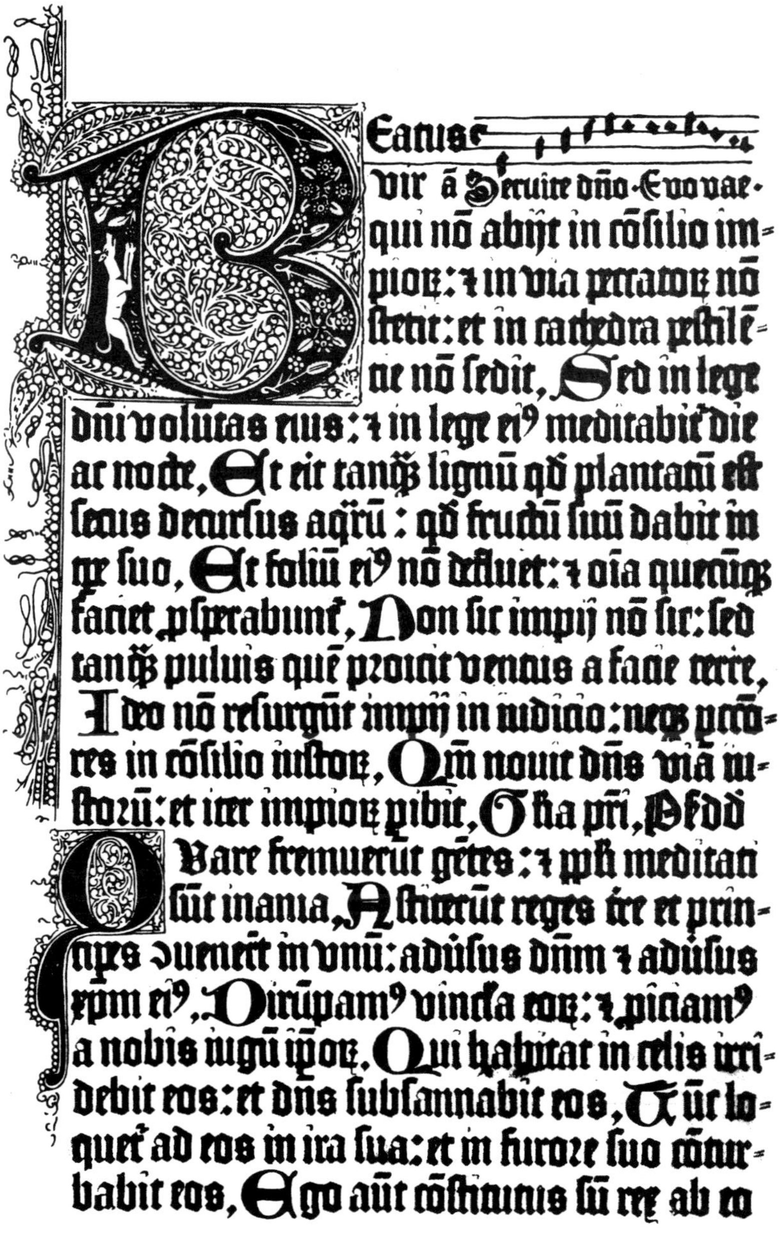
Beatus
vir q̄ Seruite dn̄o · Euouae ·
qui nō abiit in cōsilio im-
pior: ⁊ in via pccator nō
stetit: et in cathedra pestilē-
ne nō sedit. Sed in lege
dn̄i voluntas eius: ⁊ in lege ei⁹ meditabit' die
ac nocte. Et erit tanq̄ lignū qd̄ plantatū est
secus decursus aqrū: qd̄ fructū suū dabit in
tpe suo. Et foliū ei⁹ nō defluet: ⁊ oīa quecūq;
faciet psperabunt'. Non sic impii nō sic: sed
tanq̄ puluis quē proicit ventus a facie terre.
Ideo nō resurgūt impii in iudicio: neq; pctō-
res in cōsilio iustor. Qm̄ nouit dn̄s viā iu-
storū: et iter impior pibit. Gloria patri.
Quare fremuerūt gētes: ⁊ ppli meditati
sūt inania. Astiterūt reges terre et prin-
cipes cōuenerūt in vnū: aduersus dn̄m ⁊ aduersus
xpm ei⁹. Dirūpam⁹ vincla eor: ⁊ pciam⁹
a nobis iugū ipsor. Qui habitat in celis irri-
debit eos: et dn̄s subsannabit eos. Tūc lo-
quet' ad eos in ira sua: et in furore suo cōtur-
babit eos. Ego aūt cōstitutus sū rex ab eo

Opening page from the Mainz Psalter *of 1459, showing the celebrated colour-printed initials.*

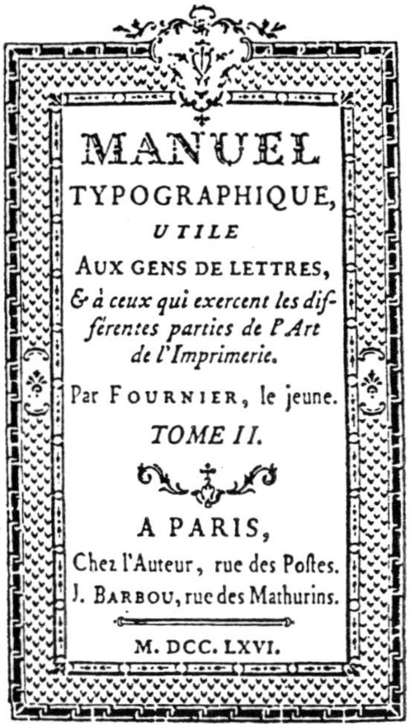
MANUEL
TYPOGRAPHIQUE,
UTILE
AUX GENS DE LETTRES,
& à ceux qui exercent les différentes parties de l'Art de l'Imprimerie.
Par FOURNIER, le jeune.
TOME II.
A PARIS,
Chez l'Auteur, rue des Postes.
J. BARBOU, rue des Mathurins.
M. DCC. LXVI.

Titles page of P. S. Fournier's Manuel Typographique, *vol. 2, dated 1766 but published two years later.*

time and place, wherever that is appropriate in book design. The text typeface, taken on its own, has to remain neutral and anonymous during the reading process; but introducing related display material and observing the design conventions of the period can open up new possibilities, ranging from subtle and controlled allusion within the book to powerful and unambiguous jacket effects. It is not suggested that book design should be allowed to turn very often into a game played with history and geography, in an effort to find the right clothing for a particular author or subject, but it is a dimension in which designers should be able to think and communicate.

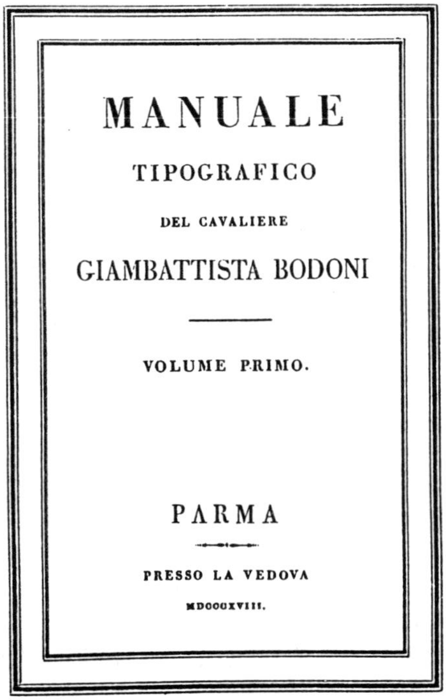
MANUALE
TIPOGRAFICO
DEL CAVALIERE
GIAMBATTISTA BODONI
VOLUME PRIMO.
PARMA
PRESSO LA VEDOVA
MDCCCXVIII.

The French Revolution and the First Empire separate the neo-classicism of Bodoni's posthumous Manuale Tipografico *of 1818 from the rococo world of Fournier's specimen of type and ornament.*

Typographic contrast in display

It has been said of both music and painting independently, that in the early twentieth century they became separated from their past as much through the intelligent use of discord as anything else: too much harmony ultimately becomes predictable and boring, and this is also true for some branches of typography. Modernism and the jazz age found exuberant release in letter forms and layout at the time, even

POETIC

GEMS

SELECTED FROM THE WORKS OF

WILLIAM

McGONAGALL

POET AND TRAGEDIAN

died in Edinburgh 29 September 1902

FOREWORD BY

SPIKE MILLIGAN

BRIEF BIOGRAPHY AND REMINISCENCES

BY

THE AUTHOR

TRIBUTE AND ODE

from three students at Glasgow University

and other

TRIBUTES AND TESTIMONIALS

DRAMATIC COLLAGES

BY

MICHAEL FOREMAN

LONDON

The Folio Society

1985

Ian Mortimer's title page design assembles an exuberant but carefully-judged display from Victorian material.

The shock of the new – Ardengo Soffici, Florence, 1915.

if all that is left is just discreet typographic cocktail mixing by comparison. The example of Italian Futurist typography dating from 1915 is typical of just one of the liberating forces active at that time, and it anticipates so many of the contrasts in scale, weight, angle and character, that have since become familiar. Identical principles of contrast can be seen to be harnessed in a more considered and concentrated form by later typographers, and similar skills remain basic to successful asymmetric design.

Galerie **Thannhauser**

These variants in the art of typographic cocktail mixing taken from press advertisements show Tschichold's attention to detail whilst working with fixed sizes of metal type: the first setting shows an intention to range the x-height levels; whereas the later version attempts to intensify the contrast yet more and also to create an alignment of cap heights.

The principle of maximum contrast was well understood and practised by Jan Tschichold, at first in relation to sanserif where extra-light is played off against ultra-bold, but in the 1930s he extended this to exploit every possible pair of opposite characteristics that could arise from the juxtaposition of two short words or statements. It is a very valid procedure but a tricky one to master.

Galerie **Thannhauser**

In these examples of effective display, it is not the letter forms themselves which are new so much as the ways in which they are used. The craft of typography often seems to progress in a similar manner; alphabets fall out of use for a while as methods and fashions change, but if they have real merit they always stand a good chance of future revival. An attempt to summarise the recent history of display faces in order to explain the current pattern of their availability would run roughly as follows:

1. as founder's type in case was rapidly disappearing from the market, type manufacturers at first supplied the display deficiency as masters on slide or spool for photoheadlining machines, which failed to establish a market beyond expensive trade typesetting as supplied to advertising agencies.
2. book designers made increasing use of rub-down lettering (Letraset etc.), since book composition houses could not at first phototypeset display to an acceptable standard.
3. type manufacturers transferred their attentions to the text and type family repertoire to the neglect of eccentric and one-off display faces, book design attention was focussed anew on the potential of the display sizes of text faces.

4. a few book designers began to take a renewed interest in authentic historical material for personal use as an alternative to the restricted, unexciting and over-used commercial repertoire.

Examples of revivals and twentieth-century designs from the historic Netherlands typefoundry: Joh. Enschedé en Zonen, Haarlem.

OPEN ROMULUS

DIDOT

OPEN KAPITALEN

MOLÉ

ROSART

Dry-transfer display lettering

The manufacturers of dry-transfer lettering have kept pace with changing markets for more than thirty years as a result of technological advances and enterprising typeface development programmes, and Letraset's policy of commissioning new designs, as well as consolidating established ones, has brought that company to the forefront as a type manufacturer. The dry-transfer concept has all the hallmarks of a classic do-it-yourself product, not least that in professional hands it will yield a result to match any other for quality. Designers find precise control over spacing and arrangement, and freedom to create and modify word-sets, invaluable when preparing titling for book jackets and display. Dry-transfer sheets and tapes enable artwork to be produced efficiently, particularly where the needs of a particular field can be met from the extensive ranges of symbols and related graphic resources. The catalogues from Letraset, Chartpak, Mecanorma and other suppliers are useful in tracking down the best solutions and for ordering sheets by reference number.

Display produced by dry-transfer is likely to outclass that which can be generated via computer for a long time to come, and so it offers great potential within DTP to anyone prepared to acquire basic skills in a versatile medium. Such simple matters as finding a suitable paper surface and burnisher make all the difference to professional and beginner alike. With practice, most people have little difficulty in keeping to a straight line, but an eye for regular and well-judged spacing between letters, words and lines will only come with a real interest in the subject. Working with sizes below 18pt (5mm capital height) or above 36pt (10mm capital height) present initial difficulties to many, and certainly the larger sizes offer very limited supplies of each letter per sheet. The cost of materials may be kept down by settling for a comfortable working size in the medium range, knowing that reduction tends to smooth out a degree of unevenness in application and that, conversely, the image will in most cases stand an enlargement as extreme as 400% without significant loss of edge definition. This presupposes access to a modern zoom copier for exact sizing (and for results that may be of acceptable reproduction quality in the right circumstances).

Dry transfer is ideal where titling calls for trial and error to get the spacing and positioning right.

Creasing, scratching and incomplete transfer from the backing sheet provided an instant solution for a theatre poster and programme.

3:5 The history and use of italics

The book designer has many uses for italics, the least of which should be thus: *for emphasis within the text*. This is frequently no more than a nervous tic on the author's part in the face of the typographic restrictions of the 'qwerty' keyboard and is normally eliminated by the copy editor, since what may pass as underlining in typescript becomes irritating to the reader if rendered as true italic, as well as complicating the traditional usage of italics for foreign words and phrases, titles of books and publications, and to make the finest level of distinction between subheading and text.

Chancery italic and text setting

Italic was devised as an alternative lower-case fount to be used – at first with roman small capitals – for continuous reading; Aldus Manutius introduced it in 1501 for the extensive series of pocket editions of the classics which he and his successors continued to publish from Venice. This innovatory typeface design, produced for him by the celebrated punch-cutter Francesco Griffo, had a number of special qualities which fitted it for this task; the most important of which being that it was based on current handwriting – on the italic hand developed in the papal chancery, taken up by the humanists, and promulgated throughout sixteenth-century Europe in a magnificent series of writing-manuals stemming from the those of the Italian masters: Tagliente, Arrighi, Palatino and Cresci. The twentieth-century revival of interest in italic handwriting inspired by Edward Johnston and Alfred Fairbank has sent schoolchildren and type designers alike back again to these unimpeachable models; whilst other hands such as the French *Civilité,* which were similarly copied as printing types but quickly fell from use, are only now beginning to attract the attention of calligraphers.

Chancery Italic (Palatino)

A second virtue of the true chancery italic lower case is that its a-z (alphabet) length should be far shorter than the equivalent roman fount so that this narrow-fitting letter accommodates more characters to a line, thus helping to avoid line-breaks and making it particularly suitable for setting poetry – a task for which it is also well adapted in other respects. The current swing away from clinical or mechanistic typefaces (notably Univers and Helvetica at the sanserif extreme) has focussed attention on those warmer and more humane letter forms that have retained hints of their handwritten or engraved origins. The chancery group of italics presents a rich field for study in this context, since – despite the unity and utility of the basic design – each version has its own unmistakable texture and quirks of personality, with the result that most people find it easier to recognise a typeface from its italic rather than from its roman spot characteristics.

It is well known that poetry by its nature has always tended to impose a more leisurely reading pace than other literary forms, and this operates in favour of italics and other less standardised letter forms in that, as the eye slows down in relation to the reading content, it may in addition have time for a peripheral awareness of distinctive and appropriate typographic dress.

Although certain other forms of italic are suitable for poetry or for concise prose extracts, the best of the chancery italic variants – and my short-list of these would have to include Arrighi, Bembo, Bembo Condensed, Blado, Cancelleresca Bastarda, Dante, Diotima, Palatino, Photina, Spectrum and Zapf Chancery – are unrivalled for their easiness on the eye in reading situations of this kind. The page from the Penguin Shakespeare, designed in Bembo Italic by Jan Tschichold in 1949, uses the Bembo Italic for precisely the same reasons and follows the same basic conventions as the page from an Aldine classic printed almost 450 years earlier.

P·V.M· AENEIDOS LIBER
SECVNDVS.

*Onticuere omnes, intentique ora
tenebant,
Inde toro pater Aeneas sic orsus
ab alto,
Infandum Regina iubes renouare
dolorem,
T roianas ut opes, et lamentabile regnum
E ruerint Danai, quæque ipse miserrima uidi,
E t quorum pars magna fui· quis talia fando
Myrmidonum, Dolopumúe, aut duri miles Vlyssi
T emperet à lachrymis? et iam nox humida cælo
P ræcipitat, suadentq́; cadentia sydera somnos·
S ed si tantus amor casus cognoscere nostros,
E t breuiter Troiæ supremum audire laborem,
Quanq̃ animus meminisse horret, luctuq́; refugit,
I ncipiam· Fracti bello, fatisq́; repulsi
D uctores Danaum, tot iam labentibus annis,
I nstar montis equum diuina Palladis arte
A edificant, sectaq́; intexunt abiete costas.
V otum pro reditu simulant, ea fama uagatur·
H uc delecta uirum sortiti corpora furtim
I ncludunt cæco lateri, penitusq́; cauernas
I ngenteis, uterumq́; armato milite complent.
E st in conspectu Tenedos notissima fama
I nsula, diues opum, Priami dum regna manebant,
N unc tantum sinus, et statio male fida carinis·
H uc se prouecti deserto in littore condunt.*

'Old Face' italic as an adjunct to roman

By the mid fifteenth-century, French punch-cutters had moved away from the idea that type was to be cut in imitation of contemporary handwriting, and freed from the need to follow the characteristic forms and rhythms of the pen in near facsimile, the engraving tools themselves began to influence the precise and detailed shaping of letters. Style can find freer expression in an italic which is no longer primarily structured for continuous reading, but designed to act as a foil or in pointed contrast to its roman, or in an almost ceremonial capacity in contriving exits and entrances. The growth of a range of alternative or 'swash' capitals with decorative flourishes, and ligature variants to the basic alphabet is part of the same story.

Old Face Italic (Garamond)

A characteristic of most of these italics is that the angles of the stems are all over the place; this certainly contributes to their vitality and sparkle on the page, and serves to contrast them admirably with roman or small capitals within the same

A LOVER'S COMPLAINT 105

*Sometimes her levell'd eyes their carriage ride,
As they did batt'ry to the spheres intend:
Sometimes diverted their poor balls are tied,
To th' orbed earth; sometimes they do extend,
Their view right on, anon their gazes lend,
To every place at once and no where fix'd,
The mind and sight distractedly commix'd.*

*Her hair nor loose nor tied in formal plait,
Proclaim'd in her a careless hand of pride;
For some untuck'd descended her sheav'd hat,
Hanging her pale and pined cheek beside,
Some in her threaden fillet still did bide,
And true to bondage would not break from thence,
Though slackly braided in loose negligence.*

*A thousand favours from a maund she drew,
Of amber crystal and of bedded jet,
Which one by one she in a river threw,
Upon whose weeping margent she was set,
Like usury applying wet to wet,
Or monarch's hands that lets not bounty fall,
Where want cries some, but where excess begs all.*

*Of folded schedules had she many a one,
Which she perus'd, sigh'd, tore and gave the flood,
Crack'd many a ring of posied gold and bone,
Bidding them find their sepulchres in mud,
Found yet mo letters sadly penn'd in blood,
With sleided silk, feat and affectedly
Enswath'd and seal'd to curious secrecy.*

It is easy enough to remove such imperfections and irregularities as slope variation, but these often impart strengths to a design for which mechanical evenness is no substitute.

MM

vv gygy

line – as happens in the setting of bibliographies and a host of similar working situations – where the reader notes distinctions in meaning or function without being made consciously aware of the visual means of differentiation.

Variation in slope affects the italic capital alphabet as well (although this has been regularised in some modern recuttings), and capitals of this class are usually best not used for setting headings and display lines. It does appear that they were primarily intended for the capitalisation of lower case as distinct from word building in their own right: the examples show the unfortunate spacing which can result and that swash characters are best used with restraint.

ELEGANCE

WILD ANIMALS

Old face italics held the stage from the late French Renaissance until the early eighteenth century, and thereafter the italic rather aped the roman and lost its true purpose and identity in the view of many designers. A fine baroque example is the so-called 'Janson' italic (taken from the Stempel specimen of 1924, which may or may not have been reproduced using restored matrices of Nicholas Kis's seventeenth-century original cutting).

The 28pt italic size from the 1924 Stempel specimen-booklet.

In einem ſchönen fernen
Reiche, von welchem die
Sage lebt, daß die Sonne

'Modern' italics

By comparison, most 'modern' or nineteenth-century italics are mechanical-looking derivatives of the romans they accompany: character widths and hence alphabet lengths are usually identical; the slope is a fixed one; and the two alphabets are contrasted simply by the displacement of the thick stroke from the vertical to the inclined. Some of the lower case hair-line serifs and strokes terminate in a hook, which acts both to stabilise and to hint at a running script – after the manner in which letters were linked in the contemporaneous copperplate hand. The result is frankly monotonous, and, just as there was great gladness when copperplate was abolished as a model in schools, there is no reason to regret the fact that the modern face is generally out of fashion for text composition. Having said that, the finest examples in historical usage have an incomparable, almost heroic quality – not for nothing did Bodoni and Napoleon belong to the same age. Noting how neo-classicism has found its way back into architecture, then it would be rational to predict an imminent revival of interest in this style of typeface and typography, not for the purposes of text composition, but used eclectically for jacket design and display.

III *III*

nature,

Copperplate, from G. Bickham's The Universal Penman, *1743.*

Modern *Modern Italic (Walbaum)*

Sloped romans

In the present century numerous roman founts of different varieties have been accompanied by italics which may be loosely described as 'sloped roman', and the proportion has increased in recent years because of the ease with which italic (as well as bold, condensed and expanded) additions to the type family may be produced by computer from the basic roman co-ordinates. Each of these designs has to be judged on its merits, but there is an inevitable tendency towards drab predictability *vis-à-vis* their romans. However, where the sloped roman convention is adopted by a master designer such as Eric Gill (Joanna, Pilgrim), a subtle symbiosis between roman and italic forms can take place which belies this crude and generalised description. The best of the sloped romans produce a clean but contrasting impression when set alongside the text, and work well for extracts – verse in particular; and the larger sizes of capitals or upper and lower can be effective in display. Romulus is a very pure instance of a sloped roman, and a good one at that:

Sloped Roman (Romulus Italic)

A final word is reserved for the pseudo italics, that is to say those forward or backward tilted distortions of the roman film or digital master which may be carried out within the actual typesetting apparatus: such fairground mirror deformations have no place in book typography.

Type modifications made on the Compugraphic system: the top four lines show increments of closer character fitting; the next four are examples of distortions to the width or slope of the italic alphabet; and the lowest two lines are slantings of the roman alphabet.

Kerning only

Yet there are also strong arguments why the des

Kerning & letterspacing track 1

Yet there are also strong arguments why the des

Kerning & letterspacing track 2

Yet there are also strong arguments why the des

Kerning & letterspacing track 3

Yet there are also strong arguments why the des

Expanded 20%

Yet there are also strong arguments why

Condensed 20%

Yet there are also strong arguments why the designer should

Pseudo italic 12° forward

Yet there are also strong arguments why the desig

Pseudo italic 12° backward

Yet there are also strong arguments why the desig

Pseudo italic 12° forward

Yet there are also strong arguments why

Pseudo italic 12° backward

Yet there are also strong arguments why

3:6 Small capitals and alternative figures

The small capital alphabet is intended for use in the text wherever it is grammatically and stylistically possible for it to take the place of true capitals. It is designed as a fount to match the weight of the lower case alphabet, since, should the normal capitals be reduced to the lower case x-height, the result is visibly lighter. This in fact is what happens with some inferior founts and typesetting systems, which offer pseudo small caps as a makeshift in text setting. The top line shows true small caps and the lower one capitals reduced to identical size; the slightly sturdier weight and structure of the former will sometimes be found preferable for display.

ABCDEFGHIJKLMN

ABCDEFGHIJKLMN

True small capitals above, enlarged for comparison with the capitals of Garth Graphic.

Small caps were traditionally never issued in typefounders' sizes above 14pt, but it is not widely realised that phototypesetting now frequently offers the designer two capital alphabets to choose between.

Small capitals arose naturally from page texture considerations for continuous reading and an awareness of how easily the reader's concentration might be thrown by poor craftsmanship in spacing and letter design. Just as slack or uneven word spacing caused holes in the fabric of the page, so overassertive characters drew attention to themselves. Capitals were prime offenders in this respect in early books printed in roman types, and they were soon lowered to less than the ascender height and also reduced in weight in order to blend harmoniously. Nevertheless problems remained wherever the incidence of capitals on the page was higher than normal for whatever reason: and small caps were devised to meet all the circumstances in which they are presently used. In display use – where headings take a line of their own – small capitals may be used evenly with confidence; but where text is to run-on, as with a conventional chapter opening, then the use of caps and small caps in combination is indicated.

Some specimen sheets show that two sets of numerals are available: those which correspond to capitals, and those which are intended to appear with upper and lower case and small caps. The former are also known as lining or modern figures, and the latter as non-lining or old style figures.

Most alphanumerical combinations – down to such details as postcodes and standard book numbers – should correspond to these examples. True small caps and non-lining figs usually look best for words, initials and dates occurring within a text.

ABCDEFGHIJKLMNOPQRSTUVWXYZ1234567890

ABCDEFGHIJKLMN 1234567890 abcdefghijklmn

A number of systems will only offer a single set of figures in any case, and certain type families are not traditionally equipped with these alternatives (sanserifs for example take lining figures only).

Most manuscripts contain a variety of numerical requirements, some of which are more immediately obvious than others: tabular or mathematical setting is apparent and a high incidence will be a key factor in choosing a typeface; but note references in superior figures are an example of the kind of detail that can easily be overlooked, and a size and style that will not function can remain unspotted even in proof.

Lining figures are the natural choice for tabular setting because, although occupying the same page area, these figures are in fact the larger and more open of the two sets. Of equal importance is the way in which the eye traverses any table both horizontally and vertically, across the columns and down them: the regularity of lining figures is a major enabling factor in all but the most elementary column setting. In order for figures to align within columns and across tables (and it is now almost universal that figures of both kinds should do so), then it is necessary for them to share the standard width of an 'en', and this simplifies checking the width of a table in relation to the page, and the overall design of tables, as discussed below.

Books with a statistical basis will incline to follow through the use of lining figures within the text, although non-lining figures are frequently to be preferred in other settings since they work particularly well in text. However there is no reason why the alternative set should not feature within any title, provided the distinction in use is a functional one and that this is made clear in the specification. Pagination is not the least of such details; even Bruce Rogers once admitted to having left the folios off simply because he couldn't think where to put them.

3:7 The use of bold type

The original bold type to be used in conjunction with roman was the black letter (some newspaper mastheads are a vestige of this device for giving weight and emphasis to titling), and this makeshift sufficed whilst usage and demand remained sporadic or insignificant. More importantly, it must have been recognised at the time that the inherent design of the roman face was resistant to 'emboldening' until the fully-developed modern face evolved at the end of the eighteenth century. This problem normally recurs whenever an attempt is made to design a related bold: in the case of a true old face roman the result is clumsy and legibility drops dramatically, especially in the smaller sizes; whereas with modern faces it is just a question of adding weight to increase the contrast between thick and thin strokes, which is fine except that even the best versions have only limited application today.

ABC g　　ABC abc
ABC g　　**ABCabc**

Baskerville with bold left, Bodoni right.

Bold type should be kept on a lead – it is too fierce to be let roam around within the text area baying staccato emphasis – every subtle gradation that is needed inside the page for continuous reading can be made without the disruptive intrusion of bold.

The designer knows that the reader can be helped to find a path through the structure of the most complicated book without recourse to bold type for signalling or signposting, and will view the bold option quite differently. Depending on the kind of volume – its format and illustration – a need may be felt for 'colour' on the page, for accents to enliven and point up the balance of the layout, which bold alone can abc

abcdefghijklmnop

nop

There are such dramatic changes in serif and curve structure between Times New Roman and its bold that the two alphabets cannot be described as truly related, but they work together excellently as the result of successful compromise.

supply. This is a valid usage, the signs of which are that the bold lines will in reality be quite small but isolated from the contingent reading areas by a sea of space. There are so many kinds of book that there must be all sorts of conventional and functional situations in which bold is the inevitable choice; it is difficult to generalise, but my point of view is that all avenues should be explored first so that bold is not introduced gratuitously into a text for continuous reading.

Immediately the reader is shifted from a situation of sitting peacefully with a book to that of standing by a shelf actively hunting information – then all our typographic premises have to be revised, and bold typefaces acquire a fresh function and perspective. I think the school textbook is also typical of this category – wherever concentration is periodically transferred to and from the printed page. Reference use involves focal distances commonly ranging from 150 to 750mm in combination with highly sophisticated scanning techniques adapted to the problem in hand; this indicates that up to three differentiated levels – bold, semi-bold, and normal – may be discriminated between and allocated functions according to the complexity of the task. The value of making comparisons in the approach to corresponding classes of book in other countries applies here as elsewhere; if there is consensus in employing a bold type in a given situation then that usage is confirmed as functional, otherwise it has only the authority of continuing custom and the designer may have a case for advancing alternative and more up-to-date thinking.

abc

abcdefghijklmnop

nop

Melior, where the open and squarely drawn 'o' based shapes (note the inner enclosed counters) give scope for a clean and legible bold even in the smallest sizes.

3:8 Typographic rule

Before writing, I suspect, came the ruling of lines. Prealphabetic clay tablets and carved inscriptions, cuneiform and hieroglyphics, display an amazing variety of directional rulings between lines, breaks, paragraphs, languages and columns; there is no doubt but that this guidance for the eye – the layout which is here being offered – is just as deliberately intended as the grids which govern today's tabloid newspaper or statement of accounts. A purist view of typographical theory would imply that rule had been rendered redundant once the means existed to order the most diverse and complex material through spatial arrangement alone; and there is certainly skill involved and satisfaction to be derived in styling tabular matter without having to resort to horizontal and vertical rulings (and at one time there were cost advantages in the practice as well.)

On the other hand, the lively introduction of rule can be fun, as this example by Imre Reiner dating from 1944 or earlier shows (the original rule printed red): no rule = no design.

Rule has the additional narcotic property of seeming to remedy weak design; it can balance a precarious layout just as a tightrope walker is preserved by his pole, it can be added as an afterthought to disguise the emptiness of a badly calculated page, or to create a semblance of unity running through unrelated spreads by its own reappearance in a standard position. But it can be used quite legitimately where the designer is sure it responds to a requirement in the brief or has something to add.

Rule is a major fashion element, rarely absent in one guise or another from book design; as Bruce Rogers, one of the earliest professionals in the field, clearly saw: 'few publishers or clients are willing to pay sufficiently for what seems to most of them "just plain printing," however well executed. They think, rightly or wrongly, that this can be done in any good printing-works without incurring designers' fees in addition to the manufacturing costs.' Rule provides a reserve of sham-functional answers without invalidating its own capacity to be used appositely and freshly.

It is fascinating to observe the current vogue in rules: whether they are used singly or in combination; across the page, down the page, or to form borders or boxes; between columns, framing the text area, or close to the trim; set to the text measure, wider, or markedly narrower; above or beneath the running head, and perhaps at the foot as well; whether square ended, mitre-jointed or of uneven lengths; with corners joined, crossed or rounded – these are just a few of the possibilities to be aware of.

From a DTP viewpoint, rules and borders are difficult to draw, or to lay accurately from dry-transfer sheets or border tapes. The basic range offered by most typesetting systems is rather mundane, although more creative and sophisticated results are possible; for example, multiple rules can be combined with a character or dingbat to produce individual borders for covers and jackets. Wherever rule is to be a key or standard element, it is worth going to a trade typesetter for precision and quality. Should fine rule be required for inter-column use or for a standard border, then artwork may be prepared for grids to be printed in two colours: in non-photographic blue for camera ready paste-up, and with the rules that are to print already present in black.

3:9 Printers' flowers, decorations and ornaments

Printers' flowers first made an appearance in 1478 (*Scientia et arte de ben morire*, printed in Verona by the brothers Giovanni and Alberto Alvise), and for five centuries these combinable type ornaments remained a standard feature of typefounders' specimens and catalogues; responding to baroque, rococo, neo-classical, gothic revival, art nouveau, art deco and other design influences, but with the early arabesques co-existing intermittently by virtue of their unbeatable versatility. Max Caflisch's book is an exercise in the permutation of just the following six units:

to form fleurons, borders and all-over patterns suitable for end-papers or bookbinding. Historical pattern can be over-used or abused, but the sources are so rich and the ways of using them so endless that they can never be said to go out of fashion *en bloc* – one only has to look at recent Laura Ashley fabrics or the replication of Victorian fireplace tiles. It is always a good sign when patterns pass out of circulation for a while, and this certainly appears to have happened to ornament with the advent of phototypesetting, when the complex method of assembling these typographic units was found to be at odds with the essentially linear nature of the new process. There is scope in the future to improve the range and quality of individual designs available for dry-transfer systems, to make wider use of the photomechanical step-and-repeat facility for producing effective and colourful pattern papers from the most basic of starting points, and, perhaps most excitingly, to generate new combinations (if not new decorative motifs) on the home micro-computer. Two factors keep ornament constantly open as an occasional resource for the designer: imagination, and the relevance of the context in which it is deployed.

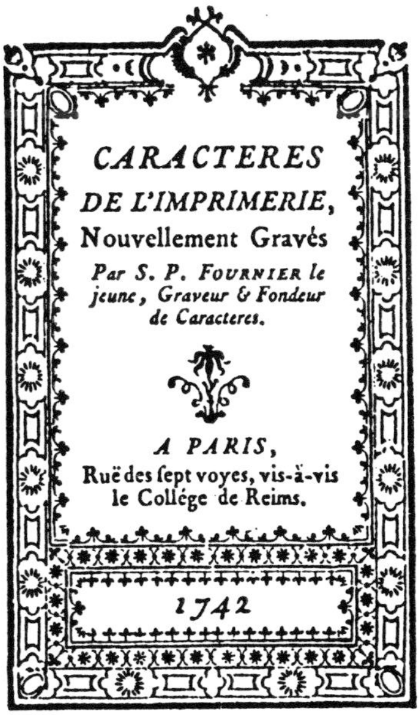

CARACTERES
DE L'IMPRIMERIE,
Nouvellement Gravés
Par S. P. FOURNIER le
jeune, Graveur & Fondeur
de Caracteres.

A PARIS,
Ruë des ſept voyes, vis-à-vis
le Collége de Reims.

1742

The decorative title to Fournier's 24mo type specimen of 1742, slightly reduced.

Dingbats and other special sorts

Most typographers are addicts of those back pages of type manufacturers' catalogues which display 'aeroplanes, anchors, angles, arrows, astronomical, automobiles, beds, braces, chessmen, circles . . .' amongst thousands of special symbols that can be used to expand the conventional alphabetic fount to the frontiers of Michelin-speak.

Zapf Dingbats are an extensive series of single-unit signs, symbols and ornaments, cleanly redrawn to work with most typefaces and now widely available. This development is to be welcomed as the first step in meeting a real demand in an area where phototypesetting can offer greater versatility than ever before in reaching the international langage market. Several ranges of these symbols are also available as dry-transfer sheets from the Letraset catalogue, which is excellent for its coverage of the conventional sign vocabularies used in producing artwork for a variety of disciplines.

ITC Dingbats Series 300.

	A	B	C	D	E	F	G	H	J	K	L	M	N
1	➀	➁	➂	➃	➄	➅	➆	➇	➈	➉	➊	➋	➌
2	➍	➎	➏	➐	➑	➒	➓	❝	❞	‟	〃	✓	✓
3	✄	♤	♡	♢	♧	♠	♥	♦	♣	◆	◇	(	)
4	←	⇦	⇨	←	⬅	➟	➠	⬅	↢	↞	↢	⇨	➳
5	➵	➭	⇨	➩	▷	➳	➵	➪	➫	➮	⇦	☎	☏
6	☞	☛	☚	☞	✍	✎	❘	❚	}	}	▮	{	{
7	✲	✿	✚	✚	✳	✺	✣	✤	✥	❀	❄	❅	✷
8	✶	✱	❤	❣	❢	✕	✖	✦	✢	✡	✹	❀	❆
9	✽	✝	✙	ↄ	⊛	❂	@	@	#	ℂ	❡	PRINTED IN USA	

Stock blocks and source books

The desktop publisher is in good company when unable to afford specially-drawn illustration or commercial rates for picture research and reproduction: the miniatures in illuminated MSS. were frequently copied from other sources, and the identical woodcut blocks used by some of the earliest printers turn up again put to a variety of uses in later books printed all over Europe. This trade became significant enough for wood and metal engravings of stock subjects to be multiplied in a range of sizes and offered for sale to jobbing printers, in exactly the way that source books of copyright-free artwork are available to advertisers, designers and printers for camera-ready use today.

From the Caslon specimen of 1785 – one of a number of type specimen facsimiles initiated by the Printing Historical Society.

Apart from specific source books – of which historical reprints in general may be of interest to book publishers, but where most contemporary out-of-copyright artwork will be found to be directed to an advertising market – there is a wealth of accessible free material in the public domain that includes decorative initials and rules, maps and city views, portraits and costume, anatomical and botanical subjects, early cartoons and photography, ephemera, family mementoes and social documentation. The zoom copier has opened a new field for experimentation to DTP, offering an instant guide to the effects of enlargement, reduction, and line treatment on various types of original on which to base camera ready artwork for paste-up alongside the text setting. Pictures that at first sight may have only a very general link to a particular title can frequently be manipulated to yield a strong and simple image through the enlargement of a telling area, which, combined with titling, can add up to an effective jacket or cover. 'Proofing', or taking trial xeroxes of image and titling at various sizes on thin coloured paper, tracing paper or clear foil allow the best impact to be built-up and judged on a trial and error basis. This can become an absorbing activity for the untrained designer who may be required to generate a series of solutions to text and title pages and covers in a particular field, and could lead into picture research proper as these 'off the peg' possibilities become exhausted.

3:10 Working with typeface specimens

Identifying a typeface can prove a tricky process even where there is access to an up-to-date library of reference material; although it may be simple enough to establish that a book has been set in Baskerville or in Palatino, it may be difficult even for the expert these days to tell quickly which version has been used. That is why it is always a good idea to give this information on the imprint page in the form "set in Clonatype

Times by ABC Typesetters, Newtown", if only for your own future reference. If the typesetter at least is known, then the quickest way to get to the answer may well be to telephone to establish at least which system is used (or was used at the time), and a list of book faces held.

The next step is to obtain an adequate specimen, since it is impossible to proceed with book design or type specification without having one to hand for constant reference; however familiar the typeface and format, no typographer should be prepared to specify even the simplest flap copy without first glancing at a specimen to check, and making rapid judgements and calculations to confirm the optimum size, leading and measure.

If the typesetter has an excuse for not having had a proper specimen printed, then a full character set in a single size should be requested; this will serve in the absence of anything better, since a zoom copier will deliver precise enlargements or reductions to any required point size; a facility that dispenses with much repetitive scaling, tracing, and lettering work in the studio. At an early stage, the editor should have supplied a list of any special characters or sorts which occur in the MS, and the designer will check these out so that the typesetter can obtain anything particularly esoteric to special order or manufacture and supply a specimen in good time.

Type specimen sheets, and the loose leaf binders in which they are stored, have always been the best answer for desk-work, but there are several other kinds of type reference material which are useful in book design. Type manufacturers' specimens come in three basic formats at present: there are the free booklets which give a comprehensive showing of newly released type families; spiral bound synopses of the full range; and gargantuan coffee table books. To receive the first it is only necessary to get onto the mailing lists, the second type are best obtained through cultivating your typesetter since many are outrageously priced to the general public, and no doubt the last mentioned are free if you want to buy the system. The individual booklets are splendid in that those that are useful can be kept and the need for the bound-up compendia will never arise; the synopses for the systems in regular use for bookwork are essential for the serious typographer. This area of typeface literature opens up what is available beyond the restricted range that most typesetters

Sabon

4pt abcdefghijklmnopqrstuvwxyzABCDEFGHIJKLMNOPQRSTUVWXYZ1234567890
5pt abcdefghijklmnopqrstuvwxyzABCDEFGHIJKLMNOPQRSTUVWXYZ1234567890
6pt abcdefghijklmnopqrstuvwxyzABCDEFGHIJKLMNOPQRSTUVWXYZ1234567890
7pt abcdefghijklmnopqrstuvwxyzABCDEFGHIJKLMNOPQRSTUVWXYZ1234567890
8pt abcdefghijklmnopqrstuvwxyzABCDEFGHIJKLMNOPQRSTUVWXYZ1234567890
9pt abcdefghijklmnopqrstuvwxyzABCDEFGHIJKLMNOPQRSTUVWXYZ1234567890
10pt abcdefghijklmnopqrstuvwxyzABCDEFGHIJKLMNOPQRSTUVWXYZ1234567890
11pt abcdefghijklmnopqrstuvwxyzABCDEFGHIJKLMNOPQRSTUVWXYZ1234567890
12pt abcdefghijklmnopqrstuvwxyzABCDEFGHIJKLMNOPQRSTUVWXYZ1234567890
14pt abcdefghijklmnopqrstuvwxyzABCDEFGHIJKLMNOPQRSTUVWXYZ12345678
18pt abcdefghijklmnopqrstuvABCDEFGHIJKLMNOPQRSTUV1234

20pt abcdefghijklmnopqrstuvwxyzçêëéèñß
ABCDEFGHIJKLMNOPQRSTUVWXYZÊËÉÈÇ
1234567890 – + × ÷ = °′ ″ · /()&% * §£$-?!ı
“”,.:;__ ⅛ ⅜ ⅝ ⅞ ¼ ½ ¾ ⅓ ⅔ ● ☎ @® ©

10/11 Centred

Yet there are also strong arguments why the designer should work in close day-to-day touch with a printing firm. What complicates the printing process is the fact that although printing employs many of the techniques of mass production each job is unique....Only through an intimate knowledge of a firm's technical facilities and the individual abilities of those it employs is it possible for a designer in

10/11 Justified

Yet there are also strong arguments why the designer should work in close day-to-day touch with a printing firm. What complicates the printing process is the fact that although printing employs many of the techniques of mass production each job is unique . . . . Only through an intimate knowledge of a firm's technical facilities and the individual abilities of those it employs is it possible for a designer in printing fully

10/11 Ranged Left

Yet there are also strong arguments why the designer should work in close day-to-day touch with a printing firm. What complicates the printing process is the fact that although printing employs many of the techniques of mass production each job is unique....Only through an intimate knowledge of a firm's technical facilities and the individual abilities of those it employs is it possible for a designer in

10/11 Indented paragraphs

Yet there are also strong arguments why the designer should work in close day-to-day touch with a printing firm.

What complicates the printing process is the fact that although printing employs many of the techniques of mass production each job is unique....

Only through an intimate knowledge of a firm's technical facilities and the individual abilities of those it

The settings above are set on track 3 automatic compensation

Ea1 24pt | Ea1 28pt | Ea1 30pt | Ea1 36pt | Ea1 42pt | Ea1 48pt

Ea1 54pt | Ea1 60pt | Ea1 66pt | Ea1 72pt

Kerning only

Yet there are also strong arguments w

Kerning & letterspacing track 1

Yet there are also strong arguments w

Kerning & letterspacing track 2

Yet there are also strong arguments w

Kerning & letterspacing track 3

Yet there are also strong arguments w

Expanded 20%

Yet there are also strong argumen

Condensed 20%

Yet there are also strong arguments why the desig

Pseudo italic 12° forward

Yet there are also strong arguments why

Pseudo italic 12° backward

Yet there are also strong arguments why

decide to install in anticipation of a general market; following up this initial information allows the customer rather than the supplier to assert individual taste and ensure that the best is widely available.

Some printers' and typesetters' catalogues include a section of specimen text pages showing incremental variations in size and leading for each typeface, and these are of much more assistance than alphabetically displayed founts in judging the look that will result from certain specifications – but only if these panels of text are photocopied and modified to simulate the page and margin areas of the format intended, since these will almost certainly differ from the format of the specimen book. Some reference of this kind is almost indispensable, supplemented as it should be by specimens collected worldwide for comparative purposes from other books which reflect a particular field of publishing interest.

I have left until last the type literature of the past, which soon establishes itself as the largest part of any working typographer's library; it is as impossible to disregard as those texts and scores which allow the historical gamut of literature and music to be reactivated on a day to day basis. It can only be regarded as obsolete in a narrowly technical sense, and there are many simple and inexpensive ways of using the finest letterforms of the past in display. The commonest involve photographic enlargement from original or facsimile specimen books, pasting-up to build the words required and to refine the spacing, sometimes a little retouching is called for but frequently not, and then the artwork is ready for reduction and reproduction. A word or short line of titling in a script, in letter-spaced open capitals or even in black letter may be involved – or some numerals and a decorative rule for part or chapter titles – or possibly the artwork for a typographic jacket and case binding. This is always very satisfying work for, although typographers are working with prefabricated units for most of their time, these at least have been authentically prefabricated. It is still unnecessary to spend a fortune on working (as opposed to collectable) copies of typefounders' specimen sheets or books, in facsimile from 1565 to about 1880, and in the original editions thereafter.

The specimen sheet reproduced, considerably reduced, on the facing page is a well-planned example from a trade typesetter. With similar italic and bold sheets, it shows the designer what is available (i.e. that small caps and non-lining figs would need to be avoided in this instance), and gives enough information to proceed with accurate copyfitting, tracing, layout and specification.

4 FORM, CONTENT AND EXTENT

This chapter considers two alternative and equally viable ways of arranging text and illustration on the page, and suggests that the designer needs to be a master of both. It then looks at the practical need for cast-off and various approaches to planning a book.

4:1 Centred and off-centred principles of layout

Until quite recently the choice between symmetry and asymmetry was an issue which split typographers into 'traditional' and 'modern' camps in a 'battle of styles', which was fought along the following general lines:

traditionalists	*modernists*
justified text setting	ragged or unjustified text setting
headings and display centred	headings and display ranged left
seriffed typefaces	sanserif typefaces
contrast by itals and small caps	contrast by weight of rom u/lc
Hart's Rules	minimal capitalisation and punctuation
traditional margins	multi-column grids with bleeds
static balance	dynamic balance
uncoated papers in 8vo and 4to	coated papers in DIN format

Here are two very distinct philosophies – to take all decisions in strict accordance with the precepts on the left would lead towards the book of the humanist Renaissance, whilst those on the right would yield an uncompromising product of the machine age. Such extreme approaches are seldom called for, and most good book design results from the subtle interplay (not the thoughtless mixing) of elements from these two traditions. The distinctions to be made between the centred and off-centred approaches to design are easily grasped and should be respected: the golden rule is to set out along one path or the other until unique features presented in the MS indicate a compromise on commonsense grounds.

The axis in typography

An axis is a backbone. It runs down the middle of symmetrical designs, but generally (although not invariably) favours the left-hand edge in off-centred ones. Asymmetrists like to accentuate this edge by contrasting it with a ragged right-hand edge, and by suppressing paragraph indents in case they break its regularity:

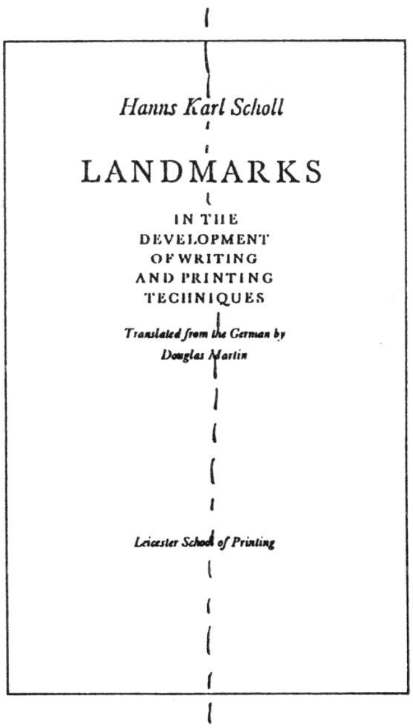

Hanns Karl Scholl

LANDMARKS

IN THE DEVELOPMENT OF WRITING AND PRINTING TECHNIQUES

Translated from the German by Douglas Martin

Leicester School of Printing

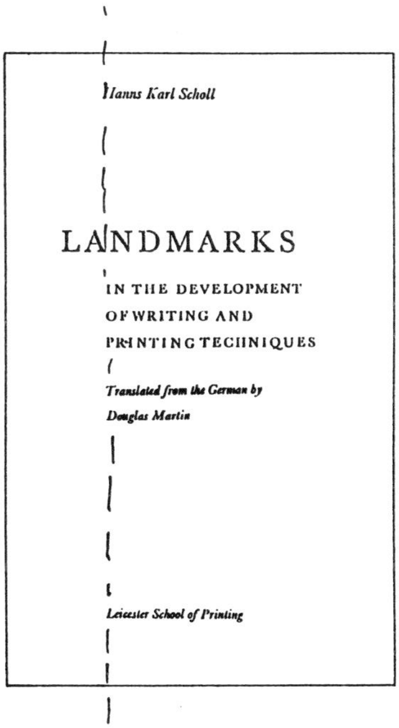

Hanns Karl Scholl

LANDMARKS

IN THE DEVELOPMENT OF WRITING AND PRINTING TECHNIQUES

Translated from the German by Douglas Martin

Leicester School of Printing

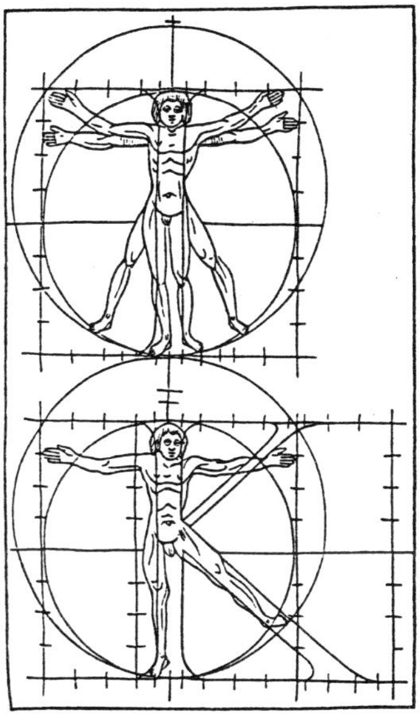

The Renaissance preoccupation with the relation of the Roman alphabet to geometry and the proportions of the human body: from Geofroy Tory's Champ Fleury, *1529.*

Designs of either kind must have balance in order to look right. Symmetrical designs have intrinsic balance – a centred title page may be compared to a vase shape, or to the human proportions (head, shoulders, feet). What happens to one side of the axis is mirrored on the other.

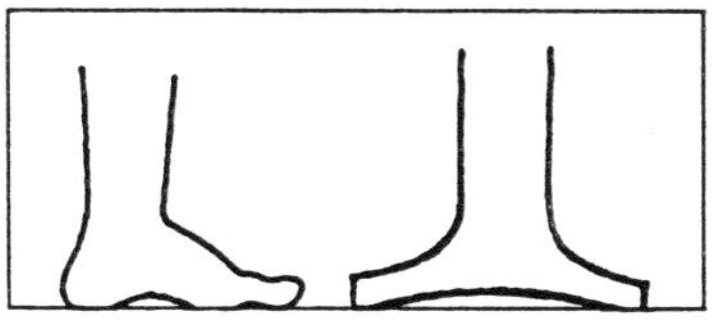

A drawing by Adrian Frutiger demonstrating that our letters, unlike those of most other cultures – arabic, indian, chinese – rest on a line and have their feet on the ground!

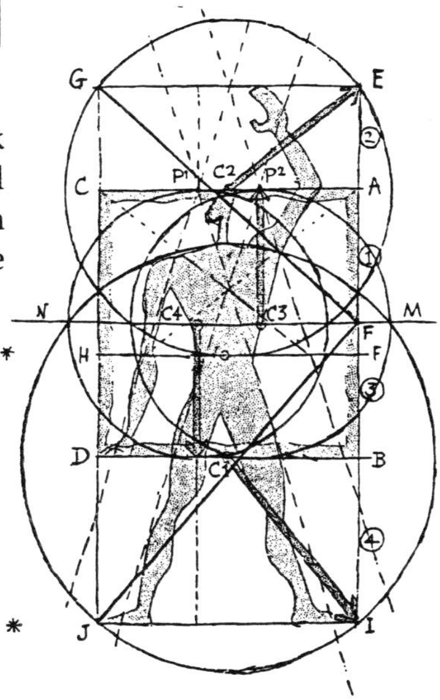

From Le Corbusier's The Modulor, *1948. Sub-titled 'A harmonious measure to the human scale, universally applicable to architecture and mechanics', this enterprise coincided with a post-war reawakening of international interest in proportion and in the aesthetic and scientific basis of all design activity, and in the Renaissance exploration of the same territory.*

Asymmetry implies a balance between unequal parts, and the diagram of a see-saw may help to explain how this is achieved. The accompanying thumb-nail sketches show how this balance between physical weights may be interpreted in terms of visual masses:

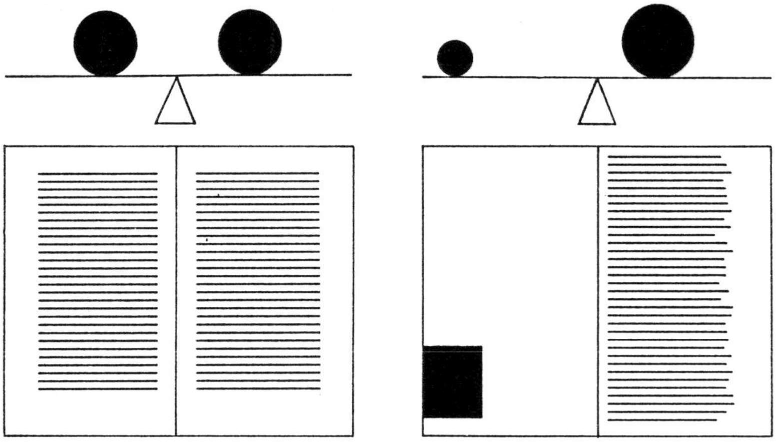

Shapes must be balanced on the page. The effect of a good title-page setting could obviously be spoiled by positioning it wrongly on the page width or by printing it too low on the page. An initial difficulty in acquiring an informed approach is to accept the role of white space in any design. In tangible terms: take an average text page, which may be made up of 60% text area to 40% white margin; but go further into the grey rectangle of text and analyse the proportion of paper that is actually covered with black ink and it may be found to be less than, say, 10%. The statement that white space is an integral part of book design is to be taken in this literal and physical sense. This is another instance (to be compared with our suppression of the mechanics of reading in order to be able to read fluently [2:2]) of a lost skill that can easily be retrieved – the ability to perceive an image successively as dark on a light ground and vice versa:

This well-known optical illusion will be seen alternatively as a Maltese cross on white and as petal shapes on black. After a few seconds' practice it is possible to subject any layout or piece of printing to a routine test of this kind in order to uncover all sorts of faults in structure and design, and to check for balance. Designers have to rely on this knack from time to time to see how well the image that is being built up relates to other parts of the design and to the page area: similar techniques involve checking the balance and scale in a mirror; folding, trimming and viewing inset or wrapped round a dummy – anything that helps to visualise the result in use (and for a jacket this may mean viewing against competition under the bookshop space and lighting conditions), and to get away from the false impression gained from viewing flat on the drawing board.

It makes both design and practical sense to take the double-page spread rather than the single page as the basic unit. This holds true even for the simplest of traditional margin schemes, where the most intractable material can usually be arranged into an acceptable sequence of facing pages. The problem of fit and extent still has only one real dimension – that of depth.

Difficulties can arise where an asymmetrical scheme is adopted with insufficient foreknowledge or control over the

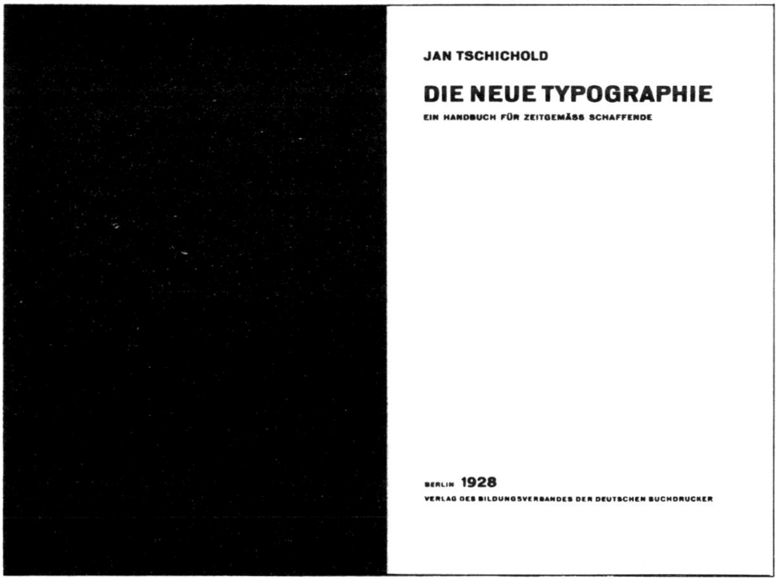
JAN TSCHICHOLD

DIE NEUE TYPOGRAPHIE

EIN HANDBUCH FÜR ZEITGEMÄSS SCHAFFENDE

BERLIN 1928

VERLAG DES BILDUNGSVERBANDES DER DEUTSCHEN BUCHDRUCKER

Title opening from The New Typography *(Berlin, 1928), a manifesto and textbook for the rational and progressive school of typography at the time: advocating standard DIN paper formats; sanserif rather than roman types; doctrinaire asymmetry in layout; and the general adoption of a machine-age aesthetic. Its young author, Jan Tschichold, rapidly foresaw the dehumanising and even fascist implications latent in the programme he had helped to build, and abandoned it for a more individual typographic stance, subsequently achieving distinction within the traditional mainstream of book design.*

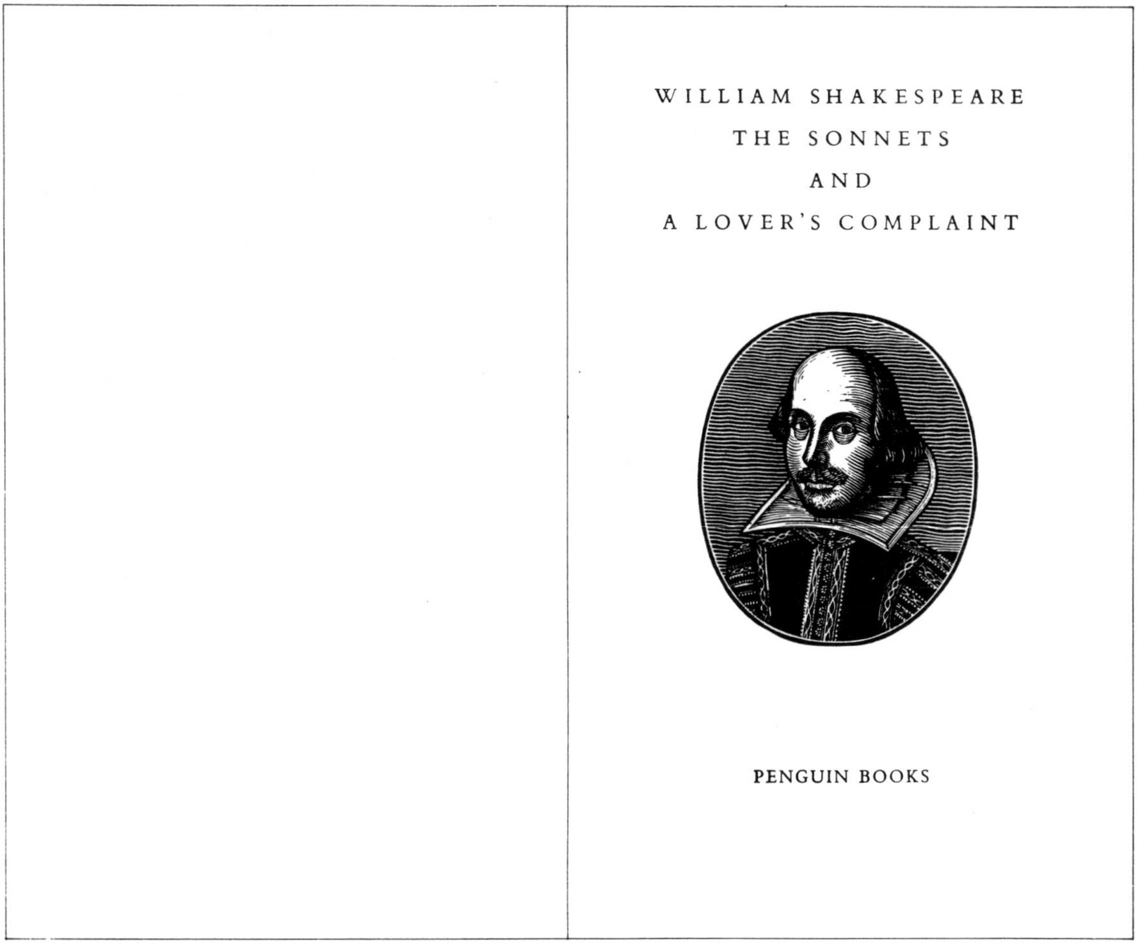
WILLIAM SHAKESPEARE
THE SONNETS
AND
A LOVER'S COMPLAINT

PENGUIN BOOKS

A typical example of Jan Tschichold's classical typography, for the Penguin Shakespeare, *1949.*

kind of material it will need to accommodate. Grids which provide a generous side-column for matter to appear in parallel with the text are particularly vulnerable where that flow is uneven: spreads fail to balance and the dimension of width has been added to the problem of fit.

Asymmetrical design is a powerful tool, although clearly it is more relevant in the design of certain categories of books than others. It not only enables heavily illustrated reference books, for example, to exist in their present form but tends to fashion them after its own image; so that a pre-plan breaks the synopsis into a sequence of spreads or 'openings' each defining the input of copy, photographs, diagrams or illustrations. Care has sometimes to be taken to prevent the controlling grid from exercising a tyranny over the work of all concerned with a publication.

The question of when and how to specify unjustified setting is an important one in the layout of these complex, multi-column pages and in straightforward situations as well.

Justified or ragged typesetting?

The case for close and even word spacing in a justified line of optimum length for continuous reading is fundamental to western MSS and printed books. Gutenberg went even further in the quest for a nearly uniform standard of close word spacing through the narrow, justified columns of his Bible, but failed to set a pattern for the future, since the plethora of contractions and variant sorts this entailed would soon have proved a greater distraction than uneven or unjustified setting. A few early printers experimented with the alternative of ragged setting in appropriate circumstances, but examples then become infrequent until the late nineteenth century.

The case for the use of unjustified setting as an alternative to be preferred to justification in conventional text measures was only made in comparatively recent times and then for a bewildering variety of technological, economic and aesthetic reasons no longer current, not the least of which was the discovery that typewritten MS (of the old-fashioned type, where a ragged right edge was mandatory) could in fact be read without undue discomfort. There is no question but that ragged setting can be made to look handsome on the page where the parameters are carefully judged, as for example by that most persuasive of advocates for its wider use, Eric Gill, in his *Essay on Typography*; but it has since been carefully established that it cannot rival the justified product over typical spells of continuous reading, and so should at all costs be avoided for that purpose. The primary difficulty consists in the onset of fatigue in picking up the correct line openings; after a short while the eye cannot cope with these irregular line lengths nearly as well as with the convention of having up to two or three successive word-breaks in justified setting.

The valid uses of ragged setting may include absolutely any or all of the interesting bits which fall outside the

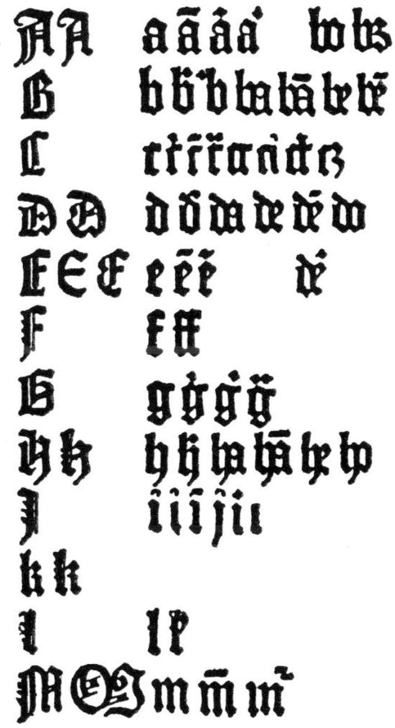

Part of the reconstructed fount dating from c. 1454, later used for the printing of the Constance Missal, *c. 1473–4 (after Otto Hupp).*

¶ Legibility, in practice, amounts simply to what one is accustomed to. But this is not to say that because we have got used to something demonstrably less legible than something else would be if we could get used to it, we should make no effort to scrap the existing thing. ¶ Goodwill may be thought to be more or less evenly spread out, like margarine or even butter, over the mass of the population, but good sense, i.e. intelligence, critical ability, and that passionate concentration upon precise perfection which is a kind of genius, is not so common. Goodwill comes from below & occasionly penetrates into studios and cabinets. Good sense comes from above & percolates thro' the mass of the people. Everybody thinks that he knows an A when he sees it; but only the few extraordinarily rational minds can distinguish between a good one & a bad one, or can demonstrate precisely what constitutes A-ness. When is an A not an A? Or when is an R not an R? It is clear that in any letter there is some sort of norm. The discovery of this norm is obviously the first thing to be done.

¶ The first notable attempt to work out the norm for plain letters was made by Mr. Edward Johnston when he designed the sans-serif letter for the London Underground Railways. Some of the letters are not entirely satisfactory, especially when it is remembered that, for such a purpose, an alphabet should be as near as possible 'fool-proof', i.e. the forms should be measurable, patient of dialectical exposition, as the philosophers would say – nothing should be left to the imagination of the signwriter or the enamel plate-maker. In this quality of 'fool-proofness' the Monotype sans-serif fount (fig. 30)

ABCDEFGHIJJK
MNOPQRRSTU
VWXYZÆŒ
12334567890

Figure 30 – Monotype Gill sans-serif

is perhaps an improvement. The letters are more strictly normal – freer from forms depending upon the appreciation and critical ability of the workman who has to reproduce them.

¶ But, as there is a norm of letter form – the bare

Trial setting for Eric Gill's An Essay on Typography, *1931.*

rectangle framing the text for continuous reading: the flaps and blurbs; prelims and display; chapter and other levels of headings; verse and parallel translation; captions; quotations and extracts; tables and lists of any type; multiple column setting of notes; bibliographies and indexes. Therefore it is almost impossible to design even the most straightforward title without recourse to some, frequently a great deal of, ragged setting; it should all be carefully specified to distinguish it from those parts of the book which are justified, for nothing can look more messy than material intended for ragged setting but which has been output as justified.

4:2 Cast-off and the control of extent

"Before building a chicken coop, decide on how many chickens you wish to coop" – as the truistic advice for architectural students runs. Given the word and character counts that are available on word processor screens, and a pocket calculator, extents can now be worked out painlessly.

The only formula needed is that the total number of characters in a job divided by the average number of characters per line in a given typeface equals the number of lines, and that this divided by the number of lines per column or page will yield columns or pages:

$$\text{i.e. } \frac{\text{Total no. of characters in copy}}{\text{Average characters per line}} = \text{Lines of type}$$

$$\text{thus, } \frac{\text{Lines of type}}{\text{Lines of text per page}} = \text{Total of pages}$$

Manufacturers and setters of type will usually be able to supply whatever tables are necessary for this and general purpose tables are also available – all of these tend to be arranged along slightly different lines, but the underlying theory is not in the least complicated. Establish a procedure to check that everything is taken into account, for there are one or two pitfalls of the kind that can give rise to an order for exactly twice as much or half as much paper as will be required for the book in question!

Character counts are actual, whereas word counts are hypothetical: the average length of the English word plus the space which follows it is customarily quoted as six characters, but that returns us to the question of whose words, Nietzsche's or Enid Blyton's? Character counts are easily made from typescript where necessary: a carefully judged vertical line averages the lengths of raggedly-set lines, and enables a series of pages to be sampled. Treat each space or point of punctuation as a single character, and regard the final line of each paragraph as a full one. This is adequate for most purposes, given a clean and consistent product from the typist. It is important to add on allowances for the drop on chapter openings and for illustrations or other matter to be inserted. Little refinements which come with practice include

```
in casting-off from typescript: match the character scale
to pica, elite or microelite. Calculate the rectangle to
the left of the vertical, which should be dropped at a
sensible point. Add on all the stray characters to the right
and on the final line of each paragraph where each paragraph
is being cast-off individually  -- within a page by page
cast-off treat the final lines as full ones, which will
recur as short lines with similar frequency in the
typesetting). Subtract any deletions that may have been made.
   Record the character totals for each chapter or passage
carefully so that these may be converted into alternative
specifications if the first trial setting does not work
out acceptably.
```

12 per inch

0 5 10 15 20 25 30 35 40 45 50 55 60 65

checking out the fit of lower-case where this may have been modified, and making allowances for ragged setting where the maximum measure may be reduced to an effective mean measure of a couple of picas less.

Where the computer supplies a character count this provides a still more accurate basis for cast-off, which can be converted on an actual rather than a sampling basis, chapter by chapter, for the book as a whole. Even word counts off computer have value for preliminary calculations to establish feasibility, or to provide a cross-check, using the rough and ready formula of a word equals six characters mentioned above.

A typescale is helpful in measuring or converting everything into line depths of the text size in use, and thus a simple but accurate map or table of the book can be built up before a line is set in type. (This has all sorts of practical uses outside pure book design, and no one should work in any editorial or publicity capacity without acquiring a basic ability to 'cast-off' or relate their copy to the space available.) The standard of accuracy which is sufficient in given circumstances must naturally vary: certainly an even working – that is to say multiples normally of 16- or 32-page sections – can be readily established and the designer can go on to work to tolerances of half a line or so in a chapter's extent, or mathematical precision in the width calculation of a multi-column table, for such information can be read off, where necessary, from the relevant tables.

The extent of copy can be related to the layout to any degree which is considered desirable in terms of concentrating material into spreads or smaller units and consolidating the visual/verbal exposition in a number of ways, and for which sophisticated techniques have been devised – some of which have been published, whereas others can be known only through close analysis of the products they facilitate. Designers and theorists such as Max Bill, Karl Gerstner, Josef Müller-Brockmann and Herbert Spencer have been in the forefront of these long-term developments which may be lumped together conveniently as the so-called 'grid system'. As a book design concept it is largely outmoded and

NOVEL FOR AGE GROUP 11+ / CAST-OFF & BOOK PLAN

based on line-by-line cast-off / go straight to page /
see layouts and detailed typographic specifications /
series style points enclosed

Metric demy 8vo: 216 x 138mm trimmed
Linotron 202 Imprint
Text 11½/14pt, justified in 24 ems, 33 lines of text
Running heads and folios 9½pt
4 lines chapter drop.

S/S artwork supplied for display lines and part titles.

Prelims: i h/title / ii other books / iii title / iv copyright
v dedication / vi blank / vii contents / viii blank
ix part title for first story / x blank

Chapter	Lines	Pages	Actual	Begins	Ends	Blanks [+ Recto Titles]
1	539	16.33	17	11	2	28/29/30
2	280	8.48	9	31	39	40/41/42
3	473	14.33	15	43	57	58/59/60
4	391	11.84	12	61	72	73/74
5	326	9.87	10	75	84	85/86
6	527	15.96	16	87	102	103/104
7	385	11.66	12	105	116	117/118
8	290	8.79	9	119	127	

[for 128pps]

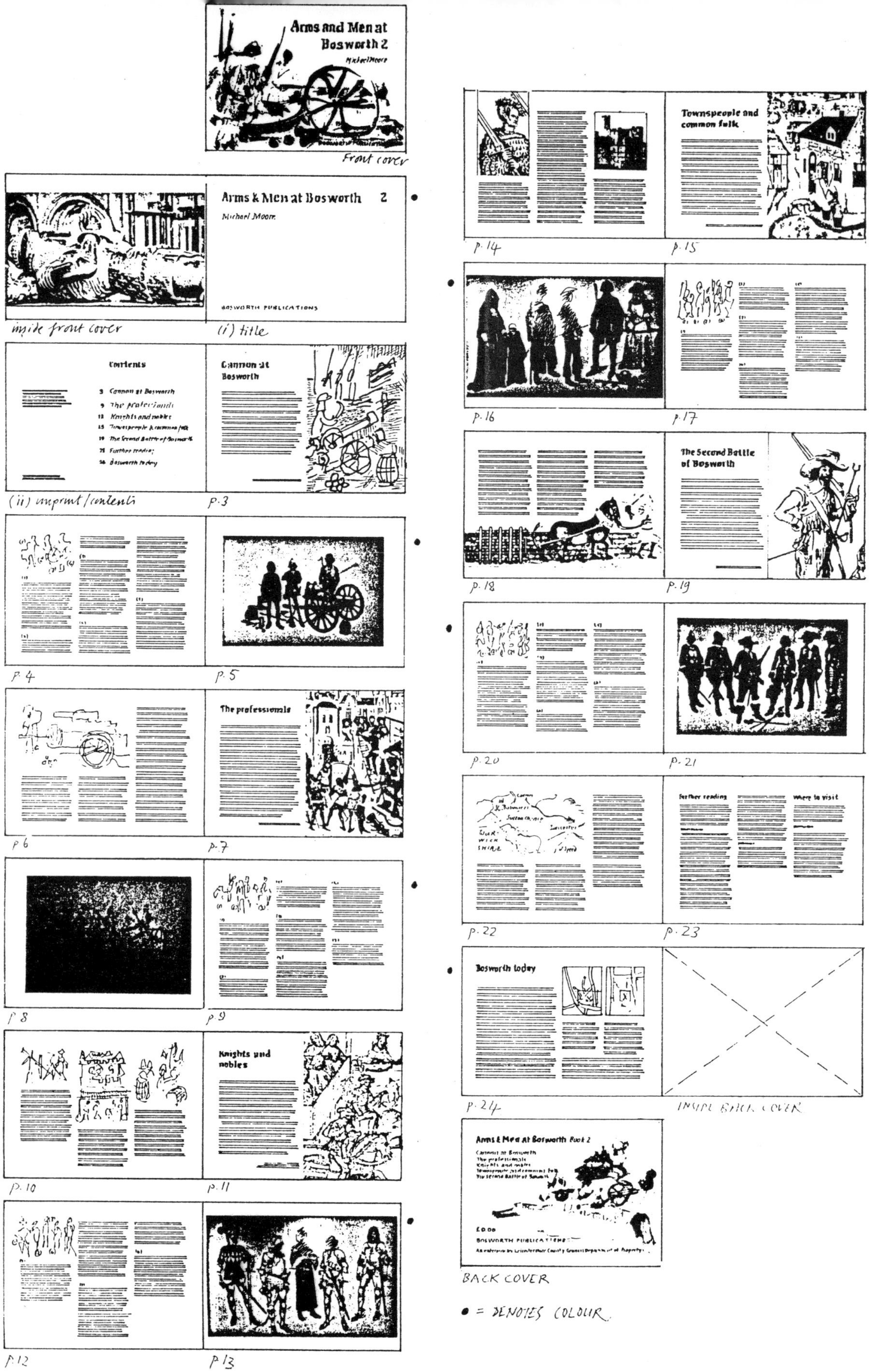

Arms and Men at Bosworth 2
Michael Moore
Front cover
Arms & Men at Bosworth 2
Michael Moore
BOSWORTH PUBLICATIONS
inside front cover
(i) title
Contents
3 Cannon at Bosworth
9 The professionals
13 Knights and nobles
15 Townspeople & common folk
19 The Second Battle of Bosworth
23 Further reading
24 Bosworth today
(ii) imprint/contents
Cannon at Bosworth
p.3
p.4
p.5
The professionals
p.6
p.7
p.8
p.9
Knights and nobles
p.10
p.11
p.12
p.13
Townspeople and common folk
p.14
p.15
p.16
p.17
The Second Battle of Bosworth
p.18
p.19
p.20
p.21
Further reading
Where to visit
p.22
p.23
Bosworth today
p.24
INSIDE BACK COVER
Arms & Men at Bosworth Book 2
Cannon at Bosworth
The professionals
Knights and nobles
Townspeople and common folk
The Second Battle of Bosworth
BOSWORTH PUBLICATIONS
BACK COVER
• = DENOTES COLOUR

unfashionable, although it retains its influence over the design of magazines, company reports and suchlike.

Through the subdivision of space into columns and cells, the grid method effectively provides a range of boxes for the containment of pictures and text, and the dangers of any such system – where the container dictates the shape and form of the content, leading ultimately and in inexperienced hands towards the cutting of text and the cropping of pictures to fit an arbitrary visual pattern – are immediately apparent. Alongside this visual rationalisation came the fresh but presently neglected idea that typing paper could be gridded or calibrated to correspond to the layout, so that author or editor might know the space they were filling as they worked.

Miniature plans

A miniature plan (reduced) for a 24-page booklet with covers.

A series of thumbnail sketches can present the whole plan of a book on a desk surface, so that continuity and variety from spread to spread or the distribution of colour or bleeds can be viewed at a glance. Quick to produce and revise, this storyboard approach is often to be preferred to a more elaborate dummy or paste-up, and it will be more intelligible to others involved in discussing the product if the plan is drawn to scale. Galley and photographs can be miniaturised on a zoom copier. Some children's book illustrators habitually prepare the initial idea for a new picture book as one long concertina fold, thus combining the advantages of being able to turn the pages as well as opening them out to see how the story has been structured.

These plans can be drawn up at any stage. Designers with dependable skills in cast-off don't need to wait for galley or repro proofs, and indeed it is the plan itself which enables the specification to be made for many sorts of book. Always have a plan for making a plan, that is to say the calculations which will guide the material into precisely the right number of pages: blind paste-up – where the first paste-up is undertaken out of sheer curiosity on this point – is far too prevalent. Anyone who already undertakes a lot of this work may find the following method of interest. In the graph the number of pages of text and illustration is plotted against the number of pages the book must make, in order to

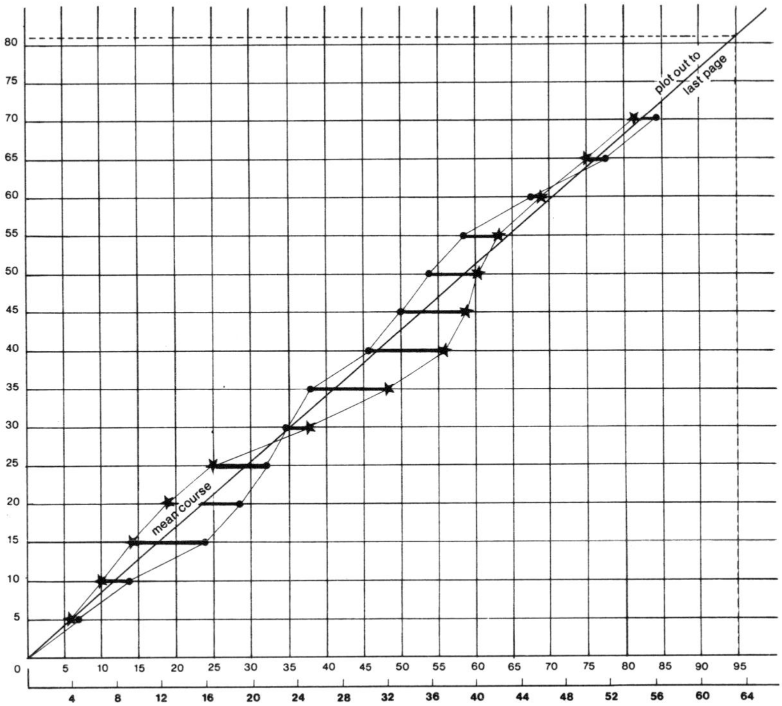

The problem here is to plan some 95 MS pages and 64 illustrations to make 80 text pages. Text and pictures are plotted at 5-page intervals to monitor progress.

set a course which can be checked and corrected every four or five pages: it works well for many kinds of material and can be elaborated to suit the problem in hand.

The standard method is to mark-off the galley, adding in illustration as it affects depth so that the page on which each chapter begins and ends is established. There are many little dodges that make for flexibility, setting out from the premise that whereas a book may make 157 pages it can scarcely be allowed to make 161. Variation of chapter drop can frequently influence matters, and the prelims (if numbered outside the text) can normally be adjusted, as can the index specification. Aim to come in a couple of pages under extent, noting any areas of flexibility where photographs might be re-scaled, so that if things are going badly as the end comes in sight there are cards left to play before firming up the pagination.

Paste-up for guidance

Rough paste-ups can be required at any stage of the game, from working with an author to arrange his material to best advantage, to issuing a blueprint for the final positioning of type and illustration at the printers'. Grids save time and can enable non-drawing-board staff to get to grips with the detailed planning of the books for which they are responsible. Where there is a strong pictorial content then, as ever, take the double page spread as the unit to view, so there is no need to worry about which is left or right and the resultant risk of mistakes.

A lot of the designer's working year can go into paste-up for presentation, but this is specialised work and is often best placed with a small studio or design group which has access to its own photography, PMTs, colour laser copiers, colour rendering systems and all the other wonders of the graphic arts industry.

Paste-up for the camera

This is printers' work by tradition, but the situation is changing with the expansion of desktop publishing and in-house composition. Most straightforward text setting can or soon will be paginated and output automatically through the typesetters' front end system, but the call for good paste-up artists can be envisaged for a considerable time to come. The requirements for the job are quite specific: it generally takes place within a studio, and is a useful step on the road to book design for some. A good eye and meticulous approach are essential, although individual temperament divides people into two camps: those who would prefer to regard it as a mechanical activity and expect a senior designer to do all the thinking and supply a guidance paste-up, and others who respond to the challenge of doing things well all round.

It takes nearly as long to produce a guidance paste-up as camera ready copy, and so the economic argument should favour going through one stage only. I have always tried to put all my effort into communicating through a detailed guidance paste-up, except when working for the very small publishing house or where there is a demonstrable advantage in supplying a finished product. I'm certain that far too much unthinking paste-up goes on when the answer would be to go straight into page, and that careful copy preparation, layout and specification can make this possible for the majority of titles.

4:3 Planning a book to page

A careful examination of the manuscript and illustration, and the opportunities and constraints surrounding it, will get the detailed layout off to a good start: some of the principal considerations are gathered or recapitulated below.

1. Are there production restrictions on bleeds or the placing of plates within the imposition? Full colour may only appear on one side of the sheet within certain sections on grounds of cost; establish how much flexibility such schemes afford. It is often proposed that black and white plates should be grouped to be wrapped or inserted into text sections; ideally the choice between this practice and integrated illustration should be based on the nature of the material, since it is now unusual for text and illustrations to be printed by different processes or on different papers.
2. Whereas plates can be planned as independent sections at almost any stage, should they call for complex integration with the text then it will generally be best to scale them after galleys become available and as the final paste-up proceeds – the placement of many types of straightforward illustration may be left to the page make-up system in accordance with guidelines and keying-in supplied; after a slow start, such systems are now improving rapidly, and there is no doubt that in the fullness of time most pre-planning and paste-up will be possible on screen for most designers rather than for the comparatively few who currently have access to these methods. Already the computer is a valuable working tool in the planning of complex books, but the drawing board will continue to be needed in perfecting the spread-by-spread design exposition of the work of a team which may also include writers, editors, illustrators, picture researchers and photographers.
3. Assess the original illustrations against the aims of the text – is considerable cropping indicated to zoom in where points are really being made, or are there reasons for respecting the dimensional integrity of the artist's canvas or the photographer's print?

4. At the earliest possible juncture the designer and all concerned should have an opportunity to look at these issues in relation to the proposed book format and the actual material to ensure that the container is in all respects suited to its contents. It is surprisingly easy for both size and number of pages to be arbitrarily laid down in advance and then blindly followed through to a flawed result.
5. Integrated books demand a pre-plan of sorts, although this can take a variety of forms. Some informational titles are planned, written and designed as a set number of double-page units from the outset. Again, the craft of children's picture books requires that they should adhere to conventions as set out in an initial paged dummy or sometimes in a precise miniature storyboard. A simple form of pre-plan for general purposes results from adding lines of galley to the *depth* to be made by illustration (also measured and expressed as lines of type) for each chapter; with allowances as necessary for space above and below each illustration, chapter drop, caption copy, etc. This routine work can be done accurately enough to iron out any wrinkles and instruct for pagination without the need for a further paste-up stage, but it can also give a sound basis for the most complicated of paste-ups. Experienced designers will confirm that first-class paste-up work can proceed at a snail's pace, and that a couple of hours' work with a typescale and pocket calculator ensuring that everything has been measured-off accurately is worth it for the peace of mind and accurate navigation in the days or weeks of work ahead.
6. If a paste-up is not adding visibly to the quality or appearance or functioning of a book at every turn then it is a waste of time and need not have been undertaken, since there are much quicker routes if all that is required are clean page proofs to the correct extent.
7. It is hard to define the circumstances in which a designer's paste-up is appropriate for various categories of book. Much will come to depend upon the printers' intelligent use of page make-up technology in eliminating the need for studio work from mainstream, and from what are at present borderline, applications. Where there is an intricate interplay between text and illustration,

then design skills within publishing will always have to be relied upon to get the product right. I also believe that there has to be a certain attitude towards the effective and sophisticated use of illustration within the book that will always require a high input of human creativity, and would like to give two instances of this. One concerns the interaction of pictures on a page, and the visual paradox by which one picture is conditioned and takes on context from the presence of another on the same spread. For instance, consider a photograph of a pair of hands gripping iron bars, which takes on an entirely different emotive charge if the facing picture implies that they belong to a spectator at a zoo or circus or, conversely, to a prisoner of political repression. Pictures interact with other pictures as well as with words, and similarly spreads with a high pictorial content react with each other in sequences forward and back, just as images in a film do. This is not an easy point to demonstrate here, but design expertise does operate powerfully in these areas where the layout of four or five spreads a day is quite an achievement, and the technology employed largely irrelevant to the processes of creative thought.

4:4 Scaling artwork and photography

Laser colour copiers and plain paper zoom copiers have improved accuracy and cut time and costs in handling flat artwork, bromides and transparencies for layout and in specifying such subjects for reproduction. It is currently only necessary to master the use of a plastic reproduction wheel to read off percentages for reduction or enlargement – which may be cross-checked on a pocket calculator for even greater precision – and to key these into the copier. Prints to size on tracing paper can be taken on the monochrome copier and positioned over the page grid to mark-up the exact area of each subject that will be required after cropping.

Where artwork is to be specially drawn for a standard reduction, the effects of sample line weights, tints and labelling can be checked on the zoom copier, which has a thousand and one other studio and DTP uses, some of which are discussed elsewhere.

Given a whole stack of originals for sizing to the page grid, it is worth noting down the main permutations of subject widths and depths which it is intended shall be used and where special problems or opportunities will arise, i.e. where the author would like to group certain subjects to view on a single spread, where true centre-section spreads will fall and where colour or bleed restrictions must be observed. It is assumed that the scaling of plates and figures will be settled as the design or paste-up proceeds from spread to spread, and it is important that decisions should always be taken with the balance of the double-page spread in view on the drawing board, together with an outline plan for the next few spreads at least, as well as having those already completed to hand for reference. The keying of illustration to text is paramount for some titles, less important for others, but it should always leave enough flexibility to keep the balance of each spread interesting and varied.

The following guidelines may help when it comes to editing, masking or cropping each subject and positioning it on the spread:

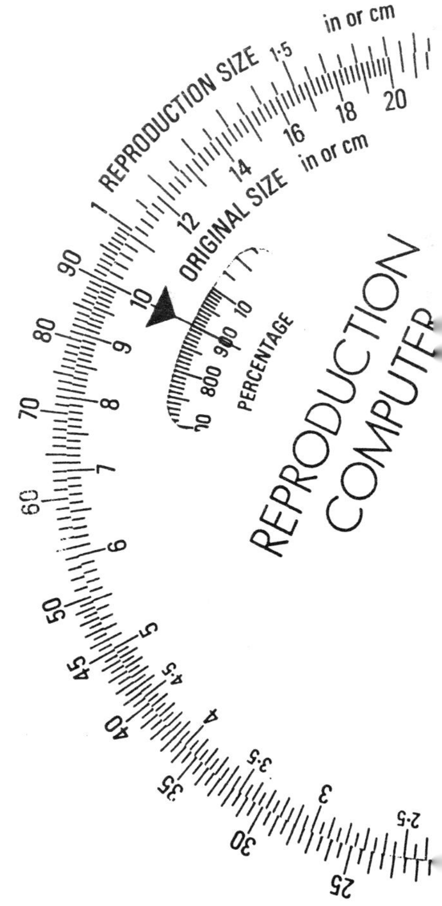

1. The informational kernel of each photograph in relation to the text should come first, and it is quite permissible to move within the photograph to focus on the essential content, particularly where the photographs were not taken for your immediate purpose or it is clear that the photographer has deliberately left a lot of surround or background. Do not close up relentlessly on all sides, however, because a little of this photographic background may be of considerable compositional or atmospheric value.
2. It ought to be immediately obvious where a photographer, exceptionally, is a master of the trimmed and finished print and where it would be vandalism for the designer to crop or do anything but provide the best white mount his margin scheme will allow. Similarly it is down-market to meddle in the slightest with paintings, drawings or other works of art except where the action is obvious and deliberate and accompanied by the use of the word 'detail' in the caption. It quickly becomes apparent where a particular subject is going to appear to best advantage on a recto rather than a verso page,

or at the head rather than the foot, and to judge where one of a pair will work best above the other, or where the appearing scale of heads and figures in successive plates needs either to be harmonised or contrasted. It is extremely difficult to convey an almost cinematographic momentum from spread to spread as designers would often like to do, in the sense of signalling a deliberate intention to do so which the reader can hardly overlook, but I think the successive spreads of Meissen Cathedral, in a book designed by the late Horst Erich Wolter – in which the camera is frequently made to zoom in inexorably – show that it can be done.

3. Develop a film director's eye for anything extrinsic to the shot or out of period or context, especially if it should be recurrent but remediable in at least some instances. There are many ways of improving the situation by cropping spectators (to the photographer) or unsightly cars or signage on the fringes of the subject area, but it will be rare to have recourse to retouching nowadays except for damage of certain types. Scanners can modify sizing and add background in interesting ways, and can sometimes render damaged or inadequate originals serviceable. Messy backgrounds to some landscapes or copy shots of museum artefacts can be removed by using cut-out halftones.

4:5 Layout techniques

Typographic layout and specification has been left until last, not because it is unimportant, but since I believe that there is a special argument to be advanced in an area in which it is impossible to be dogmatic, in that layout can be nothing more than a means of communicating with the typesetter, and in many circumstances this can be established over the telephone or by filling in a form or by submitting an explanatory sketch drawn with any degree of artistic skill. In this sense, if it works it is right: and it is certainly true that several of the great book designers of any age, including our own, are known to have dropped in to the printers' with pathetic scribbles on the backs of envelopes and, after a little chat about sizes and spacing and numerous proofs later, there has emerged a title page or whatever which attests to their unquestioned taste and insight. Others have laboured for hours to produce meticulous layouts – Beatrice Warde called it 'insulting precision', but I believe that she was wrong – calculated to produce results that corresponded to their own standards in every detail first time round.

The experienced designer, subscribing to this latter approach – where all the finer points of detail are firmly resolved in advance of any typesetting – has a whole number of advantages over working piecemeal: not least in ensuring concentration and continuity for the project in hand, but also in the ability to see and to show to others exactly how things will look. Typesetters, too, will usually welcome (but

The Nuremberg Chronicle, *1493.*

fol 27v from the Latin Exemplar (Nürnberg Stadtbibliothek Cent. II, 98), compared with fol 6v of the printed Latin edition.

do not often enough get), an accurate visual confirmation of what has been requested – although the advice for any publisher working where such layouts are not forthcoming would certainly be to concentrate on making specifications concise and watertight, possibly using a questionnaire-style form to make sure all points are covered.

Grids on semi-transparent paper can cut working time, and to paste-in lines traced from alphabet sheets is the

Prima etas mundi

quickest and most accurate way to produce professional results: these lines can be repositioned in relation to each other using a low-tack hand waxing machine, and sizes can be revised in an instant on the zoom copier without any need to retrace.

Adrian Wilson, in his fascinating study, *The Making of the Nuremberg Chronicle*, rocked the small world of book design by drawing attention to the survival of the original setting copy and layout for the edition of 1493. This page-by-page layout – still in Nuremberg City Library and until recently thought to be nothing more than a terribly mediocre manuscript – was in fact written as a line-by-line cast-off to correspond to the printing type, and the very impromptu illustrations are just a guide, and a very good one, to the positioning of the actual blocks within the page make-up. And so everything mentioned in this chapter falls into place and we would have little to teach that masterly printer and publisher, Anton Koberger, after 500 years.

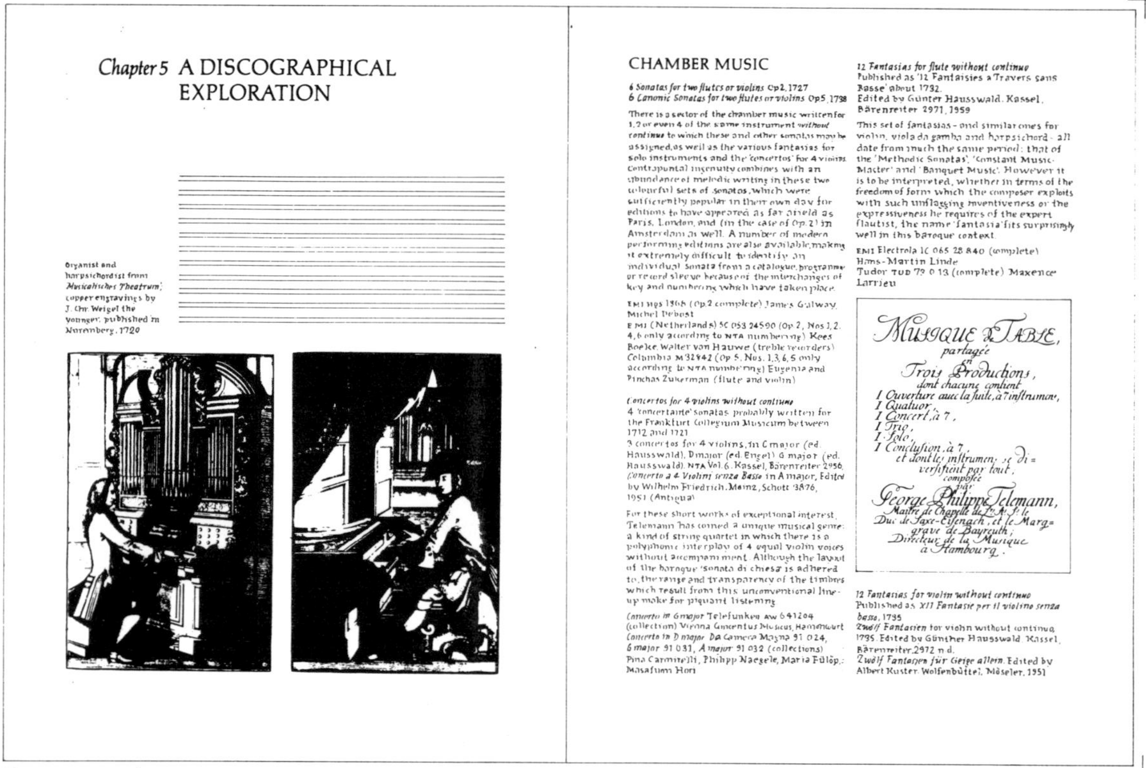

Chapter 5 A DISCOGRAPHICAL EXPLORATION

Organist and harpsichordist from *Musicalisches Theatrum*; copper engravings by J. Chr. Weigel the younger, published in Nuremberg, 1720

CHAMBER MUSIC

6 Sonatas for two flutes or violins Op2, 1727
6 Canonic Sonatas for two flutes or violins Op5, 1738

There is a sector of the chamber music written for 1, 2 or even 4 of the same instrument *without continuo* to which these and other sonatas may be assigned, as well as the various fantasias for solo instruments and the 'concertos' for 4 violins. Contrapuntal ingenuity combines with an abundance of melodic writing in these two colourful sets of sonatas, which were sufficiently popular in their own day for editions to have appeared as far afield as Paris, London, and (in the case of Op. 2) in Amsterdam as well. A number of modern performing editions are also available, making it extremely difficult to identify an individual sonata from a catalogue, programme or record sleeve because of the interchanges of key and numbering which have taken place.

EMI HQS 1368 (Op. 2 complete) James Galway, Michel Debost
EMI (Netherlands) 5C 053 24590 (Op. 2, Nos 1, 2, 4, 6 only according to NTA numbering) Kees Boeke, Walter von Hauwe (treble recorders)
Columbia M 32842 (Op 5, Nos. 1, 3, 6, 5 only according to NTA numbering) Eugenia and Pinchas Zukerman (flute and violin)

Concertos for 4 violins without continuo
4 'concertante' sonatas probably written for the Frankfurt Collegium Musicum between 1712 and 1721
3 concertos for 4 violins, in C major (ed. Hausswald), D major (ed. Engel) G major (ed. Hausswald). NTA Vol. 6. Kassel, Bärenreiter 2956
Concerto a 4 Violini senza Basso in A major, Edited by Wilhelm Friedrich. Mainz, Schott 3876, 1951 (Antiqua)

For these short works of exceptional interest, Telemann has coined a unique musical genre: a kind of string quartet in which there is a polyphonic interplay of 4 equal violin voices without accompaniment. Although the layout of the baroque 'sonata di chiesa' is adhered to, the range and transparency of the timbres which result from this unconventional line-up make for piquant listening

Concerto in G major Telefunken AW 641204 (collection) Vienna Concentus Musicus, Harnoncourt
Concerto in D major Da Camera Magna 91 024, *G major* 91 031, *A major* 91 032 (collections) Pina Carmirelli, Philipp Naegele, Maria Fülöp, Masafumi Hori

12 Fantasias for flute without continuo
Published as '12 Fantaisies a Travers sans Basse' about 1732.
Edited by Günter Hausswald. Kassel, Bärenreiter 2971, 1959

This set of fantasias – and similar ones for violin, viola da gamba and harpsichord – all date from much the same period: that of the 'Methodic Sonatas', 'Constant Music-Master' and 'Banquet Music'. However it is to be interpreted, whether in terms of the freedom of form which the composer exploits with such unflagging inventiveness or the expressiveness he requires of the expert flautist, the name 'fantasia' fits surprisingly well in this baroque context.

EMI Electrola 1C 065 28 840 (complete) Hans-Martin Linde
Tudor TUD 73 0 13 (complete) Maxence Larrieu

12 Fantasias for violin without continuo
Published as *XII Fantasie per il violino senza basso*, 1735
Zwölf Fantasien for violin without continuo, 1735. Edited by Günther Hausswald. Kassel, Bärenreiter 2972 n.d.
Zwölf Fantasien für Geige allein. Edited by Albert Kuster. Wolfenbüttel, Möseler, 1951

Typographer's preliminary study (technical pen and Letraset) to convey the intended effect.

5 THE PARTS AND THE WHOLE

This chapter takes up the story from the stage at which there is a well-resolved layout for the text opening, which in turn has resulted from a good choice of typeface in relation to the purpose of the book. To some extent the designer can now plot a course for completing the design, and, whereas much will follow on logically from decisions already made, nothing should ever be taken for granted, for however many times you may have designed such a detail as a bibliography or a binding case there is always the chance that this present candidate may turn out to be the best yet. The finished product is assuming a firmer shape in the mind, and as attention shifts from one area to another it is also beginning to focus on the wider issue of how the completed book will present itself, above all through the jacket. Architects and designers have long recognised that design proceeds from the inside outwards: first solve the inner content with honesty and the external envelope will inevitably be related and follow from it; wait for the product to emerge before deciding on how to package it . . .

Let's stand back and imagine the book on the basis of what is known about it so far – its extent and the look of the text opening. The next assignment is to complete the layout so that the manuscript can be set into page proof; and all that this entails is followed through, from the preliminary to the end pages.

5:1 The preliminary pages

Early printed books followed the manuscript in having no title or preliminary pages; instead they launched straight into the text after the Latin rubric 'hic incipit' (here beginneth), ending with an 'explicit' or colophon in which the place and date of publication and the printer's name or mark are sometimes given. It seems apparent from the scope left and the advantage taken of it that these books were intended to be 'customised'

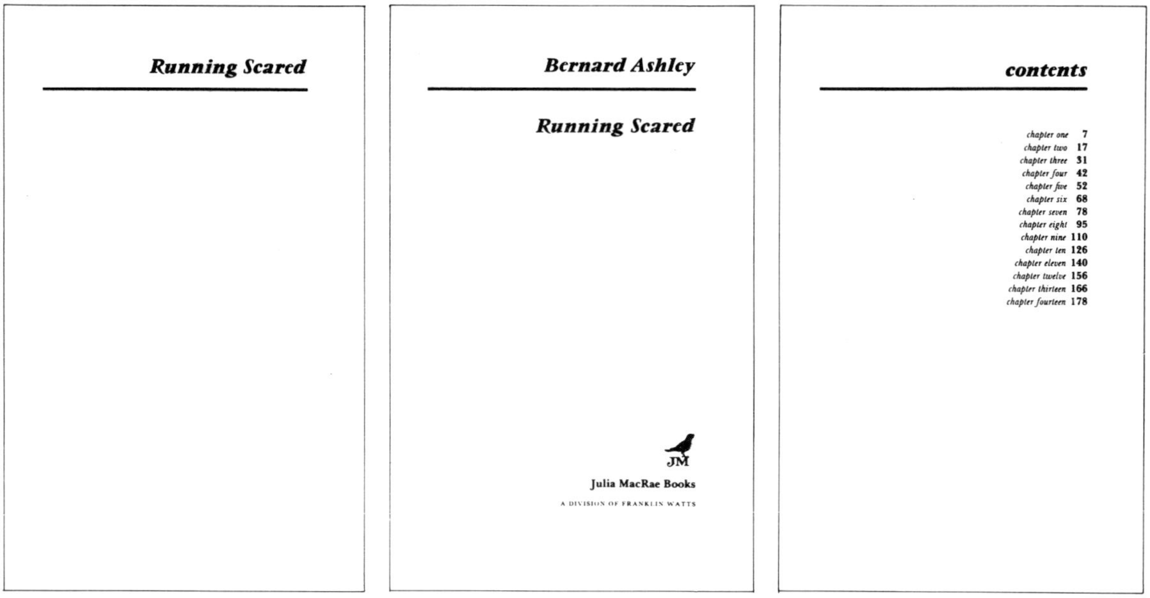

Running Scared

Bernard Ashley

Running Scared

JM

Julia MacRae Books

A DIVISION OF FRANKLIN WATTS

contents

by their owners, not only in terms of illumination and binding but in the provision of marginal notes and commentary, tables of contents and other such matter which would later come to be treated as preliminary or end pages. The main editorial task at the time was to establish and make available a clean text, to which a reference apparatus might be integral, but many other frills were considered as secondary and best added at a provincial level for the ease of reader and librarian.

This is still reflected in the working method of modern editors and designers: it is usually best to start by coming to terms with the text, and to resolve most of the detailed problems it presents, since the content and form of the prelims should then follow on logically. Much tradition attaches to the treatment of each of these pages and the sequences into which they can be arranged, but there is an immense freedom every time the problem is approached afresh. Understandably, the reader wants to press ahead, and there is a tendency to skip the prelims initially, perhaps to return later. I think designers recognise this, and that their handling of these pages almost as a formal circulation area may be in an attempt to capture this fleeting attention. Each page is discussed in a typical order of appearance in an effort to see how it relates to the book as a whole.

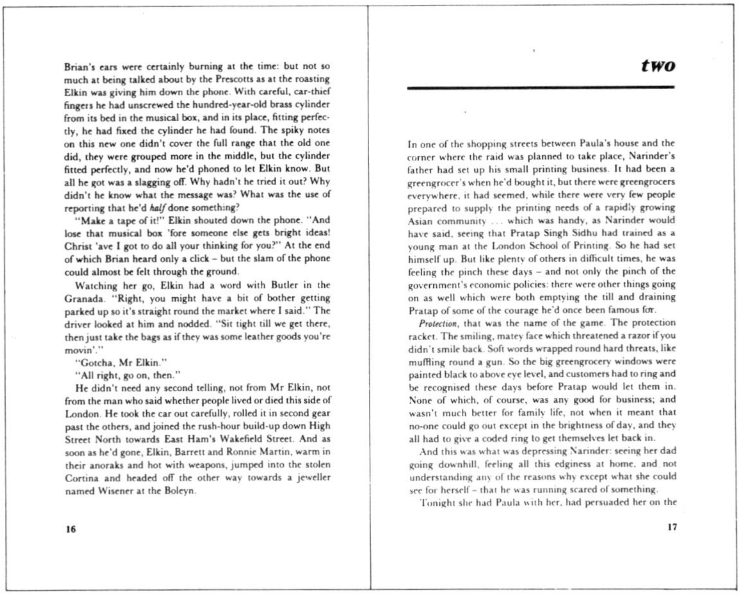

Brian's ears were certainly burning at the time: but not so much at being talked about by the Prescotts as at the roasting Elkin was giving him down the phone. With careful, car-thief fingers he had unscrewed the hundred-year-old brass cylinder from its bed in the musical box, and in its place, fitting perfectly, he had fixed the cylinder he had found. The spiky notes on this new one didn't cover the full range that the old one did, they were grouped more in the middle, but the cylinder fitted perfectly, and now he'd phoned to let Elkin know. But all he got was a slagging off. Why hadn't he tried it out? Why didn't he know what the message was? What was the use of reporting that he'd *half* done something?

"Make a tape of it!" Elkin shouted down the phone. "And lose that musical box 'fore someone else gets bright ideas! Christ 'ave I got to do all your thinking for you?" At the end of which Brian heard only a click – but the slam of the phone could almost be felt through the ground.

Watching her go, Elkin had a word with Butler in the Granada. "Right, you might have a bit of bother getting parked up so it's straight round the market where I said." The driver looked at him and nodded. "Sit tight till we get there, then just take the bags as if they was some leather goods you're movin'."

"Gotcha, Mr Elkin."

"All right, go on, then."

He didn't need any second telling, not from Mr Elkin, not from the man who said whether people lived or died this side of London. He took the car out carefully, rolled it in second gear past the others, and joined the rush-hour build-up down High Street North towards East Ham's Wakefield Street. And as soon as he'd gone, Elkin, Barrett and Ronnie Martin, warm in their anoraks and hot with weapons, jumped into the stolen Cortina and headed off the other way towards a jeweller named Wisener at the Boleyn.

16

two

In one of the shopping streets between Paula's house and the corner where the raid was planned to take place, Narinder's father had set up his small printing business. It had been a greengrocer's when he'd bought it, but there were greengrocers everywhere, it had seemed, while there were very few people prepared to supply the printing needs of a rapidly growing Asian community . . . which was handy, as Narinder would have said, seeing that Pratap Singh Sidhu had trained as a young man at the London School of Printing. So he had set himself up. But like plenty of others in difficult times, he was feeling the pinch these days – and not only the pinch of the government's economic policies: there were other things going on as well which were both emptying the till and draining Pratap of some of the courage he'd once been famous for.

Protection, that was the name of the game. The protection racket. The smiling, matey face which threatened a razor if you didn't smile back. Soft words wrapped round hard threats, like muffling round a gun. So the big greengrocery windows were painted black to above eye level, and customers had to ring and be recognised these days before Pratap would let them in. None of which, of course, was any good for business; and wasn't much better for family life, not when it meant that no-one could go out except in the brightness of day, and they all had to give a coded ring to get themselves let back in.

And this was what was depressing Narinder: seeing her dad going downhill, feeling all this edginess at home, and not understanding any of the reasons why except what she could see for herself – that he was running scared of something.

Tonight she had Paula with her, had persuaded her on the

17

In this children's novel, the horizontal level which should run through the headings of a book is stated in the simplest terms: using one size of Letraset for all display, and ranging everything right to create a sense of pace and forward momentum.

The half- or bastard title

This page was outermost when it reached the bookbinder, so it protected the true title page from soiling and also served to identify the book. Invariably it would be tipped down or hinged to an endpaper and so could not open flat, but tended rather to travel left with the board and front endpaper. Copy is restricted to the short form of title, or in the case of a series, the title and series editor; continental practice would add or substitute the publisher's mark, an attractive idea.

It should be possible in a well-designed book to draw a horizontal line from this first page through to the last at certain clearly defined levels, corresponding to the head and foot margins and the chapter drop. Much of the art of designing a good set of prelims consists in using these basic levels accurately, and in avoiding lines that stray up and down the page to produce floating or jumping effects reminiscent of those Victorian novelty books – precursors of the cinema – that create moving images as the pages are flicked over.

In a book where the overall style is centred, the half-title might pick up at the level of the first line of text, centred on the text measure, and possibly set in the small capitals of the text size. An off-centre design might suggest a drop related to that of the main line of titling on the title page and possibly thrown out to range right – clearly it must take its cue from the design of the title page.

When different typesizes and styles need to align at the head with each other and perhaps with pictures as well, then the effect of ascenders running into the heads (or descenders into the tails) may safely be disregarded; these margins are made by the x-height, and page depth is measured from top of the x-height on the first line of text to its base on the lowest line; this gives a precise depth to a full page illustration when this is to correspond to the text depth.

Alignment at head

The page depth has to be settled as early as possible, since the prelims can only be designed in relation to the text margins, which are understood to be exclusive of any running headline or folio which is to appear outside the text rectangle. Folios and running headlines are rarely printed on at least the first four or five prelim pages in any case, and then they come to take up their standard position as indicated.

In practical matters, it may help to work on a semi-transparent paper (sold as typographic detail pads), in order to check these alignments as the design takes shape. Stabbing a bodkin through a dummy at the corners of text area and drop, and joining up the dots, is effective where the paste-up is required in book form. Best of all is to work onto gridded paper, whether the aim is to produce a rough or a finished paste-up.

One common fault is to set the half-title too large and reduce the effectiveness of the title page which follows; another is to argue for the abolition of the half-title, and this has to be resisted, however severe the pressure on space or other reason. A different use has been found for this page in the case of the mass market, unsewn paperback, where it now customarily carries the blurb in the absence of a front flap.

The title opening

Frontispiece and title page form a spread, and if the book is to be structured in terms of spreads or openings as units of design, then the process should start here. American designers in particular have made an immense contribution to book design in thinking the preliminaries through by analogy with credit titles, so that the sequence unfolds naturally and with the pace and logic of film.

The frontispiece originated as a plate, often printed by a separate process (copperplate and later steel engraving, or chromo-lithography), and inserted by the bookbinder to face the title-page. This formula began to fall into disuse just at a point where British publishers – newly awakening to publicity – could spot apparently wasted space, and so it became genteelly acceptable to list other titles by the same author or in the series in this position. This survives as style for a number of literary houses, but it is not a practice that should be unthinkingly perpetuated; there may be a better case for placing a dedication here on occasion, or a citation originally intended for the title page itself.

If there is no appropriate claim on its use then page ii is best left as a blank, with the title page resolved as a self-sufficient design, either centred on the text measure or related to it by an asymmetrical scheme that runs through the book. To use the double page spread for the typography where this comprises only author, title and publisher has always seemed to me a perilous design undertaking in which few succeed, but it can sometimes work well where the copy is more complex or versatile – some kinds of publication may require a list of contributors or a résumé of contents, for example, to be featured on this titling spread. Illustrated books afford tremendous scope for the adventurous treatment of this surface, particularly where designer and illustrator or photographer are able to confer before work has started in earnest.

The title page is the front door to the book, as the magnificent architectural frames created from Holbein onwards plainly show. It has also been proscenium arch, playbill and much else besides in the time before jacket and flaps came along to share the burden of drawing the crowds. No designer tackles a title page without some sense of occasion – however rational and self-effacing the effect intended; it is an assertion of the theme of the book and its organisation through layout.

The typographic conventions used in display are still imperfectly understood, and worth a few moments' examination because they can afford a fresh angle from which to see and evaluate an item like a title page. The groups of lines that appear there are units of information visually presented, and as such no longer subject to the grammatical rules of sentence structure and punctuation. Display evolved naturally as the formal language of the copperplate invitation was modified to the ends of the modern poster, and the crowded title pages of earlier centuries were reduced to the formula: author, title, publisher. These are elements in a message that contains all that the receiver needs to know and can be expected to take in at a glance.

In practice, the designer needs to establish an order of importance for each element and to assign it a value: i.e. to clarify such matters as the market ranking of a writer or the importance of a sub-title in relation to its title, before thinking about possible sizes and styles of type, and the grouping and arrangements of these elements on the page.

NOVA BRITANNIA.

OFFRING MOST

Excellent fruites by Planting in

VIRGINIA.

Exciting all ſuch as be well affected

to further the ſame.

LONDON

Printed for SAMVEL MACHAM, and are to be ſold at

his Shop in Pauls Church-yard, at the

Signe of the Bul-head.

1609.

A delightful page, which owes its effect to the stressing of two quite arbitrary words in the title.

These elements will be reassembled into a complete message by the receiver, with the help of the order of emphasis which has been superimposed. The term 'receiver' has been used in place of 'reader', because what broadly takes place is not continuous linear reading from the head to the foot of the page so much as absorbing a total field in one span if it is a simple one, or otherwise in successive takes according to levels of importance. Hence it does not really matter, for example, whether the author's name appears below the title or above it, since relative emphasis is more effectively controlled through size and spacing than by literal order of appearance. From this it follows that such details as the use of the word 'by' preceding the author's name, as well as punctuation at the ends of lines in title page display, are not only redundant but a hindrance, serving only to draw attention to themselves. Display is a higher form of punctuation, and requires the consistent and sensitive reduction or elimination of conventional punctuation from many parts of the book where it has supplied an alternative solution.

Successful title page design hangs on the treatment of the main title, and any sub-title or subsidiary wording that stands

HAROLD EVANS
CARDIFF IN
PHOTOGRAPHS

THE WELSH COUNCIL
FOR THE ARTS
CARDIFF
1990

HAROLD EVANS
CARDIFF
IN PHOTOGRAPHS

THE WELSH
COUNCIL FOR THE ARTS
CARDIFF
1990

The eye soon becomes trained to spot the difference between a clumsy and a reasonable pattern of lines, but then the danger to be avoided is to embark on topiary or to try to fit words into preconceived shapes. Above all, letters and words should take the spacing they call for naturally, and this should never be varied to affect the line lengths (as William Morris does below in his problem line, the fourth one down).

in relation to it. The designer will look at all the possible line divisions of the titling to resolve the twin aims of stressing the sense and rhythms of the wording as well as making an acceptable shape on the page. The same process has to be repeated under different constraints for the book jacket, and the less disparity in approach between these two solutions the better, particularly in matters of capitalisation and punctuation. Agreement between the title as it appears on the jacket, case, title page and imprint – not to mention publicity – can be particularly slack where different departments and designers may be involved.

The isolation of author and title at the head of the page from the publisher's imprint at the foot is a convention we have learned to live with, but there is nothing sacrosanct about it, as various European publishers have recently shown through lively alternative solutions in series and for individual titles. Dates on title pages are untrustworthy and frequently qualified by the imprint, but where permissible they can be a helpful pennyweight to the designer seeking a fine balance on the page. It has been said that the history of the printed book is synonymous with that of the title page, and, whilst that statement might be contested on a number of grounds, it undoubtedly commands a remarkable degree of attention and any shortcomings in its design will not pass unnoticed.

A TALE OF THE HOUSE OF THE
WOLFINGS AND ALL THE KIND-
REDS OF THE MARK WRITTEN
IN PROSE AND IN VERSE
BY WILLIAM MORRIS.

WHILES IN THE EARLY WINTER EVE
WE PASS AMID THE GATHERING NIGHT
SOME HOMESTEAD THAT WE HAD TO LEAVE
YEARS PAST; AND SEE ITS CANDLES BRIGHT
SHINE IN THE ROOM BESIDE THE DOOR
WHERE WE WERE MERRY YEARS AGONE
BUT NOW MUST NEVER ENTER MORE,
AS STILL THE DARK ROAD DRIVES US ON.
E'EN SO THE WORLD OF MEN MAY TURN
AT EVEN OF SOME HURRIED DAY
AND SEE THE ANCIENT GLIMMER BURN
ACROSS THE WASTE THAT HATH NO WAY;
THEN WITH THAT FAINT LIGHT IN ITS EYES
A WHILE I BID IT LINGER NEAR
AND NURSE IN WAVERING MEMORIES
THE BITTER-SWEET OF DAYS THAT WERE.

LONDON 1889: REEVES AND TURNER 196 STRAND.

A concern for the shape of this title page led Morris first to change the line that originally read 'in prose and verse', and then to produce the poem, in his own words: 'to fill the space in the middle'.

The imprint or biblio page

The matter that for statutory reasons has to appear on the verso of the title page may have proliferated in recent years, but that only argues for its more orderly and considered presentation. The case of British Library cataloguing-in-publication data is particularly instructive. Publishers began to incorporate this information years ago, and yet only a minority of designers have yet tumbled to the fact that it is only the content and line division which are significant, and that there is nothing sacrosanct about the style and indentation of these typed slips in themselves! Clearly the arrangement of lines on either a centred or ranged left basis should follow the design principle of the page. (I treasure one early example where the publisher intimidated the printer by telephone to such effect that not only was the content printed verbatim but the notification slip as received was actually reproduced in facsimile.)

If copy threatens to overcrowd the imprint page, this may indicate that it is being used as a dumping ground and that certain credits might form the subject of a separate acknowledgements or similar heading within the prelims. Again, if the production details are of special interest, then the last page of the book (or colophon) can serve to record the printed, as distinct from the published and statutory, history of the book. These aspects – publisher's imprint and printer's imprint – are conventionally, but not necessarily, distanced to correspond and back-up to the two blocks of print at the head and foot of the title page.

The dedication

Patronage as denounced by Samuel Johnson is no more, but with it much typographic splendour also vanished. Grants in aid of publication are best either acknowledged by the author or placed on the imprint page; personal dedications should correctly occupy the recto following the title page, although the verso facing the text opening might be more frequently considered as an alternative to losing two valuable pages. The verso facing the title page is a fit place for what in the absence of definition could be called 'major' dedications; curiously this works better for some formats and titles than others. The convention that certain preliminary matter should open on a right hand page is in any case an odd one – some things invariably look wrong when handled otherwise – a list of contents for example should always open recto, but succeeding lists of illustration and so forth may well follow on.

Contents

As a map of the book, the contents should ideally open on the recto immediately following the title page unless this is taken up by a dedication or some unusual feature. Some authorities make out a case for acknowledgements and preface to precede the contents, and in certain circumstances this may be advantageous. A general if personal preference is to be able to set out these items on the contents page as part of the book to follow, since long sequences which delay the appearance of the contents page can be quite as tiresome and inconclusive in practice as a preamble to the opening credits of a film.

The designer quickly learns to ask whether the contents list is going to make a natural shape on the page, knowing that copy should never be forced into sizes of type and lengths of line to which it is not suited. Take a simple list, for example, in which all the chapter titles are exceptionally short and accompanied only by a page number, so that when titles are ranged full out left to the text measure and page numbers to the right the gap between them is immense: the solution is unlikely to be to link them by rows of dots (known as leaders), but to set in a smaller typesize in double column instead. But before making decisions on the basis of a single page, it should be routine to look systematically at all the other pages in the manuscript which may be affected (list of illustrations, notes, glossary, etc.) and to work out a specification to meet the requirements they hold in common.

Sometimes the problem of obtaining a natural fit on the page for the contents may be diagnosed as one of the depth it will make, because the copy appears to be unduly short or long. Where acceptable commonsense adjustments to size of type and to interlinear spacing have been tried and failed, the resources are far from having been exhausted: the arrangement of the copy should now be restructured. Whoever compiled the copy will have followed a pattern in setting out and typing the information, but it is important to remember that the pattern adopted – however excellent – can only be one of countless ways in which the same information can be presented:

1. In the Beginning . . . 7 is the same as Chapter One

IN THE

BEGINNING

page 7

CHAPTER IV = IV = 4 = Chapter 4 = Four = Chapter Four, and so on to Chapter the Fourth.

The designer could do worse than to consider an analysis of the contents page as the next logical point to turn to once the text page has been settled, in order to consider how it can best reflect the true structure of the book as it progresses from part title to chapter heading, and maybe down to sub-heading level.

The preliminary pages which follow, and all the end pages, are distinct from the main body of the text and may be differentiated on the contents page and in the treatment of headings, type size and styling. If the prelims are concise and relevant and the contents page itself is set in the text size then none of these measures may be needed.

Lists of illustrations and tables

Such lists show where to find visual material just as the list of contents locates the text, and so should follow the contents on the next available fresh page and in as similar a style as the nature of the copy permits.

Acknowledgements

These are of three basic kinds: those the author makes as a coda to his preface, which are therefore usually set in text size, whether following on or making a fresh page; the statutory listing of copyright permissions which may equally go at the front or the end of the book and probably in a smaller size of type; and those which may be treated alongside the author's other sources as end matter, on the grounds that only on reaching that point can the reader assess the degree of any indebtedness.

Preface

Foreword, preface and introduction are frequently and unfortunately used as interchangeable terms, and so the aim or content of such matter has to be allowed to determine its place in the prelims. A foreword, or commendatory note from an illustrious hand, should appear set in the text size as early as practical in the prelims. A preface, concerning how the book came to be written and perhaps including acknowledgements from its author, should follow any foreword and precede an introduction. The introduction – a statement of themes and scope, structure and conventions – is inseparable from the text and forms in effect its opening chapter. For most books these sections are set to the style of the text, although the foreword may be shamelessly decked out for particular markets.

5:2 Part and chapter titles

Part and chapter titles are a form of transmission from the title page down to the text – the part title being geared down from the main title, and the chapter title further still – and then within the text itself this descending order continues through headings, sub-headings and lesser headings still. The contents page should make plain at a glance how the parts and chapters hang together, and sometimes it can go further and show how the entire book has been structured, so that the reader knows what to expect. This is particularly important if there is to be no index.

Part titles are only called for where the nature of the material or the author's plan falls into distinct sections, and so they are partitions or dividing pages which must always appear recto with their verso usually left blank. Where part titles are numerous or of little importance then the paper they would occupy can be saved by placing them above the opening chapter title of each section, in which case it is essential for each section to open recto. Similarly it is possible to con-

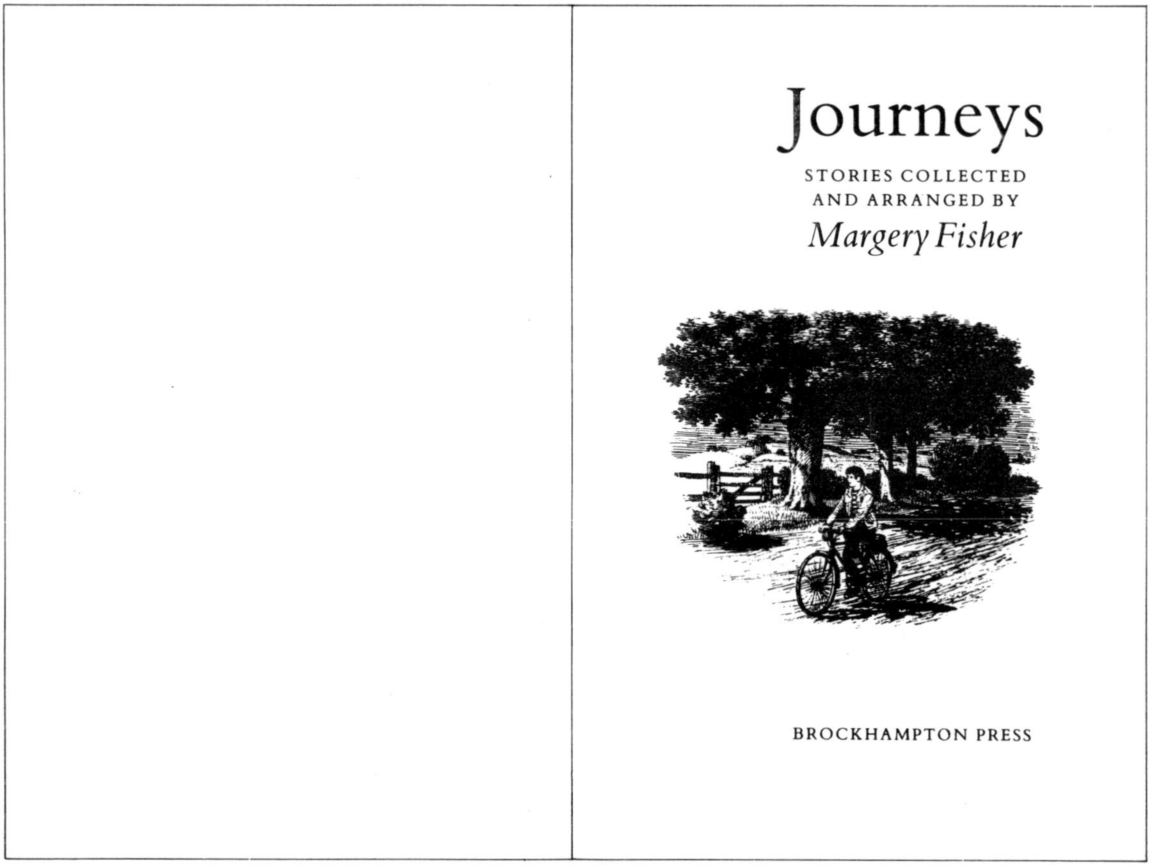

Journeys

STORIES COLLECTED
AND ARRANGED BY

Margery Fisher

BROCKHAMPTON PRESS

trive false part titles as a stratagem for disposing of unwanted blanks: the appendices may take one, for instance, and in any book where a respectable amount of prelims have appeared since the title page, the title may be re-announced on the recto before the text opening.

There may be no more to be stated on a part title than its number, but there are also precedents for all kinds of usage. A summary of the contents of each part can bring its function into focus, but the relation of such a list to the contents page proper has to be finely judged to avoid redundancy; this treatment comes into its own where indexing or colour coding – i.e. at the level of the running head or stepped down the foredge – signifies the change between parts. As the part titles are the most prominent rectos for display after the title page, it is reasonably certain that anything placed on them will not

John Masefield

lockers and a porthole covered with red curtains. A telescope hung on a rack ready for use. A canvas hammock swung from hooks in the wall, it had a pillow, mattress, sheets and blankets. The Captain showed him how to get in and tuck himself up. In a minute he was fast asleep.

JOURNEYS
ON THE WINGS OF
A BIRD

escape attention and can even be turned to dramatic account, and this may be valuable where an author needs to get across a date or a key citation. On the same grounds – that the reader is bound to be 'coming up for air' between parts – illustrations placed on these pages can have telling effect. At the other extreme, the page can be perfectly satisfying when it contains no more than a couple of words and possibly a slight rule or decoration, but used in this way it becomes a scaled-down variation of the title page design, and type and decoration should be consonant.

If you flick though the average unillustrated novel or biography the texture resembles that of a sausage, the same wherever it is cut, and the only accents of space and interest to break the monotony occur between chapters. Years ago, as consultant to one of the children's paperback lists, the depressing standard of rotary letterpress on newsprint – like so many acres of shuttered concrete – led me to think that nothing could be worse than this, and so to experiment with letting off fireworks in this chapter heading area, using the most outlandish display faces in an outrageous way to kick some life into the situation – maybe graffiti happen for the same reason.

The only lesson I subsequently derived from this situation was the need to concentrate one's fire, and if I digress briefly this is because the advent of desktop publishing has produced a tendency in some quarters to introduce fount changes, twiddly bits between paragraphs, or frames surrounding the text page, all in an effort to avoid admitting that the basic texture of the typeface is inert and inadequate. An alternative approach might be to accept the unadorned reading page and to concentrate on creating visual contrast and relief at certain key points, notably those between parts or chapters. These might be signalled, for example, by inserting leaves of coloured paper, with titling and theme treated adventurously through illustration, collage, computer or zoom copier print – all in complete contrast to the even texture of the reading pages which follow. This freedom to experiment and generate lively solutions is one of the big advantages of DTP in many fields of publishing activity.

To return to the prelims; the chapter drop, or number of lines left blank at the head of the text page except for the chapter titling, should not normally vary and will be related to a level established in the prelims and continued through the book; although it is permissible, where the number of lines of chapter titling fluctuates very noticeably, to design with a fixed separation between the lowest line and the text. Some prelim pages and all end pages normally follow the chapter opening for style.

Chapters should start fresh pages where there are few enough of them and the subject matter falls into clear divisions; but in much fiction and several other categories, where there is little more than a number, there is a free choice whether or not to allow chapters to run on after a few lines break. This practice, however, leaves litle scope when it comes to the revision of the text for subsequent editions, whereas there is a certain amount of slack at the ends of chapters where all chapters commence fresh pages.

Roman numerals should be avoided for chapters since they are unfamiliar to the modern reader, and only used – i.e. for part titles – after all the other options have been pre-empted. The prelim pages themselves ought to be paginated in roman lower case (wherever folios are required to print), and the text proper should open at arabic page 1, if for no better reason than that this gives scope to adjust the overall extent for an even working of section multiples without any call to re-number the text sequence.

5:3 Running headlines

Running headlines are as valuable an invention as cat's-eyes: a means of location and navigation through the book, that passes unnoticed on the page during the act of continuous reading. Careful positioning is essential to achieve both these aims, and a voice of type that cannot be confused with that used for any other level of heading in the text: for example, a similar size of italic or of small caps should not be used for both purposes.

The most straightforward usage is to be met with in a novel, where the running head may be centred in italic of the text size with roughly 9pt (say 3mm) extra space beneath, and the folio centred at the foot with commensurate extra space above. Observe that this heading is tucked in fairly closely to the text – paradoxically, either this practice or a marked distancing of running head from text will function, whereas anything approximating to a single line white gap in this situation can lead to the headline being picked up accidentally and recurrently in reading. Note also that there is a dilemma if the novel should have chapter numbers and no titles, since custom would have the book title on the left and chapter title on the right: in this instance it may be preferable to dispense with the running head altogether than to spell out the chapter number.

Copy for the running head requires careful consideration: the chapter titles may be too long for the measure and the editor should be advised if they require shortening; chapter numbers may be needed as well as titles, particularly where there are extensive notes in correspondence at the end; above all there are countless permutations of the matter that can appear, and it may still be possible to invent new ones on the principle that if it works, it's true. Here are just a few:

verso	*recto*
book title	chapter title
part title	chapter title
part of book	part of book (as in introduction, notes, etc.)
chapter	sub-head
sub-head	sub-sub-head
last head on page	last head on page
any of above	last head on spread
author	paper (multi-author works, and for offprints)
book/narrative	book/narrative (Bibles)
alphanumerical	alphanumerical (directories, bibliographies)
symbolic	symbolic (isotypes, as for Olympic Games, etc.)
none to appear	any copy (to appear consistently on one side only – mostly where layout is asymmetric)

The most essential task is to anticipate all the realistic ways in which the running headline may be used, and to remember that for many kinds of reference work it provides the sole or principal access to the book. For anyone involved in the design of reference works, it is fascinating to study series, such as the *British National Bibliography*, where the reference apparatus via the running head has been changed around every few years or so, as well as the various national approaches to comparable volumes in any field.

The running head is frequently found in various combinations with the folio or page number and sharing the same line; this is almost axiomatic for reference use, as is off-centred layout. The folios or the main reference element can be ranged full out left and right or even set out into the foredge margins, as well as being isolated quite high above the text area in asymmetric designs, where the designer is using it to reinforce a level on the grid which will at times be taken up by plates or other matter. For many books without an index and with no reference use envisaged then the running head can be treated as an interesting minor feature in the layout of the spread. It may appear smaller than the text face for example, or appear with the folio as a running footline: a current fashion in pictorial volumes is to 'sky', or place captions over the head of text and pictures, and this can displace the running headline to the foot, where it may look best on one side of the spread only.

The running head does not print on the opening page of any chapter nor on any of the discontinuous prelims for self-evident reasons. Where the folio is displaced from the head another position may need to be found for it – at the foot of text in the instance of chapter openings to which page references are made in the index. Headings can also be left off where bleeds or full page plates fall, and on certain pages where sub-headings, tables, figures or plates appear at the top; but even in the least demanding of circumstances it is best to try to leave no spread without some identification, either by running head or by folio.

5:4 Complexities in the text

Even when the designer has decided that a full reading of the text is not going to influence the approach to its typography, it is advisable to go through the MS. from beginning to end, noting all the points of detail which will call for special attention in terms of layout, specification or artwork. This is a priority because production issues may be raised and time must be allowed for artwork to be prepared. It is quite common for detail which looks insignificant at first glance to prove the determining factor in selecting a typeface and other major decisions.

Languages

The special languages of mathematics, science and music present similar problems and may be considered alongside those languages which have their own script or require special sorts. In setting out to capture the widest market, many phototypesetting founts now come already equipped with the full range of accents needed for most European languages, so this is rarely a problem nowadays. The Asian communities supply translation, word processing and phototypesetting to industry standards, although Urdu remains keyboard-resistant at the time of writing, and calligraphy still has to be obtained. Dry-transfer sheets for non-latin scripts are at the advertising headline stage of development, and it is doubtful whether they will progress much further since the future is so plainly with computerised systems in languages as well as for scientific purposes.

Whenever complexities or special typographic requirements arise, this usually indicates that a small but specialised readership is likely to be involved, and that the success of the venture may depend upon bringing together the right author and publisher. Authors are becoming increasingly accustomed to preparing their own MSS. on disk, using appropriate software and proof quality print-out resources, although to obtain the requisite production standard access to a high-quality laser image setter may be needed for the final output. This new participation in certain print production stages and insight into the whole process is exciting enough, but should not blind us to the fact that the mis-named 'desktop publishing' has nothing to offer in place of the traditional development of a range of basic publishing skills of which design is one.

In publishing, it is not so much the specialist use of these languages which is of concern – mathematical or musical scholars will know where to turn for expertise in any case – but rather the random requirement for a few lines of specialised setting in a general title. Dry-transfer artwork provides an answer in many such cases, and sometimes companies such as Chartpak, Letraset, Mecanorma and Zipatone among others can come up with sheets that do a specific job particularly well. Where there is a narrowly definable but recurrent problem then custom-made sheets may provide an alternative to long waits and hefty bills for specialist typesetting.

The best dry-transfer system for musical notation is manufactured under the name Notaset in the Netherlands, but here too the current intensive research into computer-based origination must eventually lead to an acceptable outcome in terms of quality and price for a desktop system.

Times New Roman was the hot metal typeface that became equipped over the years for every eventuality in terms of a related Greek and Russian and all the sorts needed for other languages and for mathematical and scientific setting; and on many systems it is still a good starting point in the search for a typeface to meet the requirement of compatibility between special material and text matter.

Marginal notes

The question of where to place the notes is discussed in the section on end pages [5.5]. Designers have to remind themselves that options and opportunities now exist to do as routine things that a little while ago they were conditioned to regard as recklessly expensive, one of which was to align a sub-column to the text. References to plates are ideally placed marginally in alignment with the point in the text they refer to, and, where the margins are generous or asymmetrical, shoulder heads could be considered more frequently. Folios can often be set out into the foredge margins to advantage, and captions may also be set marginally; but take care not to allow double booking – i.e. by material of two or more kinds which may on occasion have conflicting demands for the same position.

Extracts

Many authors make extensive use of quotations from other sources, both prose and verse, and here the reader needs to note the flow from the main text into these extracts and back again. This does not generally necessitate a drop in typesize (although this may help in avoiding turnover lines in verse, and might indeed be preferred now that there is no longer a cost differential to be taken into account), since there is an available alternative: this is to combine additional space above and below the extract with a reduction to the text measure. The extra interlinear space should be just a half-line, a full line white is excessive and will interfere with reading continuity – remember that the full white, followed by an unindented paragraph, is commonly used to make a break in the text. The measure may be reduced by indenting the text of the extract to the normal paragraph indent; again that would suffice, although it is customary to indent by that amount to the right as well as to the left for justified prose. To set the extracts unjustified makes a further contrast in texture with the text, and one that I would recommend wherever suitable, since with this procedure an extract does not lose its identity when split by a page turn. Under these conditions there is no case for retaining the quotation marks, which have been effectively replaced through this use of space.

Where the author makes frequent and extensive use of

extracts this can produce a very choppy effect on the page, which should largely be overcome through the standard editorial practice of running on those of about sixty words or less in the text. This would argue against the use of a smaller size for extracts, since it can introduce the false distinction that short pronouncements are accorded text size whilst longer ones are set down.

The setting of verse

Verse is simple to cast off since it will compose line by line except where turnover lines cannot be avoided. The art is to phase out or keep these to an absolute minimum since they spoil the natural shape a poem makes on the page. There is no reason why verse extracts should not range strictly left, since the patterns of indentation to be found are not necessarily those intended by the poet but tend instead to result from arbitrary rules imposed by subsequent editors, anthologists and designers; these are picked up by the copy typist so that whenever material is gleaned from a variety of sources one is faced with inconsistencies of indentation which only the typographer can rectify. Since this is largely a visual matter, the designer personally should check the bibliographical evidence to avoid error. A disadvantage of ranging is that there will be a column of opening capitals down the left edge, and this will be the less conspicuous if the capitals in use are small in relation to the ascenders and lower case generally.

Verse is set with a fixed word space, and this should be on the close side, adequate for the divisions between words in the typeface in question but close enough to let the rhythms of the language fall within the word as well as between words. Only the longest of stanzas should ever be broken, and then skilfully so that the true stanza structure should never be left in doubt; considerable variation in page depth is the price that should willingly be paid for this, although page break decisions also have continuity to take into account.

Line length variation is frequently extreme from poem to poem or between different sections of the same poem, and so the ability to centre each off-centre mass on the centre line of the text measure is a valuable asset – there is no rule of thumb for this: the typographer's eye quickly learns to discriminate. Where verse extracts occur here and there

20 *Chapter One: Childhood and youth*

reinforced by the addition of sexual themes (much to Charles Morin's disapproval). Indeed, the whole play is a much more 'personal' work than *Ubu Roi*: where the latter was the result of a collaboration between Jarry and Henri Morin working on a text written by Charles Morin, *Ubu Cocu* is principally Jarry's own work, and in any case certainly owes nothing to Charles Morin.

Although a detailed discussion of *Ubu Cocu* is given in Chapter Five, some explanation of the sources of its principal themes and characters is appropriate here. In it, the theme of Ubu's cuckoldry, first enunciated in *Onésime*, is more fully developed and the name of Mère Ubu's lover, originally O'Priou, becomes first Barbapoux – the nickname of a *répétiteur* at the Lycée – and then, in a subsequent version, Memnon, who is attributed with the function of *vidangeur* (night man). The implied link between sexual and faecal themes is further developed when the two lovers arrange a tryst in the latrines. Ironically, the inspiration for this scene may well have come from none other than the greatest of French tragedians, Racine. The schoolboy mind is adept at reading obscene or ambiguous meanings into the most innocent of texts – and the more sacrosanct the author, the greater is the temptation to look for such meanings. Thus the scene of Mère Ubu's rendezvous with her lover 'dans les cabinets' was quite probably inspired by the opening lines of *Bérénice*:

Arrêtons un moment. La pompe de ces lieux,
Je le vois bien, Arsace, est nouvelle à tes yeux.
Souvent ce cabinet, superbe et solitaire,
Des secrets de Titus est le dépositaire.
C'est ici quelquefois qu'il se cache à sa cour,
Lorsqu'il vient à la reine expliquer son amour.

> [*Let us pause a moment. The pomp of this place,*
> *I can see clearly, Arsace, is new to your gaze.*
> *Often it is to this room, magnificent and solitary,*
> *That the secrets of Titus are confided.*
> *It is here sometimes that he hides from the court,*
> *When he comes to explain to the queen the reasons for his love.*][30]

The most important new characters in *Ubu Cocu*, however, are those of Achras, the unfortunate 'collector of Polyhedra' whose home is invaded and taken over by Ubu, and of Ibu's Conscience. The first is an innocent and amusing parody upon Jarry's mathematics teacher, M. Périer (Périer = Poirier = Achras, the Greek word for pear-tree), who was notorious for his mannerisms of speech and his fondness for complex geometrical forms.[31] Out of these 'polyhedra' the fertile schoolboy imagination had made living creatures who were carefully nurtured and whose habits were studied by Achras. They, together

Chapter One: Childhood and youth 21

with his 'treatise on the surface of the square', are his lifelong passion, as Achras tells us in his opening speech:

O mais c'est qué, voyez-vous bien, je n'ai point sujet d'être mécontent de mes polyèdres: ils font des petits toutes les six semaines, c'est pire que des lapins. Et il est bien vrai de dire que les polyèdres réguliers sont les plus fidèles et les plus attachés à leur maître; sauf que l'Icosaèdre s'est révolté ce matin et que j'ai été forcé, voyez-vous bien, de lui flanquer une gifle sur chacune de ses faces. Et que comme ça c'était compris. Et mon traité, voyez-vous bien, sur les moeurs des polyèdres qui s'avance: n'y a plus que vingt-cinq volumes à faire.

> [Oh, but it's that, look you, I've no reason to be displeased with my polyhedra: they have little ones every six weeks, they're worse than rabbits. And it's quite true to say that the regular polyhedra are the most faithful and the most devoted to their master; except that the icosahedron rebelled this morning and I was obliged, look you, to give him a slap on each of his faces. And that way he got the message. And my treatise, look you, on the habits of polyhedra, which is coming along: there are only twenty-five more volumes to write.][32]

Ubu's Conscience, on the other hand, represents a satire upon Jarry's philosophy teacher during this year, M. Bourdon – latinized to become 'B. Bombus' – the name possibly suggesting to the pupils the 'buzz' or 'hum' of conscience, as expressed in Bourdon's moral philosophy, as a passage from the play would seem to indicate:

LA CONSCIENCE, *émergeant comme un vers au moment où Memnon plonge*: Ouf! quel choc! mon crâne en bourdonne!
MEMNON: Comme un tonneau vide.
LA CONSCIENCE: Le vôtre ne bourdonne pas?

> THE CONSCIENCE, *emerging like a worm as Memnon plunges in*: Ow! what a blow! my head's buzzing from it!
> MEMNON: Like an empty barrel.
> THE CONSCIENCE: Isn't yours buzzing?[33]

The fact of the presence in *Ubu Cocu* of Bourdon/Bombus is again an indication of the curiously impersonal nature of this parody. For Jarry referred to him twice in later life with considerable respect, remembering him as 'l'auteur de livres excellents',[34] and as having expounded to his pupils the philosophy of Nietzsche even before Nietzsche's works had been translated into French.[35] Here, notwithstanding, he appears as a tall, thin figure clothed only in a shirt, whom Ubu carries about with him in a suitcase, whom he consults concerning the fate to be meted out to the unfortunate Achras, and whose highly moral advice he then proceeds to use in a quite unintended way. The scene of this interview is one of the most brilliantly satirical passages of the play, and was considered by André Gide, along with

in a prose work the decision can be made either to centre them on the measure in this way or to let them share a fixed indent from the left, the latter being the more usual decision in an off-centred design.

An unusual solution for extracts in parallel text, in which the measure is broken in a regular pattern of overhangs and indents – it is no longer complicated or expensive to exceed the measure in this way where appropriate for extracts or tables.

The setting of plays

The text of a play makes a singular demand of typography: that it shall involve itself with the reactivation of spoken language, just as a music score is concerned exclusively with the re-creation of sounds. The conventions which have evolved historically to this end have proved remarkably successful and durable as even the first-time user will testify, and it is fascinating that there is no real advance on the techniques of the

First Folio in presenting a courtroom transcript today. There is always a boundary to be drawn between the non-spoken zones – actors' names in small caps and stage instructions in italics – and the text to be spoken. The colon (which should be preceded by a slight space) and square bracket have a special use to mark the boundaries, and the interposition of the actor's name also forces a pause which parallels the gap between speeches.

Different categories of book can operate in response to a whole variety of reading needs, ranging from learning to read in the first place to reading slowly in assimilating poetry or less familiar tongues to reading aloud for others; from being able to hear a spoken text inwardly to comparing dead languages on the page; from memorizing a passage to making a précis; and from looking up a meaning to using a catalogue. The book designer cannot limit his curiosity to a current field of activity and its presumed requirements, but must keep up an active interest in the whole since the reader passes so quickly from one state of reading to the next, often within the same book.

Listings

Wherever an author's argument breaks out from the confines of the paragraph into a listing, it is important to establish whether the intention is that such sequences of points should be made consecutively rather than coequally, since the probability is that some system of numbering will have been used in either case. Numbers are fine where an order of precedence or logical continuity is implied, but are best avoided in other cases: a list of capitalised short entries may be treated as an extract, indented and with half a line's space above and below. Longer entries which will involve turnover lines are best signalled by a punctuation mark (such as an en dash followed by a space) or a bullet, which these days may be a light open circle or square or whatever will give the right degree of emphasis.

In most circumstances it is best to set such lists with fixed word spacing and a ragged right hand edge, and with indentation and extra spacing above and below. This shows the reader what is intended, and the punctuation system within this convention – whether to regard the episode as

The basics of a healthy diet

- ■ Follow a varied diet of mixed foods
- ■ Avoid sugar and refined products.
- ■ Avoid salt, as this may cause high blood pressure.
- ■ Eat plenty of dietary fibre in your food.
- ■ Avoid too much fat and cholesterol, and keep to unsaturated fats.
- ■ Diet to remove excess body weight, but not by fasting as this reduces performance and endurance capacity.
- ■ Eat little and often throughout the day so as to keep variations in blood sugar level to a minimum.
- ■ Cook without salt, and with a minimum of fat; eat vegetables raw wherever possible.
- ■ Avoid alcohol, tobacco and caffeine.

falling within the paragraph or to have no punctuation at line endings – becomes an editorial decision.

Tables

Any sufficiently lengthy list of short items will suggest setting for downward scanning in as many parallel columns as necessary, as in the case of an index. This is distinct from the simplest setting in double column for comparative purposes, where the reading direction is across as well as down the columns. The design of any table, however complex, can be broken into four considerations:

1. arrangement into columns
2. spacing between columns
3. spacing down the page
4. the need for down or cross rules.

It is deceptively easy here for the designer to follow copy, that is to say to let the line for line appearance of a table reflect the external and quite arbitrary dress in which the author and his typist have presented the facts to the best of their abilities. Instead, the way in which the table will be used should be analysed, and surprisingly often it will be found that something as basic as transposing the vertical and the horizontal coordinates will not only improve a table's shape on the page – which in itself would never be a sufficient reason – but its comprehension as well.

Each design decision interacts with copy, and the first consideration will be to try to fit the table within the text measure and avoid turning either the table or elements within it at right angles to this. Tables, like any other copy, should never be forced to occupy a given typographic space: if it is natural for them to make less or slightly more than the text measure, or to read across the spread or even to turn on the page, well and good: simply find the sum of the maximum content of each of the individual columns plus sensible intercolumn spacing and you have a measure. (The precise measurement of numerical columns is child's play once it is realised that each figure and unit of spacing can be an en of set.) If this measure is an unworkable one at first sight, look closely again at abbreviating or turning over

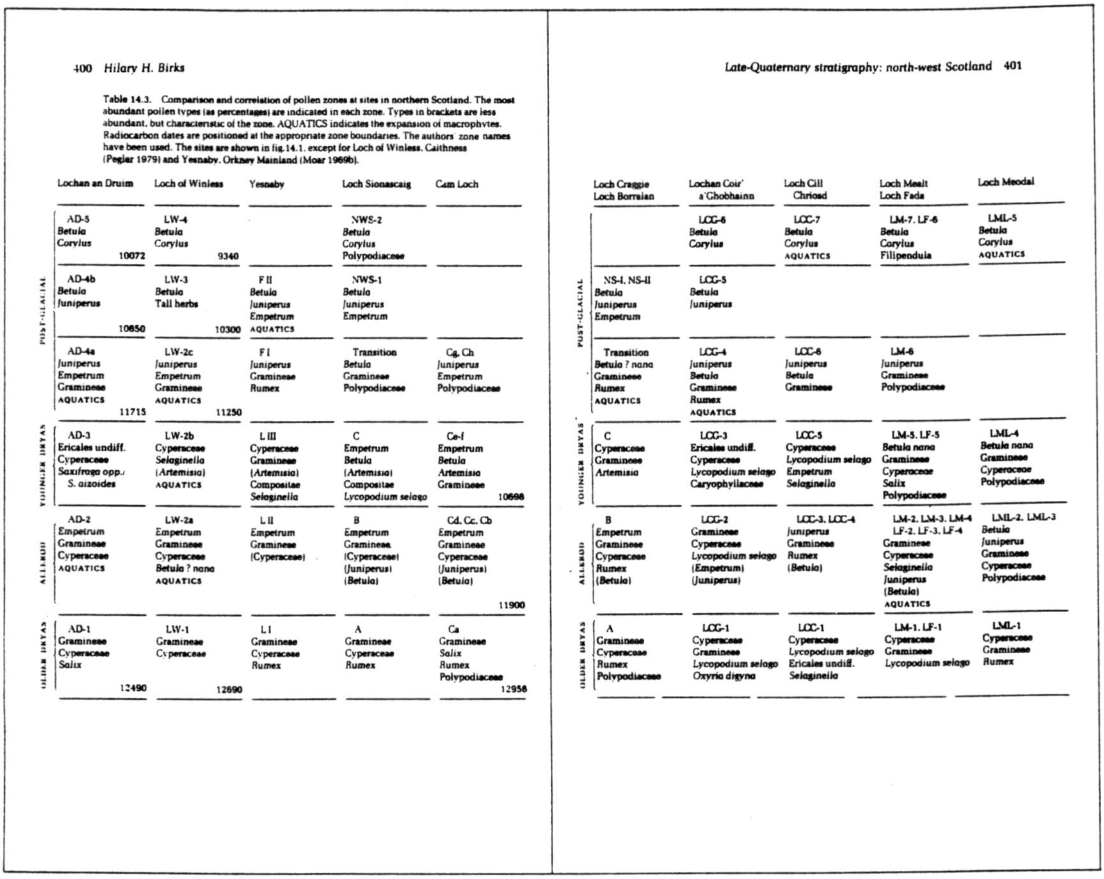

400 *Hilary H. Birks*

Late-Quaternary stratigraphy: north-west Scotland 401

Table 14.3. Comparison and correlation of pollen zones at sites in northern Scotland. The most abundant pollen types (as percentages) are indicated in each zone. Types in brackets are less abundant, but characteristic of the zone. AQUATICS indicates the expansion of macrophytes. Radiocarbon dates are positioned at the appropriate zone boundaries. The authors' zone names have been used. The sites are shown in fig.14.1, except for Loch of Winless, Caithness (Peglar 1979) and Yesnaby, Orkney Mainland (Moar 1969b).

	Lochan an Druim	Loch of Winless	Yesnaby	Loch Sionascaig	Cam Loch	Loch Craggie Loch Borralan	Lochan Coir' a'Ghobhainn	Loch Cill Chriosd	Loch Mealt Loch Fada	Loch Meodal
POST-GLACIAL	AD-5 *Betula* *Corylus* 10072	LW-4 *Betula* *Corylus* 9340		NWS-2 *Betula* *Corylus* Polypodiaceae			LCG-6 *Betula* *Corylus*	LCC-7 *Betula* *Corylus* AQUATICS	LM-7, LF-6 *Betula* *Corylus* *Filipendula*	LML-5 *Betula* *Corylus* AQUATICS
	AD-4b *Betula* *Juniperus* 10650	LW-3 *Betula* Tall herbs 10300	F II *Betula* *Juniperus* *Empetrum* AQUATICS	NWS-1 *Betula* *Juniperus* *Empetrum*		NS-I, NS-II *Betula* *Juniperus* *Empetrum*	LCG-5 *Betula* *Juniperus*			
	AD-4a *Juniperus* *Empetrum* Gramineae AQUATICS 11715	LW-2c *Juniperus* *Empetrum* Gramineae AQUATICS 11250	F I *Juniperus* Gramineae *Rumex*	Transition *Betula* Gramineae Polypodiaceae	Cg, Ch *Juniperus* *Empetrum* Polypodiaceae	Transition *Betula ? nana* Gramineae *Rumex* AQUATICS	LCG-4 *Juniperus* *Betula* Gramineae *Rumex* AQUATICS	LCC-6 *Juniperus* *Betula* Gramineae	LM-6 *Juniperus* Gramineae Polypodiaceae	
YOUNGER DRYAS	AD-3 Ericales undiff. Cyperaceae *Saxifraga opp./ S. aizoides*	LW-2b Cyperaceae *Selaginella* (*Artemisia*) AQUATICS	L III Cyperaceae Gramineae (*Artemisia*) Compositae *Selaginella*	C *Empetrum* *Betula* (*Artemisia*) Compositae *Lycopodium selago*	Ce-f *Empetrum* *Betula* *Artemisia* Gramineae 10698	C Cyperaceae Gramineae *Artemisia*	LCG-3 Ericales undiff. Cyperaceae *Lycopodium selago* Caryophyllaceae	LCC-5 Cyperaceae *Lycopodium selago* *Empetrum* *Selaginella*	LM-5, LF-5 *Betula nana* Gramineae Cyperaceae *Salix* Polypodiaceae	LML-4 *Betula nana* Gramineae Cyperaceae Polypodiaceae
ALLEROD	AD-2 *Empetrum* Gramineae Cyperaceae AQUATICS	LW-2a *Empetrum* Gramineae Cyperaceae *Betula ? nana* AQUATICS	L II *Empetrum* Gramineae (Cyperaceae)	B *Empetrum* Gramineae (Cyperaceae) (*Juniperus*) (*Betula*)	Cd, Cc, Cb *Empetrum* Gramineae Cyperaceae (*Juniperus*) (*Betula*) 11900	B *Empetrum* Gramineae Cyperaceae *Rumex* (*Betula*)	LCG-2 Gramineae Cyperaceae *Lycopodium selago* (*Empetrum*) (*Juniperus*)	LCC-3, LCC-4 *Juniperus* Gramineae *Rumex* (*Betula*)	LM-2, LM-3, LM-4 LF-2, LF-3, LF-4 Gramineae Cyperaceae *Selaginella* *Juniperus* (*Betula*) AQUATICS	LML-2, LML-3 *Betula* *Juniperus* Gramineae Cyperaceae Polypodiaceae
OLDER DRYAS	AD-1 Gramineae Cyperaceae *Salix* 12490	LW-1 Gramineae Cyperaceae 12690	L I Gramineae Cyperaceae *Rumex*	A Gramineae Cyperaceae *Rumex*	Ca Gramineae *Salix* *Rumex* Polypodiaceae 12958	A Gramineae Cyperaceae *Rumex* Polypodiaceae	LCG-1 Cyperaceae Gramineae *Lycopodium selago* *Oxyria digyna*	LCC-1 Cyperaceae *Lycopodium selago* Ericales undiff. *Selaginella*	LM-1, LF-1 Cyperaceae Gramineae *Lycopodium selago*	LML-1 Cyperaceae Gramineae *Rumex*

A table designed across the spread.

problematical headings, and only then at whether a different format or typesize is indicated.

Once it becomes possible to see how columns are going to space out across the width, then the space between lines can be calculated having regard to any bias in reading direction, or difficulty in reading either down or across because of span or absence of data. Fine adjustment to the spacing makes all the difference to the way in which a table functions, and all subgroupings of information should be articulated through differential spacing, whether lateral or in depth.

Down and cross rules are superfluous for most of the time. Box rules surrounding tables have the effect of isolating them from the text, and should be avoided where the ideal is for the reader to follow the general argument without losing contact with the text. Rules can give an intimidating look to straightforward tables, but have an undeniable use in taking over where controlled spacing is under strain in directing the eye surely. The lightest possible weight of rule discharges this task without drawing attention to itself.

5:5 The end pages

Hugh Williamson lists the sequence: *appendices, notes, abbreviations, glossary, bibliography, acknowledgements, index, colophon;* and this seems an admirable basis for academic publishing. It is difficult to comment from a design viewpoint except on: *notes, glossary, bibliography* and *index,* which are those likely to be met with in books of all kinds.

Notes

The options are to have notes on the page, notes at the ends of chapters, or notes at the end of the book; and this seems the best point at which to review the whole question.

Writers through the ages have liked shoulder and footnotes because they can do things which notes appearing in a block at the end of the book can not. The cost and complexity of manual assembly made the practice almost obsolete, but now the means of revival are at hand, and it is hoped that word of it will get about, since habit persists as tradition long after the economic or other original cause has been removed. Mere finding notes should of course continue to appear at the end where those interested will search them out. Notes on the page need not look archaic or fusty: modern equivalents are to be found in books of all kinds, but particularly in full colour works designed spread by spread – where ends are tied up and topics extended in little boxes and the like – only we no longer call them footnotes.

Notes at the ends of chapters are maddening to locate, and are unlikely to please anyone except the contributor to a multi-author volume receiving offprints.

The designer frequently needs an editor's view on the importance of notes to appear at the end of a specialised text before deciding how to set them: this will usually be two sizes down from the text, and a preponderance of short line entries may indicate setting in double column for appearance as much as for the massive saving in space.

The decisions taken for the notes will normally serve for the other end pages as well, and if double column looks the best answer throughout, then consider whether to use unjustified setting. Reference throughout the end matter is alphanumerically down the left hand edge, and short entries will tend to make the right fairly ragged in any case; justification can yield some unsightly results in narrow measures and with reduced leading, and there seems little advantage in the practice.

The reference figures used for the notes are important: lining figures are slightly easier to scan in downward column, but the important thing is to set them out sufficiently from the text block and preferably followed by a full point. Everything should be done to facilitate reference to and from text to notes: the superior figures used in the text should give clear signals of the presence of notes, each chapter should be numbered through from figure one, and in the notes section it is important to repeat the chapter number and title above each sequence of notes, and also to use the running headline to help the reader find the right section.

The glossary

Because this is a mini-dictionary, there is a tendency to think that bold type is necessary for the words to be defined, but this is not so, the italic or small caps with suitable indentation for turnover lines will be perfectly adequate. The usual rule about the relationship between parts applies here as well: turn to the bibliography as the more complex problem, resolve the typographical styling for that satisfactorily and the style for the glossary will inevitably fall into place. If bold is being deployed throughout the book, then it would be natural to use it for the glossary as well.

When the balance of the copy is right it is very occasionally possible and valuable to combine index and glossary.

The bibliography

This is of the utmost importance in scholarly books and merits careful layout based on an awareness of accepted conventions. Whereas a simple list of further reading admits a variety of typographic stylings, a true bibliographical setting involves the use of three alphabets: small caps with caps; the

CLAYTON, Thomas (and **Thomas Clayton junior**). Plasterers.
Clayton's birthplace is unrecorded, but it was probably in London. No record of his apprenticeship there has, however, been traced. As far as is known, he worked entirely in Scotland from about 1740 for at least 20 years. His son, Thomas Varsallis Clayton, born in 1743, seems to have been responsible for work at Inveraray Castle, the Edinburgh Register House in the 1780s, and possibly at Mellerstain. It has not yet proved possible to establish the exact connection of this Thomas Clayton, but it seems useful to give a conjectural pedigree. This owes much to the researches of Miss C H Cruft, who has recorded the evidence in files at The Scottish National Monuments Record, Edinburgh.

Thomas Clayton, senior = Elizabeth Wilson
(*fl.* 1710–60; married *c* 1735; lived mostly at Hamilton)

Thomas Varsallis = ? (b. at Hamilton, 8 March 1743; d. October 1793)	Archibald (b. at Hamilton, 25 December 1745)	James (?) (b. at Hamilton, April 1747)

Isabella = Rev John Reston (ordained 1783; sometime minister at Alnwick, Biggar, Kilsyth and Bridgeton, Glasgow. *See* William Hunter, 1867, *Biggar and the House of Fleming*)
(married 3 September 1778)

If Thomas Varsallis Clayton is the same person as the 'Thomas Clayton, plasterer, Edinburgh', father of Isabella Clayton, then account needs to be taken of Thomas's brother, Francis, a merchant in North and South Carolina.

Although ideal for saving space where there are a lot of short entries, multiple column setting can also accommodate carefully-styled complexities.

italic with figs; and the roman with figs. These are zoned so that authors always appear in small caps with caps; book titles in full and titles of journals (abbreviated) in italics; titles of articles, place, publisher and date of publication in roman. There are accepted orders of appearance and punctuation plays a vital role.

Although designing a bibliography is a game played within strict rules, there are enough variables [forename first, forename or initials after surname, etc.] to ensure that no two designers are likely to produce identical solutions.

The index

The index can only be completed and set after the rest of the book is in page proof; an allowance should have been made for the pages it will occupy, but there is usually quite a lot of flexibility in adjusting the styling of an index to fit the actual space available. The typesetting specification can be varied in terms of number of columns, size of type, ragged or justified setting, leading, degree of indentation, and space between letters of the alphabet. Space may be saved without shedding information by running sub-headings on, but there is greater ease of reference where each takes a fresh line.

Where page references are numerous and there is little leading, then old style or non-lining figures generally look best, but lining figures are to be preferred for their legibility in really small sizes. Italic or bold figures which contrast sufficiently with the roman can be used to denote plates.

Research has established that the average time taken to trace a reference to its source in the text is three-quarters of a minute, part of which time is taken in locating the page; thus highlighting the case for placing folios at the head and set out to the foredge, rather than centred at the foot of each page. The alphabetic thumb index (although not an index in the present sense) is an ancient means of finding one's place; and inexpensive techniques exist which, given colour-coded indexes or contents pages, could extend their sophistication and appeal in appropriate educational and popular categories.

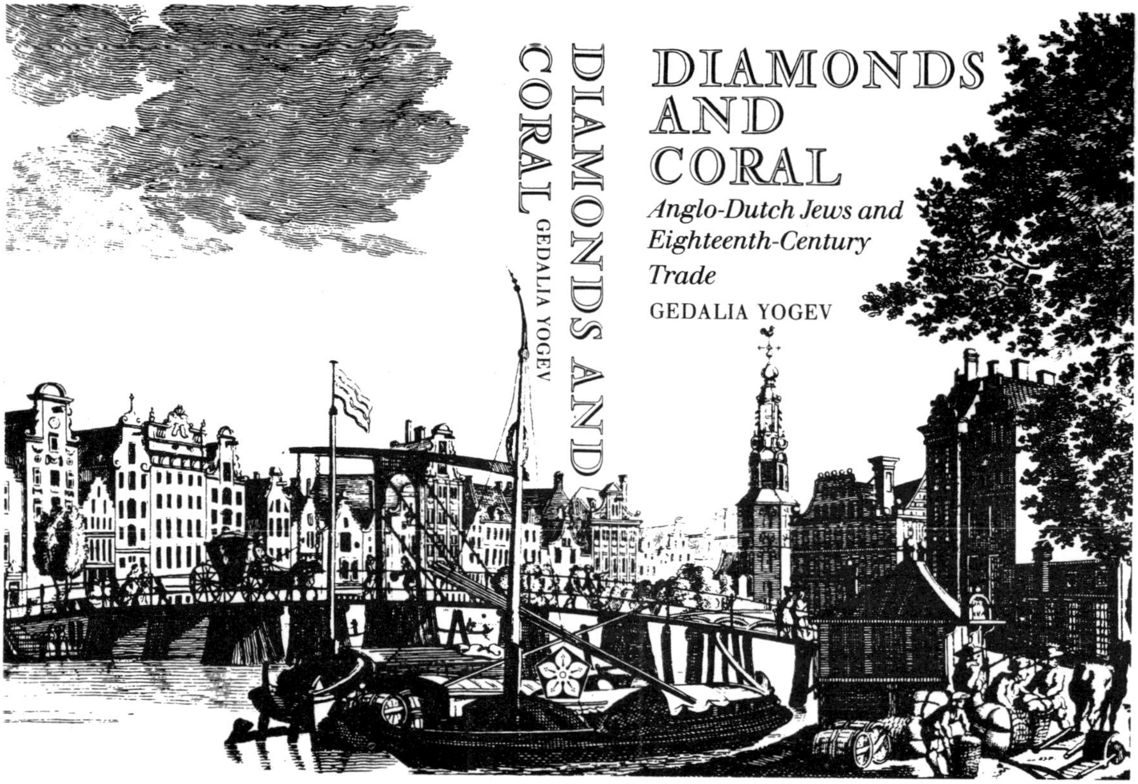

The book jacket is seen as three distinct surfaces, of which the front and spine alone have to display effectively. Wrap-round jackets are an attractive idea provided they first satisfy this criterion.

With the jacket design, one's thoughts turn naturally to binding materials and to the colour ranges in which they are available, so that the exterior of the book as a whole will present a unified appearance. Unusually, this was a black and white jacket, and so it followed that a silver blocking on a black material was chosen. The titling is a version of Rosart (shown on page 88), redrawn to meet foil-blocking requirements.

6 MATERIALS

The materials of which a book is made have to be considered as an ensemble. No designer who has seen it can ever forget the film clip of the great architect Mies van der Rohe inspecting the prototype of a window join, incidentally illustrating his own formulation: "God is in the details". The thought that anything can safely be left to chance after that is a daunting one, but in realistic terms, I have always sought to counterpose and relate this to the definition of Thomas Aquinas: "that language must be adequate for the expression of an idea, but no more". This is not a philosophical digression but a programme for action. If the designer's proposals should be more than adequate, then something may enter into the essential process of communication between author and reader that, for want of a better word, could be described as aestheticism. We in publishing need to hold to the right priorities and should never feel ashamed of the limitations within which we are compelled to work, and, in this sense, some of the books I have most enjoyed designing have been typewriter set: DTP has as proud a rationale as any learned press or bibliophile society.

Approach the evaluation and selection of materials from this angle – and materials are not something that should be added on to a specification at the last moment – and it will be seen that they interact with the design process at every stage. So the designer has to know something of the supply situation: how it developed historically, how it is constantly subject to fluctuation, and how to use it to advantage.

It can readily be seen how papyrus, parchment and hand-made paper as writing or printing substrates – and the leather or vellum, buckram or linen (and even certain plastics and synthetics) used in bookbinding – have all been successively priced out of the market for practical purposes. At each stage it is a question of looking critically at what they have been replaced by as marketable commodities, since the book designer has little or no say in their formulation, and it would appear, paradoxically, that the pace in binding and blocking materials is set by the footwear industry, of which packaging is a branch and publishers' binding only a small sideshoot.

The Victorians lived with cloth impressed to look like leather and we still accept paper impressed to resemble cloth, and this ought to inspire a degree of revulsion. The answer for our age must surely be undisguised but purpose-developed paper or synthetic, but the designer who believes this has not only the task of convincing management but of challenging an entire industrial interface. At present the British compromise solution is to sweep the problem under the carpet of the book jacket; but the seeds of more permanent solutions are often discussed between designers, and a more modern approach comes into play once the traditional area is left and we come to consider functional binding styles ranging from loose leaf to the electronic formats under development.

It would be a pity to give the impression that working within these ranges of materials, however arbitrarily they expand and contract, is anything but the greatest fun whatever the budgetary restrictions. There is a school of design, and it is well represented at the annual small press show held in Mainz, which holds that we can learn from minimal techniques in the theatre, and use offbeat and recycled resources to great effect.

The traditional book is a structure of paper, boards, thread and glue, which has been printed, blocked and finished with other materials; and it is the design properties of some of the most common of these materials that I want to consider now.

6:1 Book papers

Paper has to be right for both text and illustration, and that is not so difficult as it used to be when these requirements were in conflict under the letterpress process, and called either for compromise or different papers for each purpose. Art paper, with its high reflectivity, should be a thing of the past outside art books or photographic pictorial volumes (even here the matt qualities are generally to be preferred), and certainly any shiny finish must be avoided for the text, as should any high degree of whiteness or cold, blueish tonality. A hardly detectable tendency towards an ivory or warm tone as against grey makes for optimum continuous reading conditions, and this is only to be met with in papers of a certain quality and free of mechanical wood pulp – for acid-free papers of archival quality it is necessary to look further still. Both surfaces of the sheet should be even, and those where the sieve side (that in contact with the travelling wire mesh) differs noticeably in texture and appearance from the top surface should be avoided.

Grain direction is paramount and must run parallel to the spine. This is so widely disregarded at present that it merits a word of explanation: the fibres align themselves with the travel of the papermaking web; hence parallel filaments up to a couple of millimetres in length but of negligible diameter are highly susceptible to humidity change in respect of their width as opposed to length. This machine or grain direction of the paper is important for folding in that it is easier to fold in the grain direction than at right angles to it. When the grain direction is allowed to run at right angles to the spine this severely affects the way the pages turn and the book opens and resumes its shape, and most cases of warped and misshapen bindings and curling book jackets can also be traced back to this phenomenon, which similarly affects endpapers, all paper-based binding materials and most boards. The defence that the height to width ratio of the page format is not all that disparate is outrageous: a square format book will be correct where all the materials are rightly aligned and deformed if they are not.

Although there is a little more latitude where lines of text are backed up or perfected in precise register, relative paper opacity becomes a major factor where illustrations or solids are to print alongside the text. The use of lighter substances can prevent volumes becoming overweight and unhandy in some formats, as well as conserving fibre and the cost thereof – it is too early to comment on recycled book papers beyond identifying magazines rather than books as the primary market once the tensile strength of the web is made adequate, and residual grey is reduced to a tolerable level.

At the quality end of the spectrum, British papers have long commanded world respect, but the use of Scandinavian cartridge for B-format paperbacks and fiction in general is to be welcomed for the lightness of weight, if not for the over-whiteness, which they bring. In other respects papermakers in both America and the Far East appear to share the present initiative for interesting qualities, but the price after import and conversion is such that the British designer can only look to their use where texture and colour will really tell: on covers or endpapers, for example.

Paper is a wonderful material to work with, and it is still possible for the designer to be involved in prescribing a special making of comparatively trivial amounts – though at other times a crisis in supply or inertia about the stock situation can place the effective decisions in other hands. The designer should seek satisfactory assurances about paper from the outset – the question of overall approach as well as assessing reproduction standards in colour or otherwise are inseparable from this – and think about materials as early as possible in order to set in train a binder's dummy in the correct ones.

6:2 Endpapers

When decorated papers came into use as endpapers in the seventeenth century, someone called them 'theatre curtains' – they rise and the play begins – and it therefore seems appropriate to take them into account at an early stage in design. The separate and frequently heavier substance needed for tipped-on endpapers should either match the tone and texture of the book paper exactly or contrast markedly with it: few things can be more unsightly than a white cartridge tipped onto an ivory-toned text paper. Thus imaginative opportunities exist at relatively low cost either to extend the colour coordination of the binding ensemble through tinted or patterned papers, or to print an illustration or map in any colour or on any coloured ground over this useful spread. (Libraries will paste their own issue slips over the front surface regardless, although where the front endpaper is repeated at the back no informational loss need result.)

Self-endpapers – where the first and last pages of the outer sections are pasted down to the case – are structurally weak, a doubtful economy, and should not be used as a means of disposing of blank leaves. Again, since the endpapers are printed and added as a separate little job, it is possible at the back to contrive all sorts of ingenious fold-outs and wallets which would be prohibitively expensive as part of the book block.

Looking at the problems of matching shades between ranges of endpapers and binding papers – at the cost of this and at the risk that manufacturers' colour ranges are prone to sudden cancellations, particularly in mid-series – then there is a lot to be said for printing exact shades to order on white stock. This self-colour need not be a solid, and might include a reversal so that any of these surfaces could be used informationally or decoratively, thus circumventing above all the tyranny of routine specification for the bindery, where each spine is simply foil-blocked from a line duplicate of the titling prepared for the spine of the jacket, and the design potential of the front board is dismissed as too costly to consider.

The colourful history of decorative papers and their possible revival for endpapers and in case-binding is a personal enthusiasm, and if you should share it, spend time and enjoy the Olga Hirsch Collection at the British Library: there are good collections elsewhere, but none so fine as this one which leads the user ever onward.

Der Papyrer.

Der Buchbinder.

The papermaker and the bookbinder: woodcuts by Jost Ammann for Hans Sachs' Book of Trades, *1568.*

6:3 Colour: papers, inks and foils

The fundamental distinction that has been made between type for reading and type for display applies with equal force when colour is brought into the picture: text type was calculated in terms of black and white, and its design becomes enfeebled and its legibility reduced when colour is introduced; whereas display lettering has a range of weights and characteristics that respond to colour treatment. There are bound to be exceptions to such a sweeping generalisation, but the same broad principle is recognised instinctively in all the great manuscripts of the past, where the illuminated pages and initials have a presence and resonance of colour which surpasses, but has some common ground with, the best book jackets and paperback covers of today, whereas the text has a rhythmic, monochrome regularity. Where this simple rule is broken, and then only in the middle ground between text and display, the principal colour used as an exception is either a red or gold itself. It has remained so down to the present, and accordingly a lot of evidence may be adduced to support a theory of colour as applied to the science of typography.

Printing is the 'black art' which can exist only in reciprocation to the 'white art' of paper, and let's concentrate on that relationship as a means of approaching the question of colour. Children must always have asked "but black and white can't really be colours?", yet Goethe (but not Newton) based his colour teaching on a formulation which, although it doesn't translate well, does on reflection begin to supply the answer at both an aesthetic and a scientific level: "Colours are acts of light, its active and passive modulations."

There are all sorts of practical ways in which to make sense of this, of which one would be to collect samples of the next dozen or so pieces of white paper encountered, and to examine them under different lighting conditions – to hold them against the light, and even to photograph test strips on black and white film – to establish that no two are alike and there never can be a standard for 'white' paper. Each has an individual cast: warm or cold; greyed or ivory; bright or shaded; absorbent or reflective; neutral or coloured, and so forth. Repeat the experiment with comparable areas of solid black printing ink, and the same relativity of blackness and the quite pronounced chroma of certain examples will be revealed. So if one book typographer should say to another or to a specialist inkmaker or paper merchant: "this type calls for a warm brown matt black on a smooth ivory toned paper", a measure of understanding would be assumed; just as the dire consequences of "the printer has persuaded me that to go with the photographs the type should be a gloss ultra-black on a high-white shiny art paper" should be anticipated.

But let us return to red and gold as cited for their recurrent use through the centuries in semi-display, since they will serve to illustrate certain points in the absence of a fuller outline of colour theory, which space does not permit. It is the degree of contrast between image and ground which makes type legible, and this has nothing to do with the apparent brightness or vibrancy of a particular colour, it is a question of its tonal value – its position on a grey scale. This is best demonstrated by taking a black and white xerox of any colour chart, from which it is safe to conclude that the closer

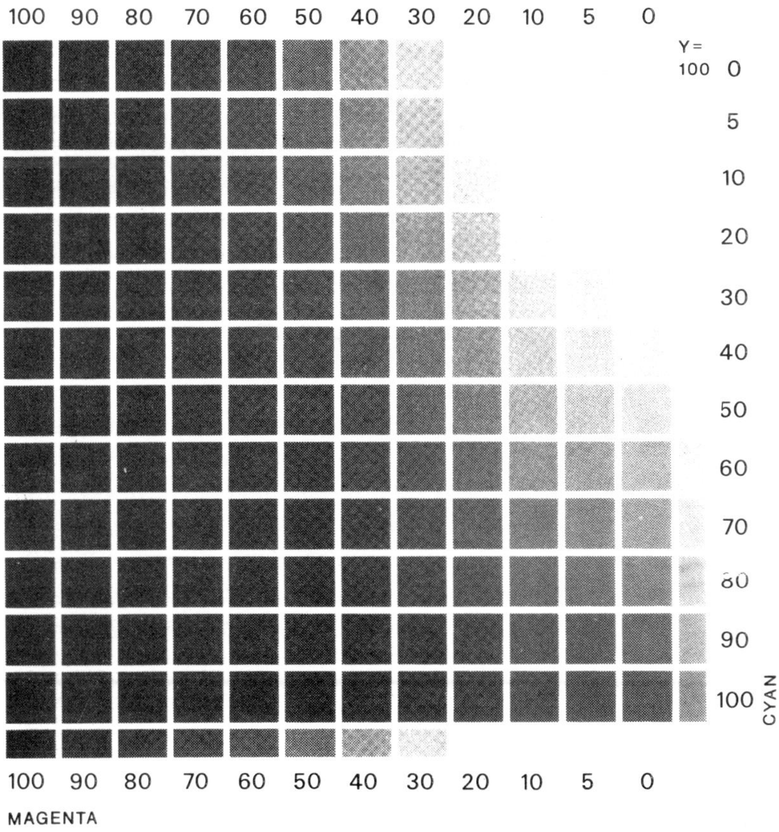

to black a colour reads the more viable it will be for printing a typeface on a white ground, and conversely the lighter the grey, the poorer its legibility will prove. Thus yellow on white, despite its vivid hue or chroma, would be the worst conceivable choice for, say, signage on a motorway. ('Legibility' and 'readability' situations are by no means synonymous, and the terms have been used here to correspond to display and text respectively.) In the intermediate situation as described above, certain reds outperform other colours because of their tonal proximity to black and because of the positive and stable edge quality they give to an image.

Real gold, applied in leaf form from early times, has always been recognised for a property it holds in common with the more recently developed ranges of metallic foils: it reflects light at two distinct levels and thus has, so to speak, two 'voices'. The designer has to pitch the tone of the background material – most commonly the binding cloth – so that both the high and low frequencies are shown to effect. This reaction of metals to light is a phenomenon aside from the accepted pigmentary colour spectrum, and the role of metallic foils is in the ascendant. As one relief process (letterpress) has declined, then another (foil blocking) has really taken off. Up to now this has been demonstrated in terms of the remarkable effects to be achieved in jacket and especially mass paperback cover design, where no future scenario can ignore the potential of holography, which is quickly establishing its place as a new method of graphic reproduction.

6:4 Bookbinding

Publishers' cased binding has become a neglected design area in England. This is all the more surprising in view of the technically adventurous if aesthetically questionable approach which followed from the introduction of bookcloth in the 1830s and lasted into the 1920s, since when it could be argued that standards in binding design have declined in inverse proportion to the rise in importance of the book jacket. Good design for the bindery as elsewhere is inseparable from taking the right production decisions and being aware of the choices that are available between alternative materials and steps in manufacture. This is an area in which there are still marked national preferences and styles, which may be compared at any international book fair, sometimes with the object of adapting the best features and practices to actual needs. The requirements of a particular book or series, whether cheap and expendable or costly and durable, will indicate those binding methods and ranges of paper, plastic, woven or non-woven bookcloth, real or synthetic leather and other coverings which may be considered. It should never be forgotten that it is the pressure of demand from informed clients that creates fashion and determines what the manufacturers and production lines have to offer.

It may be useful to review some of the considerations which determine the structure and appearance of the cased book in isolation, in order to see how these factors work in combination to make a book fit for service. An elementary thought is how a book feels: a book that is really meant to be used in a kitchen or beneath a car will set the designer thinking along the lines of wipe-clean or plastic-encapsulated paper and loose-leaf binding methods; whereas a literary or historical text will set entirely different tactile responses in motion. Equally basic is the weight of a book in relation to its size, and the current fashion in papers for colour printing is resulting in volumes that are grossly overweight. (An earlier fashion was to bulk out slender texts through the use of featherweight antique papers – but there is no evidence that the buyer equates sham bulk or weight with value for money, although excess weight clearly causes reading discomfort.) As well as keeping paper substance in scale with format, the thickness as well as the grain direction of boards is important. High quality flexible boards, much thinner that we are accustomed to, are favoured in several continental countries in graded weights for formats ranging from pocket editions up to quite large format art books, and this does make for very comfortable handling.

A question closely related to the use of lightweight boards concerns the need for rounding and backing or for a pronounced groove between spine and cover boards. There is a case for the more frequent use of the square backed as opposed to the rounded and backed style, but it is confined to shorter books; by this method even a single-section book may have a proper spine which will display its title effectively on the bookshelf. Square back binding should never be used where the bulk exceeds 25mm since the book block

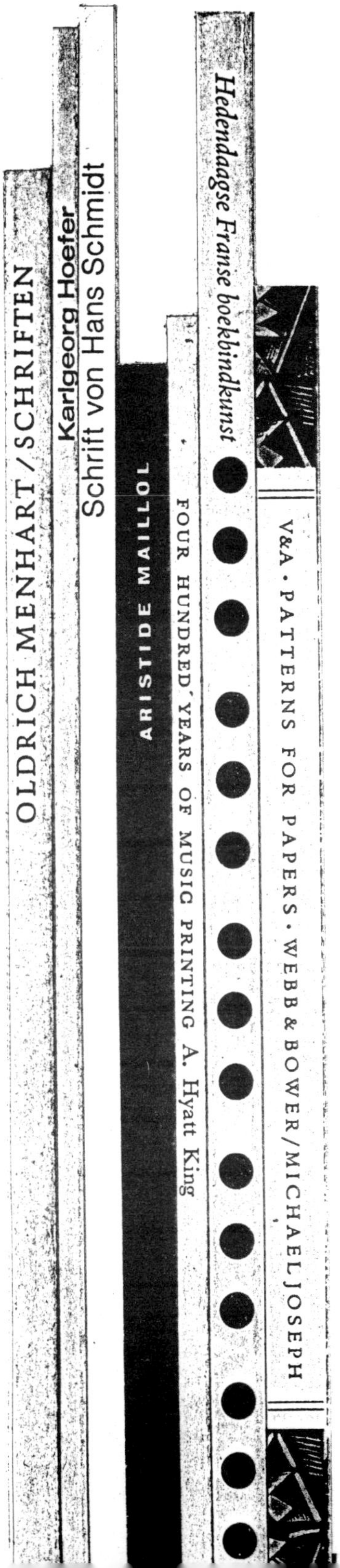

is thrown forward after use into a round which causes the centre sections to step out and protrude beyond the foredge, thus starting to part company with the case. Even a gentle rounding and backing of the spine into the opposing curve should suffice to counteract this tendency. Another detail is the 'square', or measurement by which the case is made and positioned to project beyond the book block at head, foredge and foot. This should always be specified in relation to bulk and casing materials, as well as to the page size, a 2mm square being ample for a pocket format, for example. If the designer specifies and follows up such detail within the parameters of what is structurally sound and practical, then he will develop a rapport with the industry and find that overall quality control is improved.

Treatment of the spine

There is no excuse for not blocking or printing a title on the spine. Letterspaced small capitals will facilitate this, even where the spine width is as slender as 3.5mm. Good arguments may be advanced in favour of running up the spine as against reading downwards, and these have persuaded continental Europe to opt for the former, in contrast to the *de facto* standardisation in the downwards direction that has occurred in English-speaking countries. Even that pope of modern book design, Jan Tschichold, couldn't change matters: he imposed the continental version on Penguin Books, but shortly after his reign they saw that it was necessary to conform to 'home usage', even at the excruciating cost of having stocks reading in contrary directions during the change-back period!

It is usually preferable for title and author to read across rather than down, wherever the width is sufficient to allow acceptable word-breaks and for a variety of typographic or lettering solutions to be considered. Small capitals serve well, but a narrow italic in upper and lower case, for example, may make more of the copy in the area available.

Foil blocking makes special demands of the artwork for the brass, since there is an overall tendency for the image to become thickened or emboldened and for small interstices to flood or fill in. The before and after effects – the artwork and the resultant blocked case – are readily compared, and it will be found that bold type often becomes cruder to the point of

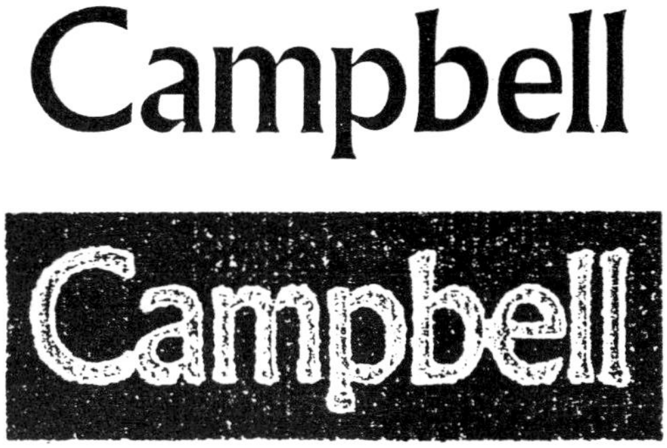

Albertus, a robust display letter, before and after foil blocking (enlargement × 2).

indistinctness. Similarly, un-letterspaced capitals or closely fitted lower case are liable to run together illegibly when blocked.

To lessen these tendencies, the weave of traditional bookcloths and the grain of some synthetics may first be crushed with a blind panel or pigment foil impression so that small typesizes may be blocked more cleanly. Attention to this detail of the behaviour of titling under blocking conditions will quickly train the eye to reject the easy option of making a routine duplicate plate from the artwork intended for the spine of the jacket where this is technically unsuited, and to become alert to the scope offered by well-spaced classic letter forms as well as of the other resources on which sound and enterprising binding design is founded.

Bookbinding and the book jacket

Two quotations from Jan Tschichold, against the current of the times: "The binding is the clothing of the book, the book jacket is just a raincoat"; "Book jackets should be printed on the cheapest possible paper to encourage people to throw them away as soon as possible and enjoy the binding."

The book jacket has become just another instance of lavish packaging within a consumerist society; it is only rarely an art form – and then mostly by accident. The book designer should be motivated by honesty to the book in attempting to convey its uniqueness through the techniques of the poster.

In many situations the jacket can effectively become the binding, or vice versa, as is the case with picture books for young children where the same pictorial design is repeated on printed case-binding and protective wrapper. This is an excellent use of undisguised paper as a binding material, and there is scope enough for harnessing this idea to other categories of book. As a constructive extension to this line of thinking, it would seem that the success of the organic lobby could lead to making a virtue of real bookbinding, packaged to show the texture of the ingredients. Certainly many people with no special interest in book design have expressed to me the feeling that having parted with a large sum for a particular volume that it could at least have been decently bound in cloth. I think that the upholders of standards – Oxford's buckram; Faber's cloth; the Folio Society's overall enterprise – have reached and retained a market all along, and that there may shortly be a general move in the direction of more considered and better quality binding design.

Finishing touches

For bookbinding automation to succeed, whether for paperback or cased books, the restriction of consumer options was essential, for a time at least. It does now seem, however, that there are suppliers round the world who are prepared to cost in extra and specialised production stages with versatility and realism. The spectacular revival of foil blocking has already been noted, but there is a whole range of possibilities from the recent history of bookbinding where the designer has to enquire whether there is a case to be made out in a particular situation: which of these additional steps in manufacture are able to contribute to the product either functionally or fashionably?

Headbanding has my vote – it is as irrational as insisting that persons of male gender should wear ties in restaurants of a certain class, but so be it. The guillotined edges of the book block merit attention, so frequently are they unsatisfactory. Edge-colouring can have value, particularly for reference books, but the light-fastness of the pigments available for this purpose remains unaccountably poor. Markers indicate the way in which a book is intended to be used – a symbolic pointer, even if the bus ticket works better in practice. Endless solutions have been proposed to aid the reader from manuscript onwards, throughout the history of the printed book, and there is no reason why any of these resources should not be revived where the need is sufficiently compelling.

Design responsibility does not end once a title has been published. The pathology of the book is an essential study, and the public library – the more old-fashioned and under-funded the better – is a free laboratory for the designer studying all the ailments to which the book is prone. The 'weakest link in the chain' theory, allied to date-stamping, explains most things – and this weakest link generally, but not necessarily, turns out to be the front endpaper. The libraries' experience tends to argue against the things which designers most enjoy (such as paper as a binding material, paper labels, square-backed binding, functionally printed endpapers and wallets of removable folding maps and so forth), but the greatest satisfaction of all is to see a volume in good shape after forty or more issues.

7 WORKING WITH ILLUSTRATORS

Two of the finest craftsmen at the agency where I was first indentured were both retouching artists. Each used an airbrush for most of the working day, but the one specialised in machinery and the other in fashion photography. It was recognised that if one were to be absent then the other would not be able to deputise, for their respective virtuosities had been developed along such antithetical lines that the merest beginner stood a better chance of producing acceptable results. I recall this since it does seem that successful art editing consists in being able to recognise horses for courses: specialists in historical costume may prove unable to draw modern dress convincingly; natural history illustrators may not draw the human figure particularly well; superb line draughtsmen frequently produce indifferent work in colour; and above all it is natural that some artists should work better at certain imaginative levels than at others.

Because of the sporadic and varied nature of their illustrative requirements, very few publishers indeed can employ illustrators on a salaried basis, and so it becomes essential to enlist the help of enough freelances with the right skills and standards. In this chapter I want to look at ways of achieving that end, taking a broad view of illustration so as to embrace photography and graphic design as well as technical drawing and calligraphy, starting with notes on picture research and artists' agents, and going on from routine and functional applications to the more creative aspect of illustration.

7:1 Picture research

As the pictorial content of books in general has increased in volume and sophistication, so picture research has emerged in recent years as a career specialisation. The rationale for this activity is based on the overwhelming probability that the picture sought is already in existence in some form or other, whether as an image from the remote past or as a press photograph which may have been taken a few hours ago. Should such a picture be unusable in its extant form, it may still be indispensable as an authentic reference for an artist's redrawing or whatever.

Experienced designers or illustrators working within specialised fields may be called upon to do their own research in some circumstances or to brief freelance researchers, and so it will help them to have an overview of reference literature and collections, picture libraries and photographic services. Some illustrators have access to specific reference collections or may even have their own, and may readily undertake to verify objective data – but in general it is unfair and inefficient to ask illustrators to make good deficiencies in the references supplied through research.

As well as locating the best and most apposite visual solutions, the picture researcher's skills consist in obtaining the material in suitable form for reproduction, without undue delays and to a budget. (The high penalties linked to damage or loss of picture library transparencies should be of concern to publishers and freelance designers alike, and indemnity insurance seems inescapable where batches valued at many thousands of pounds are circulating on a regular basis.)

The researcher should be well briefed on format and background considerations – above all for jackets, where the titling may have to be incorporated within the picture area – since these factors can and should influence the selective process or, in some instances, the instructions given for special photography. In these situations there is no substitute for a rough sketch to show the effect intended. Picture research may yield the actual artwork or photographs for reproduction, or it may provide the starting point for commissioning further illustration or photography.

7:2 Artists' agents

In some categories of publishing it may suffice to get on well with two or three freelances or small studios who can satisfy all requirements for artwork, paste-up and jacket design; but many houses, and certainly those concerned with children's books, will need extensive and up-to-date files on illustrators. At one point I had tabs on about four hundred artists for children's books, whilst working with about a score in any single year. The file will show those artists – a minority – who for reasons of their own have elected to be represented by an agent. If drawn to their work, the publisher has to make an approach through that agent. I have always insisted on meeting and briefing an illustrator directly as the need arises, whilst being happy to conduct business arrangements through his or her agent, and this has usually worked well. The agent is still providing a real service to both parties, creating the priority for the publisher's project and at the same time representing his artist's interests.

In the situation described, the art director is under a constraint to deal with the agent, but there are also circumstances in which it is worth while to seek out and be on good terms with the better agents. These act as talent scouts, and the exchange of views on portfolios and diploma shows is often helpful; it can also prove valuable to be able to look through a stack of work in privacy, without having to raise an artist's expectations. London currently has about half a dozen first-rate agents, and the *Writers' and Artists' Yearbook* lists artists' agents along with literary agents.

Photogram for a poster for Pelikan inks by El Lissitzky, 1924. The integration or fusion of type and illustration so that one scarcely exists without the other – or so that the verbal and pictorial messages arrive simultaneously – is a constantly renewed quest, and all kinds of experiment along these lines are highly beneficial to the jacket designer.

7:3 Photographic illustration

The photographic pictorial album – the visual autobiography or ego trip for the celebrated photographer – is *sui generis*. Next in line come those coffee-table books on topics such as food, homes and gardens, travel and sport, pets and natural history, where the text is subservient to glossy, magazine-style camerawork. There are top professionals specialising in most subject areas who will produce the coverage prescribed in the brief for the book as a whole, and will interpret the author's requirements (as transmitted through the art editor or designer) with fidelity. Art editors quickly come to appreciate that most photographers resent an audience, and will restrict even their own attendance to the minimum consonant with keeping the assignment on course. It is rare to encounter difficulties in working with experienced photographers in any field, provided that the quality of the proposition and the way in which it has been thought out are right.

Where a photographer's name is well known it is because at some stage the public has come to associate it with an individual style. This recollected style soon comes to refer merely to an idiom in which the artist happened to work some time ago and, as art never stands still, it is vital to examine samples in order to see the range of recent development and the scope of current styles. Only on this basis is it possible to predict the outcome of a commission within certain parameters, and to know to what extent briefing can modify or condition this.

But for the most part in book publishing we are working at a less exalted level, with photographers to whom books as a market are unfamiliar, and of whom we are making demands that are both sporadic and diverse. The working situation with a general photographer is entirely different. First one has to find a photographer with whom it will be possible to work at all. It is natural for photographers to adapt to the prevailing markets for their work, and this may entail an approach towards models that is calculated in relation to fashion and advertising, or a degree of sentimentality in the posing of animals and children. These traits are anathema in most book applications, and in their stead it may be more valuable for the photographer to have, for example, the less common skill of seeming to catch natural models absorbed in what they are doing and unaware of camera. An art editor needs to know precisely what an assignment calls for and be able to explain it to a prospective photographer. In due course and by the law of averages one or two versatile and responsive photographers will be encountered, who may be recruited into the regular team of suppliers on which any publishing house depends.

7:4 Technical illustration

Graphs, charts and diagrams were quickly identified as ideal candidates for generation on the personal computer, and maps and technical drawings of many types can now be output through high quality printers or plotters to a standard which rivals the best manual draughtsmanship. This is significant for authors preparing straightforward visual material for reproduction, since they need no longer be so dependent as hitherto on the skills of intermediary artists. However, that is not to say that the designer should not furnish guidelines and discuss samples with the author at as early a stage as possible, for in this way the overall standard of the product may be raised immeasurably in such matters as the consistent use of appropriate weights of line, properly contrasted shadings and symbols, and clear, well-positioned keys and labelling. The shapes which figures should make on the page can sometimes be defined in relation to calibrations on screen.

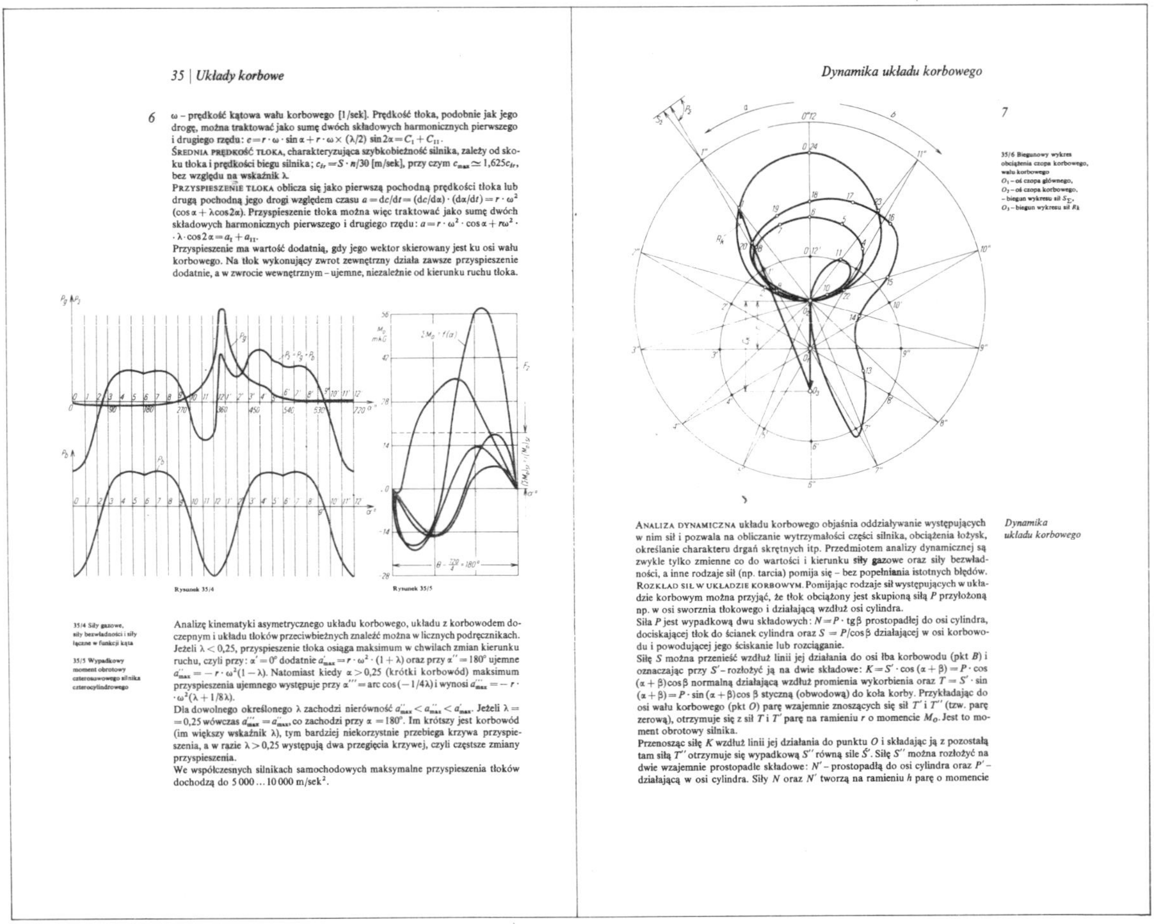

35 | Układy korbowe

6 ω – prędkość kątowa wału korbowego [1/sek]. Prędkość tłoka, podobnie jak jego drogę, można traktować jako sumę dwóch składowych harmonicznych pierwszego i drugiego rzędu: $c = r \cdot \omega \cdot \sin\alpha + r \cdot \omega \times (\lambda/2) \sin 2\alpha = C_I + C_{II}$.
Średnia prędkość tłoka, charakteryzująca szybkobieżność silnika, zależy od skoku tłoka i prędkości biegu silnika; $c_{śr} = S \cdot n/30$ [m/sek], przy czym $c_{max} \simeq 1{,}625 c_{śr}$, bez względu na wskaźnik λ.
Przyspieszenie tłoka oblicza się jako pierwszą pochodną prędkości tłoka lub drugą pochodną jego drogi względem czasu $a = dc/dt = (dc/d\alpha) \cdot (d\alpha/dt) = r \cdot \omega^2 (\cos\alpha + \lambda\cos 2\alpha)$. Przyspieszenie tłoka można więc traktować jako sumę dwóch składowych harmonicznych pierwszego i drugiego rzędu: $a = r \cdot \omega^2 \cdot \cos\alpha + r\omega^2 \cdot \lambda \cdot \cos 2\alpha = a_I + a_{II}$.
Przyspieszenie ma wartość dodatnią, gdy jego wektor skierowany jest ku osi wału korbowego. Na tłok wykonujący zwrot zewnętrzny działa zawsze przyspieszenie dodatnie, a w zwrocie wewnętrznym – ujemne, niezależnie od kierunku ruchu tłoka.

Rysunek 35/4 Rysunek 35/5

35/4 Siły gazowe, siły bezwładności i siły łączne w funkcji kąta

35/5 Wypadkowy moment obrotowy czterosuwowego silnika czterocylindrowego

Analizę kinematyki asymetrycznego układu korbowego, układu z korbowodem doczepnym i układu tłoków przeciwbieżnych znaleźć można w licznych podręcznikach. Jeżeli $\lambda < 0{,}25$, przyspieszenie tłoka osiąga maksimum w chwilach zmian kierunku ruchu, czyli przy: $\alpha' = 0°$ dodatnie $a'_{max} = r \cdot \omega^2 \cdot (1 + \lambda)$ oraz przy $\alpha'' = 180°$ ujemne $a''_{max} = -r \cdot \omega^2 (1 - \lambda)$. Natomiast kiedy $\alpha > 0{,}25$ (krótki korbowód) maksimum przyspieszenia ujemnego występuje przy $\alpha''' = \arccos(-1/4\lambda)$ i wynosi $a'''_{max} = -r \cdot \omega^2 (\lambda + 1/8\lambda)$.
Dla dowolnego określonego λ zachodzi nierówność $a''_{max} < a'''_{max} < a'_{max}$. Jeżeli $\lambda = 0{,}25$ wówczas $a'''_{max} = a''_{max}$, co zachodzi przy $\alpha = 180°$. Im krótszy jest korbowód (im większy wskaźnik λ), tym bardziej niekorzystnie przebiega krzywa przyspieszenia, a w razie $\lambda > 0{,}25$ występują dwa przegięcia krzywej, czyli częstsze zmiany przyspieszenia.
We współczesnych silnikach samochodowych maksymalne przyspieszenia tłoków dochodzą do 5 000 … 10 000 m/sek².

Dynamika układu korbowego

7

35/6 Biegunowy wykres obciążenia czopa korbowego, wału korbowego
O_1 – oś czopa głównego,
O_2 – oś czopa korbowego,
– biegun wykresu sił S_Σ,
O_3 – biegun wykresu sił R_k

Analiza dynamiczna układu korbowego objaśnia oddziaływanie występujących w nim sił i pozwala na obliczanie wytrzymałości części silnika, obciążenia łożysk, określanie charakteru drgań skrętnych itp. Przedmiotem analizy dynamicznej są zwykle tylko zmienne co do wartości i kierunku siły gazowe oraz siły bezwładności, a inne rodzaje sił (np. tarcia) pomija się – bez popełniania istotnych błędów.
Rozkład sił w układzie korbowym. Pomijając rodzaje sił występujących w układzie korbowym można przyjąć, że tłok obciążony jest skupioną siłą P przyłożoną np. w osi sworznia tłokowego i działającą wzdłuż osi cylindra.
Siła P jest wypadkową dwu składowych: $N = P \cdot \mathrm{tg}\beta$ prostopadłej do osi cylindra, dociskającej tłok do ścianek cylindra oraz $S = P/\cos\beta$ działającej w osi korbowodu i powodującej jego ściskanie lub rozciąganie.
Siłę S można przenieść wzdłuż linii jej działania do osi łba korbowodu (pkt B) i oznaczając przy S' – rozłożyć ją na dwie składowe: $K = S' \cdot \cos(\alpha + \beta) = P \cdot \cos(\alpha + \beta)\cos\beta$ normalną działającą wzdłuż promienia wykorbienia oraz $T = S' \cdot \sin(\alpha + \beta) = P \cdot \sin(\alpha + \beta)\cos\beta$ styczną (obwodową) do koła korby. Przykładając do osi wału korbowego (pkt O) parę wzajemnie znoszących się sił T' i T'' (tzw. parę zerową), otrzymuje się z sił T i T' parę na ramieniu r o momencie M_O. Jest to moment obrotowy silnika.
Przenosząc siłę K wzdłuż linii jej działania do punktu O i składając ją z pozostałą tam siłą T'' otrzymuje się wypadkową S'' równą sile S'. Siłę S'' można rozłożyć na dwie wzajemnie prostopadłe składowe: N' – prostopadłą do osi cylindra oraz P' – działającą w osi cylindra. Siły N oraz N' tworzą na ramieniu h parę o momencie

Dynamika układu korbowego

Typography and illustration by Leon Urbański, Warsaw, 1971. This design demonstrates the value of harmony of line between text and illustration, and of a lucid layout, in presenting an advanced text. In the original the drawings are printed in a red and a blue.

Once the geometric, drawing-instrument aspect of draughtsmanship is left behind, however, the need for the co-ordination of the human eye, brain and hand reasserts itself. This happens to an extent in all the sciences, and descriptive or analytical drawing has a place in most disciplines: anatomy and archaeology may be instanced in this connection, where even the most advanced photographic techniques have failed to supplant drawing in supplying the record for certain purposes. If on the one hand routine and ever more complex tasks can be undertaken on screen, whilst on the other there will remain a restricted but nevertheless real demand for skilled draughtsmanship, then it follows that a threat may be posed to the always delicate equilibrium of the illustrators' vocation and the numbers that can be kept in employment through educational and technical publishing. New entrants clearly will have to be ambidextrous – at the computer and at the drawing board – and this is asking a lot unless it is realised that the pressure will be to push forward the computerised frontiers at the expense of the quality of applied drawing, which, of its nature, requires almost daily practice. In other words, over a period of time, manual draughtsmanship skills will diminish, whereas the imaginative illustrator will take up ground where electronics can't follow.

At a practical level, artwork is normally drawn for reduction – commonly in the ratio 3:2 and rarely greater than 2:1 – in the knowledge that this will lead to a slight gain in finished quality. Weight of line, size of type, openness of tint or texture have to be judged with the effects of this reduction in view. Some early printed books reveal a conscious attempt to keep the weight of line in illustration in harmony with the averaged stroke thickness of the text face, thus giving an even colour to the page. This can still be an attractive solution in the right setting, but the amount of detail required frequently indicates a lighter weight of line to contrast with the type.

Research undertaken some years ago into lettering on maps came down strongly, if not altogether unexpectedly, in favour of sanserif as against roman type for labelling. The extended sanserif family, including bolds and condensed bolds, enables clearly gradated levels of importance to be assigned to place-names or other hierarchies of material. Legibility down to the smallest point sizes remains high, but the most impressive findings established that sanserif usually outperforms roman type when it is placed over a coloured or broken background, set curved, or placed at unconventional reading angles. These conclusions could be extended more frequently and with advantage to the labelling of diagrams of many other kinds in the smaller type sizes.

7:5 Interpretative and narrative illustration

In the case of technical illustration, the brief exists as the copy – all that is required is that it shall be organised, simplified wherever possible, and presented. This is an objective affair, unlike the two categories which I would now like to introduce: interpretative or narrative illustration, which might best be defined as illustration in the interests of the author or of the publishing concept; and imaginative illustration, in which the artist is the prime mover. In making this working distinction, it is recognised that in practice there has to be an overlap rather than a gulf between the two approaches.

Interpretative or narrative illustration is commissioned for a fee, and a partial royalty is the exception rather than the rule. Children's books, whether for school or in the home – but excluding the full-colour picture book – form the largest sector of this crowded and competitive market. The hardest part of an art editor's job is finding the right artist for a particular title since a high standard of figurative drawing, rare in itself, will not suffice: there has to be an interest in the subject matter for the drawings to come to life. Accordingly, it may be preferable to place line drawings – of, say, ponies, or the Brownies or religious tales – with a mediocre or dated artist with unfeigned knowledge or enthusiasm, than with a finer draughtsman with a disdain for such topics. This is because there should be a certain correlation of aim and level between author and artist, and there is little point in deliberately setting up a disparity in these respects.

There is no question but that until approaching the age of ten, illustration in all forms of reading matter can help make the going more credible and absorbing for all but a handful of dissidents. Fact, fiction, or comic paper – there are no barriers, and for each project it is just a matter of compiling a short list from the several hundreds of book illustrators available. (The rules are similar to casting for the theatre: you can audition new talent but it would be preposterous to request samples before commissioning someone established or at the top of their profession – it's your business to ensure you are up-to-date with their work.)

It follows from the notion of keeping text and illustration on similar planes that the better the writing the better the illustration needs to be, and that rather than have routine or

These examples of work by the typographer Malcolm Harvey Young highlight the scope of a graphic approach to cover design. Graphic design in a sense occupies the ground which links typography to illustration: it is concerned with symbolic and universal rather than with subjective aspects of communication. The British Council covers are drawn from an extended series, and show how design attention to a publishing problem as a whole can create a strong visual identity or framework within which present and future diversification may occur. The horizontal bands make provision for details of topics, venues and dates to be inserted when known within the appropriate pre-planned subject categories to complete each cover design.

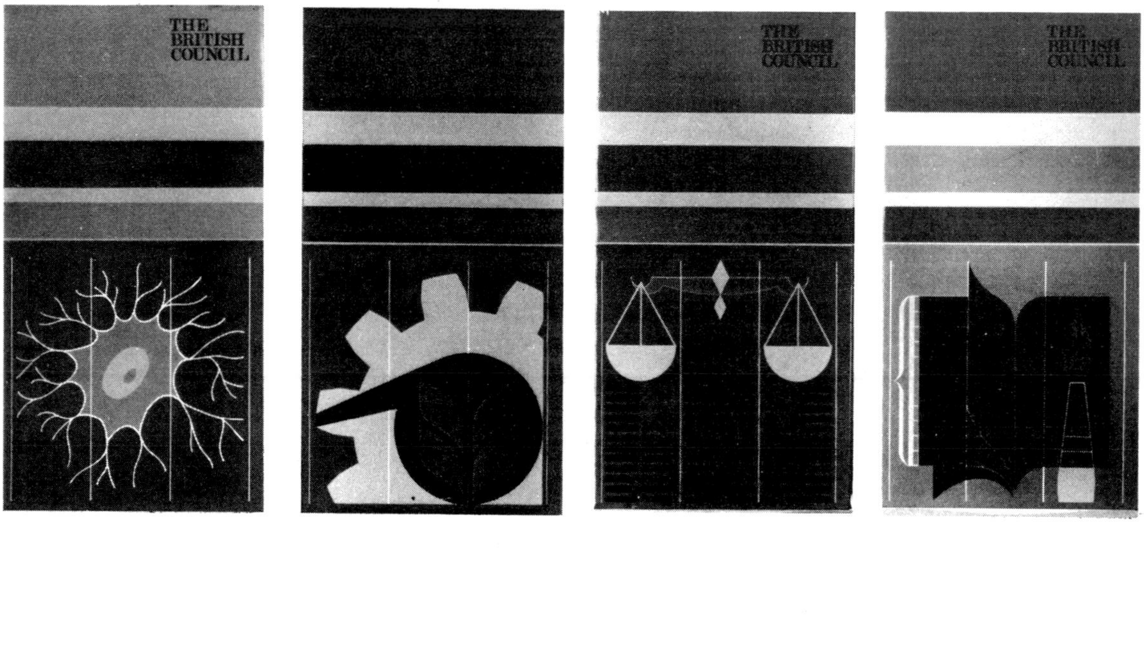

perfunctory drawings it is preferable to have none at all. I think that there are three aspects to what has happened with the novel for older children over the past twenty years: first, writing for this group has improved immeasurably and at its best is indistinguishable from the adult novel; second, children no longer expect these books to carry illustration; third, a generation of splendid black and white narrative illustrators has not been replaced. The focus on full-colour reproduction has been at the expense of black and white, but this situation may be changing and accomplished line artists could soon be at a premium once again.

7:6 Imaginative illustration

Book illustration has come to mean the illustration of children's books, whether the illustrator is accompanying another's text or acting as soloist in creating colourful picture books for the very young. There is little or no adult counterpart to this activity in some countries including the British Isles, and wherever this is so it seems to me that the situation cannot be altogether healthy, and well-balanced. 'Real' illustration is confined to a ghetto, and commercial artists take over the packaging of paperbacks.

In the present context, I would argue for greater awareness of the riches on our doorstep, and of some of the possibilities for renewal and diversification that are at hand. Short of the full-scale illustration of the classics, there are endless ways in which drawings may contribute to book design, ranging from jacket design to the layout of the title spread, part titles or chapter openings. Some of these resources are worth mentioning as viable means of escaping the stereotypes which prevail in certain overcrowded fields of publishing, and in the belief that the tide may already be turning in favour of such initiatives.

Many children's book illustrators concede that the prefix 'children's' came to be tacked on to them through the accident that no other market existed for their work, but that they would like nothing better than to illustrate at an adult level from time to time. It would be exciting to take a suitable paperback sub-series down that particular path in contrast to the contorted hyperrealism plus elaborate foil blocking which is the current orthodoxy.

Line drawing by Rigby Graham for Values *by Spike Milligan (Offcut Press, 1969).*

Apart from the colouristic, painterly approach which holds the most promise for the revitalisation of jacket and cover design, there is a black and white line tradition which surfaced most tellingly in the immediate postwar decades in the way that it had throughout most of the eighteenth and nineteenth centuries. Its recent unfashionability can be attributed to a decline in printing standards (notably with the rotary letterpress paperback production line), publishers' cost-cutting at a time of chronically declining print runs, and art school trends that ran counter to figurative drawing. All these tendencies are now being reversed, and there are

The difference between calligraphy and creative lettering is essentially that between writing and drawing, and David Howells has written all the examples on this opening, either with pen or brush. The tempo and spontaneity of writing involves the happy use of accident that comes of immense experience. Sometimes a little retouching is necessary but frequently none at all, before calligraphy can be used on the book jacket to generate an immediacy and excitement obtainable in no other way.

already some excellent line practitioners of a younger generation on the scene.

Wood engraving is another aspect of black and white line artwork, and the British school is one of the finest in the world. Whereas a number of members of the Society of Wood Engravers and their work would feel most at home in the placid backwaters of the private press tradition, there is no lack of vigorous and forward-looking engraving. It is only necessary to visit a show to spot the exciting potential and relevance for the printed book. The same might be said of the work of members of the Society of Scribes and Illuminators, for the role of lettering and calligraphy in relation to book

jackets and general book design has always been significant. Again, a period of comparative neglect by publishers has seen the rise of a new and highly competent group of craftsmen, with ideas that could prove stimulating in the right place.

7:7 Commissioning jackets and paperback covers

There is much to be said for thinking out a jacket solution at the earliest possible stage – in fact just as soon as the titling and the marketing guidelines have been finalised. If the book is illustrated and there is to be a drawing on the cover or jacket, then it may be wise to request the artist to break off and produce at least a rough for this before the artwork for the book as a whole is completed, otherwise there is a danger that all the energy and ideas may have been expended on the inside of the book, leaving little in reserve for the cover. It is for this reason that so many compromise solutions have to be reached along the lines, for example, of reproducing the most suitable of the interior drawings again as part of a makeshift cover design.

Before commissioning a cover drawing, a designer may find it useful to spend a few minutes playing about with the actual words that are to appear on the front and spine. It will

These two pages of drawn lettering for publisher's jackets are by Michael Harvey, demonstrating an expressive range and variety which begins where the impersonal nature of typefaces breaks off and extends to the freedom of pure calligraphy.

usually be found that certain arrangements are more effective than others, that some word divisions are altogether unacceptable, or that the titling set in upper and lower case has a more positive presence than when set in capitals. Sketches or traces of the sort of lettering the designer has in mind should be supplied, ideally to the size at which the artwork will be drawn, to show the illustrator the area required for titling. Communication can be poor over this issue, and the artist's proposed background to the titling area may prove too broken or disturbed in tone and colour for the titling to read with sufficient clarity and impact. (A well-known picture book artist admitted recently that only after his first book had gone through the press did he come to appreciate the need to leave spaces in his pictures for the text.) For co-edition purposes it may have been agreed that all language changes to the titling shall be confined to the black plate, and the illustrator needs to be aware of what this entails.

It is customary to request a rough for cover artwork, but I have always held that it is sufficient to know the lines along which an artist intends to proceed, and am usually quite happy to approve an idea jotted down in a restaurant or explained over the telephone. This is because I recognise that many artists detest presentation roughs in full colour, since they either start something going in the rough which then has to be aborted, or find that when required to pick up the threads – perhaps weeks or months later – they feel constrained by an old idea and would prefer to tackle the problem afresh; or worse still, that they cannot recapture spontaneous qualities present in the rough. Some established illustrators now refuse point-blank to supply roughs and pre-

fer to play everything for real, being prepared for a full repeat on the rare occasions that they misfire. Of course there are illustrators of different temperament, but no more nor less professional, who would much rather present a finished rough and then follow it through implicitly.

Unillustrated books on every topic under the sun all need selling covers, and the whole gamut of visual presentation ought to fall beneath one person's overview within each publishing house, great or small. A freelance designer or illustrator is a problem solver like any other professional, and when called in should be permitted to make an individual diagnosis and submit recommendations on the basis of the symptoms exhibited or disclosed. The mistake that is so often made is for the client to feel that he or she has first to solve the visual conundrum and then find an artist to produce the prescribed drawing: i.e. the artist may be under-briefed and over-directed. At a mundane level this

is sometimes unavoidable, but it is a waste not to reap the benefit of an independent specialist input – one's own thoughts on the matter can always be held in reserve should they be needed at a later stage.

The illustrator of first choice for a particular title is often immediately plain, but there will always be special cases where there is no obvious answer. Such titles afford a special opportunity for breaking new ground, and for reviewing the relative merits of solutions entailing the use of typography, calligraphy, graphics, photography, illustration and other possibilities, singly or in combination. Working with illustrators is a constantly renewed challenge and privilege for any book designer, and it is satisfying when alphabet and image can be seen to work together on the page as planned.

BIBLIOGRAPHY

GENERAL SUBJECT REFERENCE WORKS

Aldis, Harry G.: *The Printed Book* (3rd edn, Cambridge University Press, 1951)

Baudin, Fernand: *How Typography Works: And Why it is Important* (Lund Humphries, 1989)

Carter, Harry: *A View of Early Typography up to About 1600* (Clarendon Press, 1969)

Day, Kenneth (ed.): *Book Typography 1815-1965 in Europe and the United States of America* (Benn, 1966)

Garland, Ken: *Graphics, Design and Printing Terms: An International Dictionary* (Lund Humphries, 1989)

Gaskell, Philip: *A New Introduction to Bibliography* (Oxford University Press, 1972)

Glaister, Geoffrey Ashall: *Glaister's Glossary of the Book* (2nd edn, Allen & Unwin, 1979)

Jennett, Seán: *The Making of Books* (5th edn, Faber, 1973)

Kapr, Albert: *Schriftkunst: Geschichte, Anatomie und Schönheit der Lateinischen Buchstaben* (Dresden: VEB Verlag der Kunst, 1971), translated as *The Art of Lettering* (London and New York, 1983)

Kapr, Albert and Schiller, Walter: *Gestalt und Funktion der Typographie* (Leipzig: VEB Fachbuchverlag, 1977)

Krimpen, Huib van: *Boek: Over het Maken van Boeken* (revised edition, Veenendaal: Gaade, 1986)

Lewis, John: *The Twentieth Century Book: Its Illustration and Design* (new edn, Herbert Press, 1984)

McLean, Ruari: *Modern Book Design: From William Morris to the Present Day* (Faber, 1958)

—*The Thames and Hudson Manual of Typography* (Thames & Hudson, 1980)

Simon, Oliver: *Introduction to Typography* (1945, revised edn by David Bland, Faber, 1963)

Steinberg, S. H.: *Five Hundred Years of Printing* (2nd edn, Penguin, 1961)

Thomas, Alan G.: *Great Books and Book Collectors* (1975, reprinted, Spring Books, 1988)

Tschichold, Jan: *Meisterbuch der Schrift* (2nd edn, Ravensburg: 1965), translated as *Treasury of Alphabets and Lettering* (reprinted, Omega Books, 1985)

Turner Berry, W., Johnson, A. F. and Jaspert, W.P.: *The Encyclopaedia of Type Faces* (4th edn, Blandford, 1983)

Updike, Daniel Berkeley: *Printing Types: Their History, Forms, and Use* (2 vols, 2nd edn, Cambridge, Mass.: Harvard University Press, 1937, reprinted New York: Dover Publications, 1980)

Vervliet, H. D. L. (ed): *The Book Through Five Thousand Years* (Phaidon, 1972)

Whalley, Joyce Irene: *The Art of Calligraphy: Western Europe & America* (Bloomsbury, 1980)

Williamson, Hugh: *Methods of Book Design: The Practice of an Industrial Craft* (3rd edn, New Haven CT: Yale University Press, 1983)

1 INTRODUCTION

1:1 *What is design?*

Brill, Hans: *100 Best Books on Design* (Trefoil, 1989)

Frutiger, Adrian: *Type, Sign, Symbol* (Zurich: ABC edition, 1980)

Gropius, Walter: 'Is there a science of design?', reprinted in *Scope of Total Architecture* (Allen & Unwin, 1956), 35-49

Le Corbusier: *The Modulor* (Faber, 1954)

Lewis, John and Brinkley, John: *Graphic Design* (Routledge & Kegan Paul, 1954)

1:2 *The book designer*

Dair, Carl: *Design with Type* (Toronto: University of Toronto Press, 1967)

Rogers, Bruce: *Paragraphs on Printing* (New York: William E. Rudge's Sons, 1943, reprinted New York: Dover Publications, 1979)

Spencer, Herbert: *Pioneers of Modern Typography* (Lund Humphries, 1969) [for those aspects of typography not rooted in the printing industry, but which parallel modernist movements in the arts and architecture]

Willberg, Hans Peter: *Buchkunst im Wandel: Die Entwicklung der Buchgestaltung in der Bundesrepublik Deutschland* (Frankfurt am Main: Stiftung Buchkunst, 1984) [recent trends in West German book design viewed in relation to aesthetic and technological change]

Wilson, Adrian: *The Design of Books* (Studio Vista, 1967)

Individual designers

Cinamon, Gerald: 'Hans Schmoller 1916-1985, typographer, his life and work', *The Monotype Recorder* (new series, 6, April 1987), 1-64

Dreyfus, John: *The Work of Jan van Krimpen* (Haarlem: Joh. Enschedé en Zonen, 1952)

Mardersteig, Giovanni: *The Officina Bodoni: An Account of the Work of a Hand Press, 1923-1977* (Verona: Edizioni Valdonega, 1980) [this is Mardersteig's work, a life is awaited]

Meynell, Francis: *My Lives* (Bodley Head, 1971) [in conjunction with Dreyfus, John: *A History of the Nonesuch Press* (Nonesuch Press, 1981)]

Moran, James: *Stanley Morison: His Typographic Achievement* (Lund Humphries, 1971)

Leben und Werk des Typographen Jan Tschichold (Dresden: Verlag der Kunst, 1977) [reprints major essays with bibliography and 200 illustrations, and supplements McLean, Ruari: *Jan Tschichold: Typographer* (Lund Humphries, 1975)]

Berthold Wolpe: A Retrospective Survey (Victoria & Albert Museum and Faber & Faber, 1980)

Hermann Zapf & His Design Philosophy (Chicago: Society of Typographic Arts, 1987) [selected writings on calligraphy and contemporary type design, splendidly illustrated, full list of his typefaces]

1:4 *Design in interaction*

Butcher, Judith: *Copy-editing: The Cambridge Handbook* (2nd edn, Cambridge University Press, 1981)

Clark, Giles N.: *Inside Book Publishing: A Career Builder's Guide* (Blueprint, 1988) [design in a career setting]

Hart's Rules for Compositors and Readers at the University Press, Oxford (revised edn, Oxford University Press, 1983)

Sanders, Norman: *Graphic Designer's Production Handbook* (David & Charles, 1984) [successfully anglicised by Roy Brewer]

2 THE TEXT PAGES

Dowding, Geoffrey: *Finer Points in the Spacing and Arrangement of Type* (3rd edn, Wace, 1966)

Hochuli, Jost: *Das Detail in der Typografie* (Langen: Compugraphic Deutschland GmbH, 1988)

Miles, John: *Design for Desktop Publishing: a Guide to Layout and Typography on the Personal Computer* (Gordon Fraser, 1987)

2:1 *Selecting a format*

The Print and Production Manual (4th edn, Blueprint Publishing, 1989)

2:2 *How reading works*

Caflisch, Max: 'Typography needs type' (paper read at Lausanne: Association Typographique Internationale, 1977) [constants in arranging a text traced back to earliest inscriptions]

Ovink, G. Willem: *Legibility, Atmosphere-value and Forms of Printing Types*, (Leiden: Sijthoff, 1938)

Spencer, Herbert: *The Visible Word: Problems of Legibility* (2nd edn, Lund Humphries, 1969) [useful subject bibliography to date]

Visible Language (P. O. Box 1972 CMA, Cleveland, OH 44106: 1970ff, formerly The Journal of Typographic Research, 1967ff) [see in general]

Zachrisson, Bror: *Studies in the Legibility of Printed Text* (Stockholm: Almqvist & Wiksell, 1965)

2:3 *Typographic measurement*

Bigelow, C. and Day, D.: 'Digital typography', *Scientific American* (August 1983), 106-119

Hutt, Allen: *Fournier: The Compleat Typographer* (Muller, 1972)

Jammes, André: 'Académisme et typographie: the making of the romain du roi', *Journal of the Printing Historical Society* (1, 1965), 71-95

Karow, Peter: *Digital Formats for Typefaces* (Hamburg: URW Verlag, 1987)

Kindersley, David: 'Optical letter spacing', *The Penrose Annual* (62, 1969), 167-176

—*Optical Letterspacing for New Printing Systems* (2nd edn, Lund Humphries, 1976)

Maag, Bruno: 'Typeface design on the Apple Macintosh', *Typografische Monatsblätter* (2/1989), 1-24

'Monotype 96-unit copyfitting system' (Monotype Typography, n.d.) [8pp leaflet containing theory and tables]

Ovink, G. Willem: 'From Fournier to metric, and from lead to film', *Quaerendo*, (9/2 & 9/4, 1979), 95-127, 283-307

Zimmermann, Roland and Fleischhacker, Heinrich: 'Balancing type widths and the different effects of metal, photo, CRT and laser setting systems'. *Typografische Monätsblätter* (6/1982), 1-18

2:4 *Margin schemes*

Gerstner, Karl: *Programme entwerfen: Designing Programs* (Teufen: Niggli, 1963) [good exposition of grid theory]

Hurlburt, Allen: *The Grid* (Barrie & Jenkins, 1979)

Müller-Brockmann, Josef: *The Graphic Artist and His Design Problems* (2nd edn, Teufen: Niggli, 1964)

—*Grid Systems in Graphic Design: A Visual Communication Manual for Graphic Designers, Typographers and Three Dimensional Designers* (Teufen: Niggli, 1981)

Rosarivo, Raúl M.: *Divina proportio typographica: Das Buch vom goldenen typographischen Modul* (Krefeld: Scherpe, 1961 [proportional canons traced in late mediaeval MSS.]

Ruder, Emil: *Typography* (Teufen, Niggli, 1967) [treatise on what has come to be called the 'Swiss dogmatic style' of the period]

Tschichold, Jan: 'Non-arbitrary proportions of page and type area', *Print in Britain* (September 1963) [key essay on margins in MSS. and early printed books]

3 TYPEFACES

3:1 *Choice of typefaces – basic working ranges*

A.Typ.I. Index of Typefaces (Frankfurt: Committee of Type Manufacturers, Association Typographique Internationale, 1975) [lists 3600 typefaces, giving manufacturer, designer and year of issue]

Carter, Sebastian: *Twentieth-Century Type Designers* (Trefoil, 1987)

Dowding, Geoffrey: *An Introduction to the History of Printing Types* (Wace, 1962)

Fine Print On Type: The Best of 'Fine Print' Magazine on Type and Typography, 1977-1988 (Lund Humphries, 1989) [*Fine Print* is published from P. O. Box 3394, San Francisco, California 94119, USA]

Haiman, György: *Nicholas Kis: A Hungarian Punch-cutter and Printer, 1650-1702* (San Francisco: Jack W. Stauffacher, 1983) [extensive account of the creator of the 'Janson' type; qualified by John A. Lane in 'The types of Nicholas Kis', *Journal of the Printing Historical Society* No. 18 (1983-4), 47-75]

Johnson, A. F.: *Type Designs, Their History and Development* (3rd edn, Deutsch, 1966)

Morison, Stanley: *A Tally of Types* (new edn, Cambridge University Press, 1973) [historical background to twenty celebrated 'Monotype' faces]

Pardoe, F. E.: *John Baskerville of Birmingham: Letter-founder and Printer* (Muller, 1975)

Ryder, John: *Printing for Pleasure* (revised edn, Bodley Head, 1976) [letterpress printing explained]

Schumacher-Gebler, Eckehart (ed.): *26 Letters: An Annual and Calendar* (Typostudio Schumacher-Gebler, Goethestrasse 21, D-8000 München 2, 1989) [168pp packed with lively specimens, information and views from type designers, manufacturers and users]

Tracy, Walter: *Letters of Credit: A View of Type Design* (Gordon Fraser, 1986)

—*The Typographic Scene* (Gordon Fraser, 1988)

3:2 *Factors in selecting a typeface*

Dowding, Geoffrey: *Factors in the Choice of Type Faces* (Wace, 1957) [letterpress oriented]

Knuttel, Gerard: *The Letter as a Work of Art: Observations and Confrontations with Contemporaneous Expressions of Art from Roman Times to the Present Day* (Amsterdam: Typefoundry Amsterdam, 1951)

Perfect, C. and Rookledge, G.: *Rookledge's International Typefinder* (Sarema Press, 1983)

Wallace, L. W.: *Type Design: Developments 1970 to 1985* (Arlington, Virginia: National Composition Association, 1985)

3:3 *The display sizes of text faces*

Sutton, James and Bartram, Alan: *An Atlas of Typeforms* (Lund Humphries, 1968, reprinted, Wordsworth Editions, 1988)

Type for Books: A Designer's Manual (revised edn, W. & J. Mackay & Co, 1965; new edn, Bodley Head for Mackays, 1976) [the repertoire of a fine book house in the last days of letterpress – founders' type in all sizes for display – specimen pages of text]

3:4 *Faces intended for display use only*

Gray, Nicolete: *Nineteenth Century Ornamented Typefaces* (new edn, Faber & Faber, 1976)

Hlavsa, Oldřich: *A Book of Type and Design* (Peter Nevill, 1960)

Hornung, Clarence P.: *Handbook of Early Advertising Art: Typographic Volume* (New York: Dover Publications, n.d.) [Dover reprints, distributed by Constable, include wide-ranging source books on typography, calligraphy and decorative art]

Letraset Graphic Design Handbook (Esselte Letraset, annual) [catalogue of dry-transfer lettering range and related products of DTP interest]

Lewis, John: *Printed Ephemera: The Changing Use of Type and Letterforms in English and American Printing* (paperback version, Faber & Faber, 1969)

Reiner, Imre: *Typo-Graphik: Studien und Versuche* (St Gall: Zollikofer & Co., vol 1, 1944; vol 2, 1950 [also trans. as *Modern and Historical Typography*]) [Reiner explores the frequently out of the way uses of type and ornament in books and ephemera over the centuries, and then creates similar effects in an original and up-to-date way]

3:5 *The history and use of italics*

Fairbank, Alfred: *A Book of Scripts* (revised edn, Penguin, 1968)

Osley, A. S.: *Scribes and Sources: Handbook of the Chancery Hand in the Sixteenth Century* (Faber, 1980) [how the writing-masters taught – translations and introductions]

3:6 *Small capitals and alternative figures*

Peignot, Jérôme: *'du chiffre': Aspects typographiques historiques et plastiques* (Paris, Damase, 1982) [a jumbo illustrated thesis]

Tschichold, Jan: 'Kursiv, Kapitälchen und Anführungszeichen im Textsatz des Buches und in wissenschaftlichen Zeitschriften', *Börsenblatt für deutschen Buchhandel* No. 20 (1964), 1213-18

3:9 *Printers' flowers, decorations and ornaments*

Caflisch, Max: *Kleines Spiel mit Ornamenten* (Bern: Angelus-Drucke, 1965) [an essay and set of variations on the Granjon arabesques]

'Monotype' Ornament Broadsheets: 1.*The Arabesque*, 2.*The Fleuron*, 3. *The Border*, 4. *The Nineteenth-Century Ornament*, 5. *Type Flowers in the Twentieth Century* (Monotype Corporation, n.d.)

Ryder, John: *Flowers & Flourishes: including a newly annotated edition of 'A Suite of Fleurons'* (Bodley Head for Mackays, 1976)

4 FORM, CONTENT AND EXTENT

4:1 *Centred and off-centred principles of typography*

Gill, Eric: *An Essay on Typography* (1931, the 2nd edn of 1936 reprinted Lund Humphries, 1988) [referred to only for the case for unjustified setting]

Tschichold, Jan: *Typographische Gestaltung* (Basel: 1935), translated by Ruari McLean as *Asymmetric Typography* (Faber, 1967)

4:2 *Cast-off and the control of extent*

Brown, Bruce: *Brown's Index to Photocomposition Typography* (Greenwood Publishing, 1983)

Fyffe, Charles: *Basic Copyfitting* (Studio Vista, 1969)

4:5 *Layout techniques*

Tschichold, Jan: *Typographische Entwurfstechnik* (Stuttgart: 1932) [English translation by Ruari McLean, as *How to Draw Layouts*, not yet published]

Wilson, Adrian: *The Making of the Nuremberg Chronicle* (Amsterdam: Nico Israel, 1976)

5 THE PARTS AND THE WHOLE

Kapr, Albert: *Hundertundein Sätze zur Buchgestaltung* (2nd edn, Leipzig: VEB Fachbuchverlag, 1977) [maxims on each aspect of book design briefly and expertly formulated, unillustrated]

Tschichold, Jan: *Ausgewählte Aufsätze über Fragen der Gestalt des Buches und der Typographie* (Basel: Birkhäuser, 1975) [selected articles on most aspects of book design]
—*Designing Books* (New York: Wittenborn, Schultz, Inc., 1951) [written shortly after Tschichold's reform of Penguin typography and including his 'house rules for composition']

5:1 *The preliminary pages*

Johnson, A. F.: *One Hundred Title-pages: 1500-1800* (Bodley Head, 1928)
Morison, Stanley and Day, Kenneth: *The Typographic Book: 1450-1935* (Benn, 1963) [subtitled: a study of fine typography through five centuries, exhibited in upwards of three hundred and fifty title and text pages drawn from presses working in the European tradition]

5:5 *The end pages*

Knight, G. Norman: *Indexing, The Art of* (Allen & Unwin, 1979)

6 MATERIALS

6:1 *Book papers*

Eves, Ian: *The Publisher's Guide to Paper* (Blueprint, 1988)
Hunter, Dard: *Papermaking: The History and Technique of an Ancient Craft* (2nd edn reprinted, New York: Knopf, 1957)
Turner, Silvie and Skiöld, Birgit: *Handmade Paper Today: a Worldwide Survey of Mills, Papers, Techniques and Uses* (Lund Humphries, 1989)

6:3 *Colour*

Goethe, Johann Wolfgang von (ed Matthaei, Rupprecht): *Goethe zur Farbe und Farbenlehre* (Weimar: Goethe-Nationalmuseum, 1955)
'Pantone' colour matching system (see *Letraset Graphic Design Handbook*, annual)

6:4 *Bookbinding*

Potter, Geoff: *The Publisher's Guide to Binding and Finishing* (Blueprint, 1988)

6:5 *Decorated papers*

Loring, Rosamond B.: *Decorated Book Papers* (3rd edn, Cambridge, Mass: Harvard College Library, 1973)
Mick, E. W.: *Altes Buntpapier* (Dortmund: Harenberg, 1979) [splendid colour plates in popular series – worth hunting]
Victoria and Albert Colour Books: *Decorative Endpapers* (1985), *Patterns for Papers* (1987)

7 WORKING WITH ILLUSTRATORS

7:1 *Picture research*

Evans, Hilary and Mary: *Picture Researcher's Handbook* (4th edn, Van Nostrand Reinhold, 1989) [an international guide to picture sources – and how to use them]
—*Sources of Illustration: 1500–1900* (Adams & Dart, 1971)
Wall, John: *Directory of British Photographic Collections* (1st edn, Heinemann with the Royal Photographic Society, 1977)

7:2 *Artists' agents*

Writers' and Artists' Yearbook (A & C Black, published annually)

7:3 *Photographic illustration*

Evans, Harold and Taylor, Edwin: *Pictures on a Page: Photo-journalism, Graphics and Picture Editing* (Heinemann, 1978)
Gernsheim, Helmut and Alison: *The History of Photography* (Thames & Hudson, 1955) [under Helmut Gernsheim's revision, so far published as *The Origins of Photography* (1982), *The Rise of Photography* (1989)]

7:4 *Technical illustration*

Cherry, David: *Preparing Artwork for Reproduction* (Batsford, 1976) [how to do it, artist's methods and materials]
Lockwood, Arthur: *Diagrams: A Visual Survey of Graphs, Maps, Charts and Diagrams for the Graphic Designer* (Studio Vista, 1969)
Tufte, Edward R.: *The Visual Display of Quantitative Information* (Cheshire, Connecticut: Graphics Press, 1983)
Wildbur, Peter: *Information Graphics: A Survey of Typographic, Diagrammatic and Cartographic Communication* (Trefoil, 1989)

7:5 *Interpretative and narrative illustration*

Brett, Simon: *Engravers: A Handbook for the Nineties* (Silent Books, 1987) [survey of work of members of the Society of Wood Engravers]
Harthan, John: *The History of the Illustrated Book: The Western Tradition* (Thames & Hudson, 1981)
Hodnett, Edward: *Five Centuries of English Book Illustration* (Scolar Press, 1988)
Hogarth, Paul: *The Artist as Reporter* (Gordon Fraser, 1986)

7:6 *Imaginative illustration*

Martin, Douglas: *The Telling Line: Essays on Fifteen Contemporary Book Illustrators* (Julia MacRae Books, 1989)
Whalley, Joyce Irene and Chester, Tessa Rose: *A History of Children's Book Illustration* (John Murray with the Victoria & Albert Museum, 1988)

7:7 *Commissioning jackets and paperback covers*

Child, Heather (ed): *The Calligrapher's Handbook* (A. & C. Black, 1985)
Harvey, Michael: *Calligraphy in the Graphic Arts* (Bodley Head, 1988)
—*Creative Lettering: Drawing and Design* (Bodley Head, 1985)
—*Lettering Design* (Bodley Head, 1975)
Reiner, Imre and Hedwig: *Lettering in Book Art* (St. Gall: Zollikofer & Co, 1948)
Rosner, Charles: *The Growth of the Book Jacket* (Sylvan Press, 1954)
Schauer, Georg Kurt: *Kleine Geschichte des deutschen Buchumschlages im 20. Jahrhundert* (Königstein im Taunus: Langewiesche, 1962)

USEFUL ADDRESSES

Manufacturers of founders' type, analogue and digital typefaces for phototypesetting, and dry-transfer letter products

Adobe Systems Incorporated
1585 Charleston Road
P. O. Box 7900
Mountain View CA 94039-7900
USA

Agfa-Compugraphic GmbH
Ohmstrasse 2
D-6070 Langen
West Germany

H. Berthold AG
Teltowkanalstrasse 1-4
D-1000 West Berlin 46
Germany

Bitstream Incorporated
Athenaeum House
215 First Street
Cambridge MA 02142
USA

J. Bobst & Fils SA
division Bobst Graphic
CH-1001 Lausanne
Switzerland

Esselte Letraset
St George's House
195-203 Waterloo Road
London SE1 8XJ
UK
(publish *Baseline*)

Fundición Tipográfica Neufville, SA
Travesera de Gracia 183
E-08012 Barcelona
Spain

Haas'sche Schriftgiesserei AG
Gutenbergstrasse 1, Postfach 611
CH-4142 Münchenstein
Switzerland

Dr.-Ing. Rudolf Hell GmbH
Grenzstrasse 1-5, Postfach 62 29
D-2300 Kiel 14
West Germany

International Typeface Corporation
(ITC)
2 Hammarskjold Plaza
New York NY 10017
USA
(publish *U&lc*)

Linotype AG
Mergenthaler-Allee 55-57
Postfach 56 60
D-6236 Eschborn bei Frankfurt
West Germany

Linotype Limited
Chelham House
Bath Road
Cheltenham GL53 7LR

Mecanorma International
14 route de Houdan
F-78610 Le Perray-en-Yvelines
France

Monotype Typography
a division of The Monotype
Corporation plc
Salfords
Redhill RH1 5JP
UK
(publish *The Monotype Recorder*)

Scangraphic Dr. Böger GmbH
Rissener Strasse 112-114
D-2000 Wedel bei Hamburg
West Germany

D. Stempel AG Schriftgiesserei
D-6000 Frankfurt am Main 70
Hedderichstrasse 106-114
West Germany

Stephenson Blake
Broombank Road
Chesterfield S41 9QJ
UK

URW Unternehmensberatung Karow
Rubow Weber GmbH
Harksheider Strasse 102
D-2000 Hamburg 65
West Germany

World Typeface Centre Inc. (WTC)
303 Park Avenue South
New York NY 10010
USA

Booksellers

European and American books, catalogues and magazines of interest to the book designer appear in this country from time to time: A. Zwemmer are the most likely booksellers to be able to help through their shops at 78 Charing Cross Road WC2, or 24 Litchfield Street WC2 for mail order; the bookshop in the Design Centre, 28 Haymarket SW1 is also good. Several antiquarian booksellers specialise in typography and send out lists, and I have filled many gaps over the years with informed help by post and telephone from: Keith Hogg, 82 High Street, Tenterden, Kent TN30 6JJ; Adam Mills Rare Books, 328 High Street, Cottenham, Cambridge CB4 4TX; and S. P. Tuohy, 86 Hurst Street, Oxford OX4 1HF.

A selection of specialist libraries, collections and organisations concerned with the arts of the book

Association of Illustrators
1 Colville Place
off Charlotte Street
London W1P 1HN
UK
(publishes *Illustrators* and *Despatch*)

Association Typographique
Internationale (ATypI)
Secrétariat
B.P. 611
CH-4142
Münchenstein
Switzerland
(a lively forum for new thinking and a link with international colleagues, publishes *Letterletter*)

Basler Papiermühle
Schweizerisches Papiermuseum &
Museum für Schrift und Druck
St. Alban-Tal 37
CH-4052 Basel
Switzerland

The Chartered Society of Designers
(formerly SIAD)
29 Bedford Square
London WC1B 3EG

Deutsche Bücherei
Deutscher Platz 1
DDR-7010 Leipzig
German Democratic Republic
(a reference collection of well designed books from all over the world fully indexed under their designers, illustrators and even typefaces)

Deutsches Museum
Postfach 26 01 02
D-8000 München 26
West Germany
(impressive section on print and paper history and technology)

Gutenberg-Museum
Liebfrauenplatz 5
D-6500 Mainz
West Germany
(international museum for the history and present practice of printing and the book arts)

Klingspor-Museum
Herrnstrasse 80
D-6050 Offenbach am Main
West Germany
(archive and regular exhibitions of modern lettering, printing and book illustration)

Museum Plantin-Moretus
Vrijdagmarkt 22-23
B-2000 Antwerp
Belgium
(a unique museum of a company where building and equipment, books and archives have survived intact to give a detailed picture of book production as it was conducted in the sixteenth and seventeenth centuries)

St Bride Printing Library
St Bride Institute
Bride Lane
Fleet Street
London EC4Y 8EE
(also centre for membership of the Printing Historical Society, which publishes *Journal* and *Bulletin*)

Society of Scribes and Illuminators
54 Boileau Road
London SW13 9BL
(publishes *The Scribe* and *SSI Newsletter*)

Society of Typographic Designers
21-27 Seagrave Road
London SW6 1RP

Stiftung Buchkunst
Sophienstrasse 8
D-6000 Frankfurt am Main 90
West Germany
(the foundation organises the selection of the best West German books of the year and issues illustrated catalogues)

GLOSSARY

align to range type and/or pictures, either horizontally or vertically – e.g. alignment to the base or mean line.

alphabet length the length of the lower case alphabet in a given typeface and size.

ampersand monogram (&) derived from the latin *et*, meaning 'and'.

antique laid a twin-sided writing paper, the top surface of which emulates the raised laid and chain lines of handmade paper – book applications should be restricted to endpapers, and to jackets where wearing properties may be safely disregarded.

antique wove denotes a matt, rough-surfaced paper of reasonably good quality, unsuitable for halftones, but can be used for its bulking properties.

appearing size as related to nominal point size: types of identical point size vary considerably in apparent size; depending above all on their x-height – thus 10pt types of large x-height such as Times and Plantin will appear bigger than other 10pt types such as Bembo and Perpetua where the x-height has been kept down to leave room for taller extenders.

art paper a paper having a coating of china clay, unrivalled for quality halftone and colour printing by letterpress, but with unacceptably high reflectivity for continuous reading from its gloss surface; it need rarely be used for offset presswork, and then the matt qualities should be considered first. Further disadvantages include its contribution to the excessive weight of outsize books, and the tendency of jackets to slip unless machined on single-sided art.

ascender stroke of a lower case letter which extends above the *x-height* (q.v.), as in the ascending letters b, d, f, h, k, l, which, together with the *descenders* (q.v.) comprise the *extenders*.

backing in binding, see *rounding and backing*.

backing-up where text pages printed on either side of the sheet correspond, so that one line falls on the back of the other when held up to the light; this preserves the colour of the paper and keeps 'show-through' to a minimum.

backs the combined back margins of a book, which need to be determined with the proposed method of binding in mind; see *gutter*.

base line the foot of the x-height, giving the common level at which different sizes of type will align; it forms the horizontal from which the true foot margin is measured (regardless of descenders), and with which squared-up illustrations may range.

biblio, or imprint page the verso of the title page where bibliographical details of edition appear.

binder's board various grades of grey board and chip board are stocked, but true millboard or flexible boards (i.e. for small format classics on india paper) are hard to procure; caliper and weight should always be kept in scale with the format and thickness of the volume.

black letter, or gothic a group of broad-pen vernacular scripts dating from the twelfth century, of which the thirteenth-century textura was later to become the type of the Gutenberg Bible. Black letter delayed the ascendancy of the Renaissance roman in several European lands for a long period before it settled down in its Fraktur and Schwabacher forms as the dominant type in use for German language publications, being briefly challenged during the Enlightenment and finally ousted from that role after 1941. The ecclesiastical and legal overtones it aquired in England in the wake of the Gothic Revival still inhibit the wider use of this vigorous and decorative letter.

blad the initial or sample pages of a title in preparation, presented as a dummy for promotional purposes.

bleach-out where a lightly-developed photographic print is used as a basis for a line drawing, and this bromide is then bleached away after the over-drawing is finished.

bleed to extend an illustration beyond one or more of the trimmed edges of a page – the bleed, or allowance for trim, is normally 3mm.

blind blocking impressing letters or a design on to a binding case without the use of pigment or foil – blind panel-sinking may also be used to crush the grain of the material and create a smoother surface to receive foil-blocked titling.

blow up of photographs, see *enlargement*.

body the original metal cube carrying the printing surface of a piece of type, and specifically its fixed measurement from top to bottom, i.e. from above to below whatever character it carried (which incidentally never came to these very edges lest characters in printed lines should touch): thus a 12pt body = 12pt type. Phototypesetting inherited this basis for measurement, although the body had become purely notional.

body copy or body matter text setting, that is all matter to be set as the text pages, as distinct from prelims and endmatter to be set as display or set down in size.

bold heavier version related to a typeface – in the case of some founts this medium/bold differentiation has to be selected and specified with care nowadays from among a scale of weight values which may include: light, book, medium, demi-bold, bold and black.

book-block the sewn or perfect bound book before any rounding, casing-in or covering.

brace a bracket for grouping items, usually within a table.

bracket to the typesetter a bracket will be square or angled – the curved form is a parenthesis.

bracketed serif where the serif form is a smooth, curved transition from its point (or the thinnest part of the stub) into the thick stem of the letter – a characteristic of old face and transitional typefaces.

brass engraved brass die for blocking on binding case; largely supplanted by less expensive, photomechanically etched plates such as 'Chemac', or zincos.

broadside full size of sheet from which the subdivisions folio, quarto, octavo, etc., derive.

bromide a print or filmsetting on bromide (or light-sensitive, photographic) paper, suitable for use as CRC.

bulk (1) the thickness of a sheet of paper; (2) thickness of the *book-block*, also known as *bulk between boards* to avoid confusion with the *round* when preparing artwork for jacket and case. bulking dummy – a blank book made up in correct paper and materials to confirm all dimensions and allow jackets to be printed.

bullet photosetting term for an open or solid circle or similar geometric sort, frequently used to highlight individual features within a listing.

calligraphy writing or penmanship of a high order. Calligraphy differs from drawn lettering in terms of speed, spontaneity and the influence exercised by writing instrument and surface.

camera ready artwork or copy (CRC) or camera-ready paste-up (CRPU) complete type and line artwork pasted up into final page position for photographing, usually for lithographic platemaking.

cap height the height of capitals within a fount, specifically the level at which they align at the head, which is normally slightly lower than that of the ascenders.

caption copy which identifies or describes an illustration, also called a legend or underline (USA), and usually set smaller than text matter.

cartridge printing or drawing paper with good opacity, bulk and dimensional stability – smooth or coated offset cartridges are popular for colour printing.

case-binding the case (previously manufactured from boards covered in a paper, synthetic, or natural binding material) is attached to the book-block on a hardback production line; see *specimen case*.

casting-off determining the area copy will occupy when set in a given typeface, size and measure. The character content of the typescript is first measured or calculated, and then converted by means of averaged tables into pages or lines of the style to be specified for typesetting.

centre spread the two facing pages at the centre of a section or signature, hence the only place where the paper is continuous and the alignment of a subject placed 'across the spread' is ensured.

chancery italics named after their origin in the Vatican Chancery – models for numerous types as well as for good handwriting.

chapter-drop the number of blank lines left between the head of the page and the first line of text on a chapter opening page, which is normally a uniform allowance.

character compensation a facility on many type composition systems which closes up or opens out the spacing between all letter combinations incrementally. Generous 'plus' compensation may be used for the letterspacing of caps and small caps, and a small degree of 'minus' compensation may possibly improve the fit of certain typefaces on specific systems, but the indiscriminate modification of fit can reduce readability as well as altering the copyfitting factors for a typeface; see also *kerning*.

character count total number of characters and spaces in copy to determine (1) whether a heading will fit or turnover; (2) the area text will occupy.

'Chemac' proprietary etched copper plates for bookbinder's blocking; see *brass*.

cicero equivalent of pica within the Didot system of typographic measurement used in most European countries.

civilité an obsolete cursive typeface attributed to Robert Granjon and based on the current French court hand of the mid-sixteenth century.

club line strictly where the last short line of a paragraph falls at the foot of a page, but nowadays used equally of an *orphan* (q.v) or opening line as well; see also *widow*, as the most unsightly and least acceptable of these faults.

collating checking correct sequence of gathered sections, usually with the aid of a stepped black mark on the back fold of each section.

colophon (1) where the production details of a volume are of particular interest – e.g. a limited edition – then details appearing at the end of the book constitute a colophon; these are extra to those which appear on an imprint or biblio page; (2) also now used for a publisher's mark or device.

colour cast poor colour balance, giving predominance to one particular hue in a transparency or proof.

colour distribution pages available for colour use according to the imposition or production plan for a title.

colour laser print an economical alternative to a photographic print where an uncorrected colour blow-up is required for design presentation.

colour-matching system the 'Pantone' system is the most widely used: numbered colour swatches may be attached to artwork or specifications, to permit the printer to look up the ink-mix formula.

coloured edges or tops the dyed edges of the book-block, which can form an attractive finishing touch and a practical one for reference volumes; some top edge colours are prone to uneven fading, and seepage where poorly applied.

combined line and tone where a monochrome original drawing has both linear and tonal characteristics to a marked degree, it is possible to combine these in a single piece of film to yield a closer printed facsimile.

condensed faces narrow versions of a typeface design, marketed as such where the design lends itself to such treatment and may meet a need but can also be generated as, say, 10% or 20% distortion in width to any typeface on certain filmsetting systems.

continuous tone the presence of a range of relative greys on a scale from white to black is immediately obvious in a photograph but not so in all types of artwork, where the choice has to be made between *line, half-tone* or *combined line and tone* (q.v.). (Engravings and pencil drawings, for example, can turn out to be perplexing borderline cases, even calling for trial proofs at times.)

copperplate script a product of the flexible steel pen, a writing instrument that has only recently attracted renewed interest from calligraphers who have found it to generate, when held at special angles, a range of thick to thin stroke transitions to be encountered in swash letters and flourishes as well as in the italic versions of such modern faces as Bodoni – in other words, results have wrongly been ascribed to the influence of metal engraving which in fact flow naturally from this neglected and traduced school of penmanship.

copyfitting relating copy to a practical typesize and to the space available through calculations – *see* cast-off.

counter wholly or partly enclosed part of a letter: the inner shape of an 'o' or 'p', for example.

CRC see *camera ready copy.*

crop marks right angle marks near outer edges of artwork to show where the finished print is to be trimmed – also known as tick marks or cut marks.

cropping to mask or show where extraneous areas of a photograph or illustration are to be removed to improve composition or fit available space.

cross-head a centred heading or subheading.

cut-line mark caused by shadow from edge of patched-in artwork on CRC.

cut-out a half-tone illustration with background painted out or removed by process work.

descender stroke of a lower case letter which falls below the baseline or x-height: thus the regular descending letters are f, g, j, p, q, y, which, together with the *ascenders* (q.v.) comprise the *extenders.*

digital fount electronically stored fount in which the characters are stored as computer instructions for the typesetting machine rather than as film images or in other physical form.

dingbats recently developed and extensive ranges of signs, symbols and printer's ornaments designed to work as special sorts with founts of any design – similar to, but not synonymous with, *pi founts* (q.v.).

display face a type designed primarily for effect in its larger sizes, and not usually available or suitable for use in text sizes.

display sizes those sizes from a text face design which are effective in sizes 14pt and above, either used in conjunction with the smaller sizes or in their own right.

dot-for-dot reproduction of an already screened half-tone by photographing it as if it were fine line, to avoid the moiré pattern which the superimposition of screen on screen induces.

double-page spread a pair of facing pages considered as a unit for design purposes, and across which pictures or tables may be extended on occasion.

drop initial see *initial.*

dry transfer lettering translucent plastic sheets carrying dry-ink images of characters or motifs on the underside, which may be released by rubbing down onto a finished artwork surface.

dummy rough or prototype made-up in book form by an illustrator or designer for evaluation or sales presentation; see also *bulking dummy.*

duotone, or duplex half-tone a process whereby a monochrome photograph or illustration is printed in two colours – two negatives are made at different screen angles and to different contrast ranges, one normally for a black which conveys the greatest detail, and the other for a dark shade which reinforces the dot but at the same time colours the lighter tints.

E-height the height of the capital 'E' expressed in millimetres is the standard advocated for the metrication of typesizes.

egyptian display typefaces characterised by squared or slab serifs.

electronic scanner machine which scans full-colour transparencies or artwork wrapped around a drum and, by reading colour densities, produces separations.

elite small size of typewriter type, with 12 cpi (characters per inch); see also *pitch.*

em (1) the 12pt em or pica is the standard unit of typographic measurement, used to express the width and depth of the text area on a page irrespective of the sizes of type in use; (2) the em or 'square' of each individual point size, as it conditions character proportions and spacing.

en half the width of the em in any specific context – it is also taken to represent a keystroke or the width of the average type character for the purposes of measuring and costing keyboarding output.

endmatter or end pages the final parts of a book following the main text.
endpaper a folded sheet, one leaf of which is pasted down to the front or back board and the other, the fly leaf, tipped by a narrow band of adhesive in the backs to the first or last page of the book.
enlargement may be calculated as a percentage of original size using a calculating wheel portentously described as a 'reproduction computer' and available from a good artist's materials shop.
even small caps small capitals without full capitals: avoid for text openings.
even working where the extent of a book is made to fit a given number of sections, each of 16pp or 32pp etc., according to the production plan.
expanded extra wide version of a display face.
extenders see *ascenders* and *descenders*.
extent the eventual number of pages it is decided that a title shall make – this should normally be an *even working*, and may require a number of accurate calculations and adjustments to achieve.
extract a quotation displayed or differentiated from the text by means of spacing, indentation or a smaller typesize.
family all variants of a roman typeface (in terms of italics, light or bold weights, narrow or wide versions) designed and issued as a series by the type manufacturer, comprise a fount or family.
feathering adding or subtracting fine increments of leading to modify the depth of a page, also known as *vertical justification* – a facility which can operate automatically on some typesetting systems, but which the designer should monitor and regard with caution.
figure (1) an illustration printed in the text, as opposed to *plate* (q.v.); (2) a numeral: see *lining figures, non-lining figures, roman numerals*.
film advance instruction for the distance between lines of type, as measured from base line to base line, i.e. body size of type plus any leading required; see *white line*.
fitting the fit, or standard spacing between characters, should never be modified as a means of justifying badly spaced lines; see *character compensation, kerning*.
fixed space constant word space as found through ragged setting, and which should be specified in units of the typesetting system in use.
flat artwork colour illustration which will require separations; if drawn on a surfaced board it may present difficulties to a drum-type scanner as opposed to a flatbed model.
flat, or square back, binding where rounding and backing operations are omitted; stylish for slender book-blocks in various formats, and practical as a binding method for single-section children's picture books which would otherwise have little or no spine to display.
flush left or right in alignment with the left or right margin.
flyleaf see *endpaper*.
foil blocking titling or decoration impressed on a binding case or paperback cover through metallic or pigment foils using a heated die or brass; see also *blind blocking*.
fold-out a folded sheet in or at the end of the book which opens out beyond the page-size, usually to contain a large plate or map.
folio the page number of a book.
font see *fount*.
foot or tail margin traditionally greater than the other page margins (just as a properly mounted picture will have more space at the foot than at top and sides), the foot margin follows from imposing the text area as specified at the head and trimming the book-block precisely, and therefore its depth measurement does not need to be stated.
footnote see *notes*.
foredge the outer vertical, trimmed edge of a book, opposite the spine.
foredge margins the outer left and right margins of a spread – with an asymmetrical margin scheme these will not necessarily be equal in width.
format (1) the trimmed page size – but also loosely adopted for a containing concept or style of presentation, as in 'coffee-table format'; (2) frequently occurring set of typographic commands stored as a code on a typesetter.
foundry type metal type in case for hand composition.
fount in terms of metal type this consists of a set of alphabets and ancillary sorts *of a single size* and based on one design (thus a 9pt Times type found in a 10pt Times case would be a 'wrong fount'); but the meaning of the word has shifted radically with the development of typesetting, and it has come to refer to the same vocabulary of characters but in the *whole range of sizes* which may now be generated from a single master.
french groove in binding, the free-hinging joint between the boards and the shoulder produced by rounding and backing.
frontispiece a plate facing the title-page; on occasion a subject which has to be printed separately from the text may still be tipped-in here by hand.
full bound completely bound in the same material, in contrast to a quarter binding where the spine is of one material and the rest of the case another, and half binding where the corners are also strengthened by the spine material. Traditional materials are leather with cloth or paper boards, or cloth with paper sides.
full out not indented, but aligned with the left (as for an opening paragraph) or with the right margin.
galley an unpaginated proof or bromide, as supplied to the designer for use in a rough or camera-ready paste-up.
grain direction the alignment of fibres with the travelling web of the papermaking machine. For a book to retain its shape and serviceability, this grain or machine direction in text papers must run parallel to the spine.
grid accurate drawing of the proportional system for margins and positioning elements in a book design; gridded paper may be printed in non-photographic blue as a base for preliminary design and paste-up or CRC.

gutter strictly the spacing *between* the visible back margins of the finished book, an allowance made for a given binding method; but applied loosely to the *backs* themselves.

hair-lines the fine unbracketed serifs and other thin strokes of typefaces classified as moderns.

half binding see *full bound.*

half-title the first printed page of a book, which normally contains its title only, and from which the pagination of the prelims commences as (unprinted) roman p.i, or that of the book as a whole from (unprinted) arabic p.1.

half-tone reproduction of a tonal range from white to black as present in a photograph or drawing, by means of a pattern of dots of various sizes.

hanging indentation the entry-line for the paragraph starts at the left margin, and subsequent lines are indented, like this glossary.

head margin white space at the head of a page which needs to be carefully measured and expressed as: 'from trim to the mean line (the top of the l.c. x-height) of the first line of text'. Any running headline is ignored for the purpose of specifying the head margin, although its presence will exert an optical effect which has to be taken into account.

headband cotton or silk cord attached to the top (and occasionally the tail as well) of the spine of the book-block prior to lining.

heading the graded levels of titling, heading and sub-heading are not always clear from the author's MS, and editorial clarification and coding are helpful in assigning the right degree of typographic emphasis to these distinctions.

headliner machine which is basically a photographic enlarger mechanically linked to a film or slide fount so that individual characters may be fitted and exposed to produce headlines in display sizes; advantages (shared with custom dry transfer sheets) include the designer's optical control of spacing and the availability of founts or custom lettering in recurrent use.

hollow space between the case and the back of the book-block, achieved by steps in binding which permit the spine to hold its convex round, whilst the sewn sections open on the opposing curve.

imitation art an unpleasant and unnecessary paper where china clay is added as a loading to the pulp rather than as a coating.

imposition arrangement of pages in a sequence which will read consecutively after the printed sheets are folded, gathered and trimmed – relevant at the design stage as it affects where bleeds, halftones or colour may fall.

imprint see *biblio.*

incunabula books printed prior to 1500, i.e. in the infancy of printing.

indentation to set type further in from the left margin than the standard measure of surrounding text. An em space of the typesize in use, sometimes more, helps to signal fresh paragraphs; several fixed levels of indentation may be necessary to show the pattern of sub- and sub-subheadings, in an index for example; see *hanging indentation.*

india paper properly an ultra-thin opaque rag paper, but used loosely of alternative papers of similar substance used for religious books, dictionaries and standard classics.

initial large capital as used for chapter opening: either ranged with the base of the first line of text and *raised*, or *dropped* and fitted to the depth of two or more lines of text and ranged with the lowest base line.

in pro in proportion – artwork drawn for common reduction or transparencies grouped for same enlargement.

insert, or *inset* a plates section placed and bound into the centre of a text section, contrast *wrap.* [Note that pre-printed material which is insetted is anchored in some way, whilst inserting means it is loosely placed inside.]

integrated book where text and illustration may be juxtaposed, free of production constraints requiring the zoning of plates or colour; also used to describe a particular kind of co-edition book or partwork created by a team of specialists.

interlinear space a term used by designers to describe the total white space visible between lines, as measured between the base line of one line of text and the mean line of the next. Interlinear space is *not* synonymous with leading: it is what happens when leading, if any, is added to the space already present when lines of type are set solid and so it should never be used in connection with actual specification.

ISO (formerly DIN) paper sizes the international A series does not challenge the metricated traditional sizes preferred for book formats from one European country to another, although its adoption as a standard for books and publications in certain specialised fields has to be respected.

jacket paper high quality one-sided coated paper used for dust wrappers, so that the inner surface will not slip against the case material, and so that the printed result may safely be laminated provided the grain direction of the paper is correct.

justification causing text to be composed in lines of equal length through adjusting the spaces between all words to a like degree within each individual line – so that both left and right margins are straight, in contrast to *unjustified setting* (q.v.) where one edge, normally the right, is ragged.

kerning adjustments to improve the spacing and fitting of certain letter combinations in word-building. With metal types this was confined to those parts of a letter (i.e. the extremities of the lower-case italic '*f*') which were made to overhang the body of adjacent letters; but the term is used more loosely now that automatic kerning programmes are featured on many photosetting output systems; see also *character compensation.*

key in to indicate the approximate position of illustrations or other matter in the margins of the typescript or galley proof for guidance.

keyline artwork in which tints or colours are to be laid or fitted at reproduction stage to the edges of a basic line drawing; the line itself may or may not be required to print.

lamination thin plastic film applied by heat and pressure to a book jacket or cover for protection and appearance. It is generally inadvisable to laminate jacket flaps as curling and folding back may occur.

landscape artwork or a format that is wider than it is deep, as opposed to *portrait*.

lead-in a newspaper or advertising term for capturing the eye's attention through introductory setting in a larger, bolder or different type style which then 'funnels' into the body text.

leading lines of type were formerly spaced out with strips of metal (leads), hence the expression 10pt, 2pts leaded (or 10/12pt). Nothing has changed beyond the gradual obsolescence of the term leading, which may be replaced by 10pt, 12pt line feed, or *film advance* (q.v.).

letterspacing additional spacing needed between all capitals and all small cap letter combinations: optically adjusted in the case of lettering which is drawn or uses dry transfer or headliner founts, and in the revised spacing of display typesetting; but added as specified fixed unit increments in photocomposition down to the smallest sizes.

ligature two or more letters joined together as one sort to improve awkward fitting.

light box portable, back-lit, translucent glass screen for viewing transparencies.

line artwork a subject consisting of solid black lines or dots only, and having no intermediate grey tones; see also *dot for dot*.

line conversion reducing a suitable continuous tone subject to line by photographing it without a half-tone screen: intermediate tones must resolve either to pure white or to black, yielding a frequently dramatic but hit-or-miss line result, which may benefit from some line retouching before use.

line feed see *film advance*.

lining reinforcement of the spine of a casebound book with paper and glue.

lining figures (also known as *modern* or *ranging figures* as distinct from *non-lining* or *old style* figs, q.v.) – arabic numerals of even height ranging with or slightly below the cap line; used in preference with capitals, in tabular setting, and with those typefaces which they were originally designed to accompany.

make-up converting typeset galley and other matter into final pages.

margins the space surrounding the text area at back, head, foredge and foot of page.

mark-up designer's instructions for typesetting and make-up entered into setting copy or proof, as distinct from layout and specification.

mask an overlay which eliminates or instructs to eliminate the unwanted areas of artwork or transparencies.

matrices moulds from which types for hand composition are cast; also used of masters for film or digitised founts.

mean line the level of the top of the lower case x-height, to which the true head margin is measured from trim, and at which the heads of squared-up illustrations etc. may align.

measure the width of the column within which type is set, whether justified or ragged; this is invariably given in pica or 12pt ems so that various typesizes may share a common line length.

mechanical composition describes the composition of metal type using typecasting equipment, just as *photomechanical composition* would describe that generation of filmsetters which adapted the same mechanical principles to compose from film matrixes.

mechanical tint patterned or textured tints that can be added to the artwork from dry transfer sheets or laid by the printer to instructions supplied with keyline artwork.

mechanical wood pulp produces papers that deteriorate and become brown and brittle on exposure to light; *chemical wood pulp* (also known misleadingly as *wood-free*), which has had oils, resins and ligneous matter removed, gives whiter and stronger qualities.

modern face category of typefaces having vertical stress contrasted with hair line serifs, current c. 1790–1900, but have retained popularity in latin countries.

modern figures see *lining figures*.

non-lining figures (as distinct from *lining* or *modern* figs, q.v.) accompanied *old face* types, to which they were integrated by a common x-height and the deployment of extenders; they are therefore unobtrusive in text and work best with small caps or upper and lower case.

notes ideally the function and extent should determine whether these are best set (normally in a smaller size of type than the text) at the foot or shoulder of the page, or at the end of chapters or of the text.

numerals see *lining figures, non-lining figures, roman numerals*.

octavo abbreviated as 8vo, the eighth part (16pp section) of the traditional *broadside* (q.v.) sheet sizes.

oddment a signature with fewer pages than the others and requiring separate printing, in contrast to *even working* (q.v).

offprint a separately printed copy of a single article from a book or journal.

old face roman types in use from Aldus (1495) to Caslon (c.1720), as revivals of varying degrees of authenticity and as examplars in twentieth-century type design.

old style figures see *non-lining figures*.

old style typefaces Victorian interpretations of old face designs: in general larger in x-height at the expense of the extenders, with oblique serifs but vertical stress, and lighter in colour than the originals – excluded from systems of type classification, these types are likely to remain unfashionable for text composition.

opening a pair of facing pages, also known as a double-page spread.

optical centre that point above the mathematical centre at which an element within a design appears to be centrally placed.

optical letterspacing the manual adjustment of the gap between each pair of capitals to achieve even spacing throughout titling; mechanical increments of letterspacing improve evenness and increase legibility for all sizes of caps and small caps elsewhere.

original a photograph or drawing supplied as camera ready copy.

orphan the first line of a new paragraph or, more seriously, a sub-heading which appears at the foot of a page: the former is usually acceptable, whereas the latter should be resolved; see also *club line, widow.*

overlay a transparent flap covering the front of a photograph or drawing, and containing instructions or separated artwork.

overrunning re-adjustment of word spacing through a paragraph, caused by a correction or by the need to improve spacing or to make or save lines.

page make-up manual or computer-aided assembly of the elements in a page into their final design.

pagination inserting folios, i.e. page numbers.

'Pantone' see *colour-matching system.*

paper-covered edition used (in preference to 'limp' or 'soft') of thread-sewn books in any format with drawn-on paper covers, and to distinguish these from mass market paperbacks.

part a group of related chapters, which may be preceded by a displayed part-title (wrongly called a half-title), usually with verso blank.

paste-up a scissors and paste job undertaken to resolve the integration of text with illustration and/or other complexities either to provide guidance for page make-up or to provide CRC.

perfect binding adhesive binding method widely used for mass edition paperbacks. The backs should be sufficiently wide to compensate for the process and attendant difficulty in opening the pages flat.

photogram print made by exposure of object directly on photographic paper – a graphic technique in occasional use.

photolettering method of setting display-sized type from photographic founts, favoured by designers capable of evolving their own lettering for jackets, etc.

pi fount an ancillary fount containing special sorts. There is no agreed standard for the composition of such founts: but some provide for mathematical signs with Greek; and others for miscellaneous accents, arrows, brackets, fractions, stars and the like; see also *dingbats.*

pica (1) unit of typographic measurement equal to 12 points (0.166044", therefore 6 picas = approx. 1"), synonymous with *12-point em* – and used in multiples as a common denominator for measuring page and column widths and depths irrespective of the sizes of type being composed within such parameters; (2) size of typewriter face having 10 character widths to the linear inch.

pitch measurement of the size of typewriter or printer faces by the number of standard character widths to the linear inch; common pitches are 10 characters (pica), 12 (elite), and 15 (microelite).

plate an illustration printed separately from the text, but the distinction between *figures* (q.v.) and plates should be made on grounds of utility rather than of custom.

PMT, or photomechanical transfer paper negative which produces a positive print by a process of chemical transfer; this economical process is extensively used to produce line artwork and screened prints to size.

point system the printer's system of measurement, where 1pt = 0.352mm (0.013837"); see also *cicero, pica.*

portrait artwork or a format which is deeper than it is wide, as opposed to *landscape.*

presswork quality of printing, brought about through regulating inking, impression, register and back-up on the press in order to transfer an optimum printed image to paper; commonly called *machining.*

proportional spacing used of typewriter head where the width or set of each character varies according to design, the 'm' being wider than the 'i' and so forth – one of the means by which word processor output aspires to approach typeset quality.

pseudo italic or small caps italics produced by slanting the roman alphabet digitally or through a lens, and small caps by reducing the cap alphabet to match the lower case x-height.

punchcutting traditionally, a master for each character in type was produced by engraving and filing on steel, which was then tempered and struck into a matrix, from which in turn metal printing types could be cast. Benton's punchcutting machine (1884) worked on the pantograph principle in following an enlarged template to engrave the steel punch at the requisite reduction; today's typical equivalent of this stage is for the computer to store the digitized data for direct type generation or to drive a plotter which cuts a large-scale master in film.

quad (1) spacing material, in subdivisions or multiples of the em of the size in use, used to fill out lines of type; obsolescent for filmsetting, where the expression 'quad, left or right or centre' is replaced by 'set flush (or range), left, right or centre'; (2) paper terminology for a sheet four times the size of the traditional broadside sheet.

quarter binding see *full bound.*

quarto a page one-quarter of the traditional broadside sheet size, e.g. crown 4to.

ragged right see *unjustified setting.*

raised initial see *initial.*

range to align.

recto a right-hand page, acknowledged to take visual precedence over a *verso* or left-hand page – thus the opening of the text and certain preliminary and end-pages should fall on rectos.

reducing glass the opposite of a magnifying glass; invaluable in assessing artwork which is to be reduced.

reduction most artwork is flattered by reduction, and many artists prefer to draw for a reduction in the ratio 3:2 (known colloquially as $^1/_2$-up) or 2:1 (twice-up); artwork, bromides or transparencies for reduction or enlargement are best specified as percentages.

register marks fine corner crosses in the same relative position on artwork, overlays, film or plates to ensure that subsequent printings are accurately superimposed.

retouching skilled handwork on a photographic original prior to reproduction to remove blemishes, accentuate highlights and deepen dark tones, or to correct colour separations in the course of reproduction.

reversal distinguish between (1) positive to negative, i.e. black to white; (2) lateral (known also as wrong-reading, reverse reading), i.e. left to right.

reverse out commonly to cause type or a panel to read white out from a colour or 4-colour set.

river a fault resulting where several wide and adjacent word-spaces in successive lines of type cause a distracting white channel to lead the eye down the page.

roman numerals research has shown how unfamiliar these have become: they are serviceable in lower case as a contrasting system for numbering the prelims independently of the text, but otherwise best avoided unless there is a functional or historical case for their use.

rough the author's reference, or an artist's visual, for any subject that will have to be redrawn.

round, or spine width the measurement of the covered back strip of a case binding; this, or a *bulking dummy* is needed by the designer to ensure the fit of the jacket etc.

rounding and backing shaping a book so that the back is convex and a joint or shoulder is formed on either side of the spine (the continental European style favours rounding the book-block only, without joints – see *french groove*).

rub-down lettering see *dry transfer*.

rules originally strips of metal available in a range of thicknesses measured in points, and printed in tabular or displayed setting; now any lines of specified thickness to print.

run-on chapters instead of beginning a fresh page each time, chapters follow on the same page as the conclusion of the preceding chapter and after a break of a set number of lines.

run round where the text measure is reduced to allow an illustration to be dropped in.

running headline a line which appears in the head margin of pages other than chapter heads, and which may give the book, part, chapter, section or subsection title or other reference; the folio may sometimes be combined with this running page head.

same size abbreviated as 's/s'; used where an original is to be reproduced at 100%.

sanserif types without serifs; their pure yet mechanistic, near-monoline construction has led to their description as *lineal types* in the more recent classifications.

scanner see *electronic scanner*.

screen pattern of lines that creates the dot formation in *half-tones* (q.v.) – normally of crosslines and angled at 45 degrees, although there are a range of other geometrical and textural screen configurations which may be used to occasional graphic effect.

screened original see *dot-for-dot*.

script a typeface which sets out to capture the character of formal or informal handwriting: see *chancery italics, civilité, copperplate script*.

section a printed and folded sheet (or signature), together with any inserted or wrapped plates, ready for gathering and sewing.

self-ends where the first and last pages of a book-block are pasted down to the boards instead of attaching a proper or 'made' endpaper.

separated artwork where the artist makes a drawing in black for each additional colour in turn, usually on an acetate overlay which is registered to a base or keyline drawing.

series a complete range of sizes in the same typeface.

serif the horizontal structure of stroke termination in letter form – this may be absent (sanserif), a hair line (modern), bracketed (old face), slab or square (egyptian), and so forth.

set a measurement of the width of the notional rectangle (originally a piece of type) assigned to each individual character in a particular fount: the set widths for individual characters relate to the em of set for the fount as a whole; which itself has to accommodate the width of the widest letter in the design; see *unit*.

set flush matter composed without any indented lines.

show-through where print from the reverse side of a leaf is visible due to poor positioning (back-up) or paper opacity.

sizing scaling originals for reproduction, i.e. determining the percentage reduction or enlargement that will bring illustrations to final appearing size.

sloped roman a classification of italic faces designed to resemble their respective romans at a fixed angle of inclination: this involves inherent suitability and skilled modification, for which reasons these are to be distinguished from the so-called *pseudo italics* (q.v.).

small caps an alphabet of roman capitals designed to relate to the x-height and weight of lower case and non-lining figures.

solid (1) type set to strict point or body size without any leading (or additional spacing between the lines); (2) areas of the page with full ink cover, and which may cause problems of show-through with poor opacity papers.
sort any individual alphanumerical character, punctuation mark or sign from a complete fount.
special colour a printing ink obtained by mixture rather than made up from the process colour set, thus an additional working to 4-colour printing, or a natural alternative to process inks for 2- or 3-colour printing.
special sort any character or symbol outside the normal make-up of a fount. This may be found as a *dingbat* (q.v.) or from a *pi fount* (q.v.) or among peculiar accents or the specialised symbolic vocabularies for astronomy, botany, chess, medicine, meteorology, etc.
specification the designer's written instructions which enable a book to be produced to a detailed styling and in materials as prescribed; the specification consolidates, and in some circumstances may even supplant, the layouts.
specimen case the binder should submit a flat specimen case so that the covering material, blocked titling, boards, size and squares may be approved by the designer and others before the binding cases are manufactured.
specimen pages in times past a 4-page sample, showing proposed style and specification for the text page and treatment of chapter and sub-heads, would accompany the printer's tender for a title, but this service fell into disuse as soon as a charge was made for it; however, the designer should insist on seeing a few lines of trial setting where needed to confirm a tricky styling and the typesetter's grasp of it.
square, or slab, serif rectilinear serif formation characteristic of the egyptian group of typefaces (e.g., Rockwell, Playbill).
square-back see *flat binding*.
squared-up half-tone a rectangular or square photograph as distinct from a *cut-out* or *vignetted* one (q.v.).
squares the measured projection of the binding case beyond the book-block at head, foredge and foot respectively – for protective purposes and precision in manufacture.
swash alternative flourished capital or lower case character, supplied particularly in the italic alphabet, and best used sparingly and in accordance with the type designer's original intention in display: i.e. at the beginning or ending of a word or line and at specific conjunctions within words.
tabular setting matter to be set in columns, with or without rules.
tail foot of page, see *foot margin*.
tail-piece an illustration or decoration placed at the end of a chapter.
text, or type, area the rectangular panel made on the page by the typesetting – both a consequence and a determinant of the margin scheme or grid.
text type that size of typeface used for the main text of a book; and, more generally, those typeface designs which, in a given range of their sizes, could reasonably be considered suitable for text composition purposes.
tint see *mechanical tint*.
tip-in to attach a single leaf to the adjoining page by a narrow line of adhesive along the backs; this will usually be a plate which folds, or is printed in colour or by a different process to the book itself.
titling capitals only alphabet, and thus able to appear large on body – for use as fitted initials and for formal titles.
trade typesetting a livelihood centred on the typesetting supply stage only, and thus complementary when planning work with the large number of book houses that have dispensed with typesetting in order to concentrate on a print-bind service.
transitional typefaces of the eighteenth-century movement from old to modern face, in which the vertical stress to inner curves and the weight differential between thick and thin strokes are already apparent, although the refined bracketed serif has still to give way to the horizontal hair line characteristic of the full-blown modern.
turning (on the page) where a table or illustration is rotated through 90 degrees so that its left-hand side is at the foot of the page.
turnovers the second and subsequent lines made by an entry, which may call for special styling such as indentation.
type classifications systems which group typefaces into families according to shared design characteristics. Both the BS and DIN standards reflect most features of the pioneering Vox method.
type family roman, italic and bold together with any further variants of one typeface design.
typefounding the activity of devising, *punchcutting* (q.v.), typecasting, and marketing matrices or supplies of metal printing types cast therefrom.
typescale the most useful kind is a slotted plastic rule calibrated in ems of all $^1/_2$-pt typesizes from 6pt to 14pt – of which the pica or 12pt scale will be needed most.
unit smallest subdivision into which the em character width measurement of a fount is divided. Used as the counting basis for all character widths in a fount – the number of units varies with the manufacturer's system, but the designer quickly becomes familiar with systems in regular use and these units of set facilitate precise copyfitting calculations and the specification of preferred degrees of fixed letter and word spacing.
unjustified setting where an uneven right-hand edge is allowed to result from the use of fixed word spacing throughout and the general avoidance of word breaks – sound practice in narrow measures and tabular setting and for contrast, but undesirable for text typesetting in standard measures (unjustified or ragged text output, however, remains the recommended norm for typewriters and most computer printers at present).
unsewn binding see *perfect binding*.

varnish an alternative to lamination, where a high gloss may be undesirable, as a protective finish for jackets or paperback covers.
venetian types because of the focus of interest on the 1470 roman of Nicolaus Jenson by William Morris and others, a separate type classification grew up around the roman types of the Italian printers prior to Aldus.
verso a left-hand page; see also *recto*.
vertical justification see *feathering*.
vignette a half-tone which is softened and faded-out at its irregular edges.
visual an advertising and publicity term for a designer's *rough* (q.v.).
wash drawing, or water colour a brush drawing necessarily containing grey tones as well as black and white; where used with certain qualities of black line, *combined line and tone* (q.v.) may need to be considered.
weight the degree of blackness of a typeface design, where versions may be cut on a scale extending from extra-light to ultra-bold – in a similar sense, weight is a factor when book designers use the term 'colour' in discussing the overall character of a page of type, even though it is printed in black.
white line line of space in photosetting and make-up – as though a line of text had been painted out leaving those above and below in position; when a line of white falls at the foot of a page its unaided effect as a break in the text may largely be lost.
widow where the short line ending a paragraph falls at the head of a page: this is unsightly and disruptive for the reader, and should be phased out. see also *club line, orphan*.
woodcut the broader printmaking technique, where the side grain of the wood is worked with a knife – as distinct from wood engraving, where a burin or graver is used on the end grain.
word breaks, or division unacceptable word breaks should be scanned for in proof, since these are known to disrupt reading concentration and continuity.
word count supplied on certain word processing software, and can be a useful aid to estimating extent, although a character count provides the best foundation for accurate copyfitting.
word-sets an advertising term drawing attention to the finesse with which the letters which comprise a specific name, title, or headline may be combined. This close consideration goes further than ordinary word-building but not as far as the creation of logos or trademarks – it explores the modification of individual letter design and the creation of new ligatures through hand drawing or on screen and is relevant to similar problems encountered with book jackets and titling.
working see *even working*.
woven material linen or buckram as used infrequently for case covering, in contrast to non-woven synthetics and papers.
wrap a plate section placed around the outside of a folded text section and bound into a book; contrast *insert*.
x-height the relative appearing size of a given typeface design depends upon the height of the lower-case letters (ignoring the extenders) as represented by the 'x', since this is an easy letter to measure – in the case of different 12-point typefaces this height may well vary between 0.055″ and 0.080″.
zoom copier xerographic copying process which delivers accurately sized plain paper prints – essential studio equipment when working with highly-illustrated books.

INDEX

Italic numerals refer to the pages on which illustrations appear as well as or instead of references in the text.

Copyright permissions

Every effort has been made to trace the copyright holders of illustrative material reproduced in this book and acknowledgement is made to the following: Angelus Druck, Bern 100; De Arbeiderspers, Amsterdam 184, 185; Armitage Typo/Graphics Ltd 106; John Bartholomew & Son Ltd 156; The Bodley Head Ltd 184; The British Council 179; Mary Evans Picture Library 158; Faber & Faber Ltd 109; The Folio Society 85; Hodder & Stoughton Ltd 142,143; Leicester University Press 55, 79, 89, 151, 154, 158, 182; Leicestershire County Council Department of Property 118; Little Theatre, Leicester 89; Julia MacRae Books 132, 133; Michelin et Cie 102; Monotype Typography 38, 114; Stadtbibliothek Nürnberg 128, 129; Offcut Press 181; Penguin Books Ltd 91, 112; Springfield Books Ltd 50, 54, 152; URW Verlag, Hamburg 43; Verlag der Kunst, Dresden 126, 127; WKŁ, Warsaw 176; Yale University Press 184, 185, Zollikofer & Co, St. Gallen 99.